# The Olmecs

# THE OLMECS

## The Oldest Civilization in Mexico

🕱🕱🕱🕱🕱🕱🕱🕱🕱🕱🕱🕱🕱🕱🕱🕱

# Jacques Soustelle

TRANSLATED FROM THE FRENCH BY
HELEN R. LANE

University of Oklahoma Press : Norman

# Acknowledgments

The following Mexican and American institutions:

Instituto Nacional de Antropología e Historia, Mexico City
Museo Nacional de Antropología, Mexico City
Parque-Museo de La Venta, Villahermosa, Tabasco
Museo de Antropología de la Universidad de Veracruz, Jalapa, Vera-
    cruz
Dumbarton Oaks (Trustees for Harvard University), Washington, D.C.
Smithsonian Institution, Washington, D.C.
American Museum of Natural History, New York
Museum of the American Indian, Heye Foundation, New York
Brooklyn Museum, Brooklyn, N.Y.
have kindly aided me in the research that enabled me to write and illustrate this book. I hereby extend them my most grateful thanks.

I should also like to express here my sincerest thanks to my eminent colleagues Ignacio Bernal and Michael D. Coe, and honor the memory of two great archaeologists: Alfonso Caso and Matthew Stirling.

Jacques Soustelle

ISBN: 0-8061-1962-4 (pb.)

Originally published in French as *Les Olmèques* by Librairie Arthaud. Copyright © 1979 by Les Éditions Arthaud, Paris. Translation copyright © by Doubleday & Company, Inc. All rights reserved. Manufactured in the U.S.A. University of Oklahoma Press paperback edition published by arrangement with Doubleday & Company, Inc. First printing, 1985.

# Contents

# Illustrations

## MAPS AND PLANS

# Abbreviations

| | |
|---|---|
| A.M.N.H. | American Museum of Natural History, New York |
| I.N.A.H. | Instituto Nacional de Antropología e Historia, Mexico City |
| M.A.I. | Museum of the American Indian, New York |
| M.N.A. | Museo Nacional de Antropología, Mexico City |
| U.N.A.M. | Universidad Nacionsl Autónoma, Mexico City |

# Dimensions of Certain Monuments

*La Venta:*

Altar no. 1: height 1.85 m., width 2.65 m., depth 2.80 m.
Altar no. 2: 0.99 m. × 1.34 m. × 1.29 m.
Altar no. 3: 1.50 m. × 1.65 m. × 1.40 m.
Altar no. 4: 1.60 m.  × 3.19 m. × 1.90 m.
Stela no. 1: height 2.51 m., width 79 cm.
Stela no. 2: height 3.14 m., width 1.93 m.
Stela no. 3: height 4.26 m.
Colossal head no. 1: height 2.41 m., circumference 6.40 m., weight 24.3 tons
Colossal head no. 2: height 1.63 m., circumference 4.24 m., weight 11.8 tons
Colossal head no. 4: height 2.26 m., circumference 6.50 m., weight 19.8 tons
Monument no. 19: height 95 cm., width 76 cm.

*San Lorenzo and Potrero Nuevo:*

Monument no. 2, Potrero Nuevo, atlantes altar: height 92 cm., width 1.29 m.
Monument no. 3, Potrero Nuevo, jaguar and woman(?): 1.25 m. long
Colossal head no. 1: height 2.85 m., circumference 5.90 m., weight 25.3 tons
Colossal head no. 3: height 1.78 m., circumference 4.02 m., weight 9.4 tons
Monument no. 10, San Lorenzo, humano-feline figure: height 1.19 m., weight 8 tons
Monument no. 11, the "Scribe": height 68 cm., width 74 cm.
Altar no. 14, San Lorenzo: Height 1.83 m., width 3.48 m., depth 1.52 m.
Monument no. 34, San Lorenzo, kneeling figure: height 79 cm., width 55 cm.
Monument no. 58, San Lorenzo, fabulous fish: 1.30 m. × 60 cm.

General map of Middle America.

# Introduction

⊠⊠⊠⊠⊠⊠⊠

Coming suddenly to light within a few decades from the depths of time, a civilization totally unknown to us has emerged, with its compelling evidence and its mysteries, with its style and its gods, forcing us to recognize it as being the earliest of all those that man has built on the American continent, and perhaps as the "mother civilization" of the New World.

The Aztecs have often been compared to the Romans, the Mayas to the Greeks. It has been said that the Toltecs played in Amerindian antiquity a role comparable to that of the Etruscans in Italy. The Olmecs, for their part, remind us of the Sumerians: like them long unknown, like them precursors, like them buried beneath ruins many thousands of years old and hidden from our eyes by the traces of peoples who succeeded them. Whereas vast portions of ancient Sumer are today parched and deserted, it is in the loneliness of the jungle, beneath a thick veil of tropical vegetation, and in the marshlands of low-lying coastal plains that Olmec monoliths and altars are hidden. It seems almost inconceivable, at first sight, that man prospered, worked, erected buildings, developed an art and a religion in this setting where nature is so overpowering. However, in an era contemporary with that of the Trojan War, the first monuments of American antiquity took shape beneath the hand of man, in valleys not far from the sea that were periodically inundated by rivers with lazy meanders, in this country of the rising sun and torrential rains that today forms a part of the Mexican states of Tabasco and Veracruz.

When the Spaniards invaded the continent at the beginning of the sixteenth century, the Aztecs reigned over their empire from one ocean to the other and from the Pánuco River to the Isthmus of Tehuantepec; farther toward the southeast, their outposts in Soconusco and the expeditions of their warrior-traders spread the renown of Moctezuma and the glory of their god, the solar Hummingbird, as far as Central America. But this empire was of very recent date. Less than a century had passed since the "Obsidian Serpent," the emperor Itzcoatl, had first lent impetus to the expansion of Mexico and its allies. Moreover, the Aztecs, latecomers to central Mexico, could scarcely be said to have been in a position to reap the benefits of a long tradition. For them, as the Indian historian Ixtlilxochitl, among others, noted, the past consisted of a golden age, that of the Toltecs, preceded by a vague, mythical era, that of the Giants, lost in the mists of legend. And it was the gods themselves, they believed, who had built the colossal pyramids of the Sun and the Moon at Teotihuacán. If we situate the major phases of Mexican history within our own chronology, the Aztecs may be said to have left their distant place of origin, Aztlán, in the twelfth century A.D. and to have arrived in the Valley of Mexico in the thirteenth century, founding their capital there at the beginning of the fourteenth; before them, Toltec civilization reigned on the high central plateau and beyond for a period of about two hundred years, beginning in the second half of the ninth century A.D.; and finally, Teotihuacán had been the center of a powerful civilization from the beginning of our Christian era until its collapse eight centuries later.

It has been Mexican archaeologists such as Manuel Gamio, and their North American colleagues such as George Vaillant, who have broadened our perspective; thanks to their work, our reconstruction of indigenous history can now be extended much farther back into the past. It became apparent that a so-called archaic period preceded the era of great cities and monuments: a period in which men cultivated maize, lived grouped in villages, fashioned artifacts of clay. This period and its subdivisions have been named after sites in the central valley of Mexico: Zacatenco (900–400 B.C.), Ticomán (400 B.C. to the beginning of the Christian era).

Thus Mexican or, rather, Mesoamerican[1] antiquity seemed divisible into three phases: archaic or pre-classic before the Christian era; classic during the first thousand years A.D. (Teotihuacán, El Tajín, Oaxaca, Mayas); post-classic (Toltecs, Yucatán, Aztecs) from A.D. 1000 to the Spanish Conquest. Naturally this chronological picture could be—and in fact was—reworked, refined, and filled out in greater detail time and again; it nonetheless remained basically simple and clear, not to mention satisfying to the mind because of its ternary structure.

Yet the curiosity of archaeologists and prehistorians remained unsatisfied. Two great problems, or two series of problems, invariably confronted them. The first: were there men in Mesoamerica before

[1] "Mesoamerica" has become the customary designation for a zone that covers the whole of Mexico with the exception of the subdesert regions of the North; Guatemala; Belize; El Salvador; and part of Honduras, Nicaragua, and Costa Rica. Beyond political boundaries and geographical demarcations (North America, Central America), this vast zone is characterized by a remarkable cultural homogeneity.

the pre-classic phase, and therefore before agriculture and villages, and if so, where did they come from? The second: the origin of agriculture. There is no doubt that in Mesoamerica maize was the most important factor in the transition to sedentary life, the prerequisite of all civilization. But where did maize itself come from? Where had it first been domesticated, first brought under cultivation, thereafter to become the very base of Indian life?

To answer the first question in a vastly simplified manner, we may say that, as far as is known at present, the people who populated the American continent came from Asia, first setting foot on it more than twenty-five thousand years ago and probably less than forty thousand years ago. What we now call the Bering Strait constituted, for long periods, a "bridge" between Siberia and Alaska, the sea level being much lower then than it is today: enormous quantities of water, in fact, were trapped in the form of ice in glaciers. The first man to set foot on the American continent was a Paleosiberian, a hunter hardened to the rigors of the Arctic climate. His equipment was limited to the stone weapons and tools he needed to kill and to cut up the carcasses of the animals he chased. We can easily imagine that small bands of these nomadic Asiatic hunters traveled without realizing it from one continent to the other amid the ice and snow, gradually venturing farther and farther south. From one millennium to another, these men reached various isolated pockets lying between the mountain ranges and the rivers of this vast new world. They encountered a great number of very different climates and extremely varied environments. Certain of them settled down in regions that they found propitious, rich in game and in wild plant species from which food could be gathered; others of them continued to migrate. There were humans in Peru around 13,000 B.C. and in Chile around 7000 B.C. In central Mexico, we find traces of man's presence over twenty thousand years ago; here he fashioned stone spearheads and killed mammoths on the swampy shores of the great lagoon that covered a large part of the valley.

These "Indians" all unquestionably belonged to the species *Homo sapiens*, that is, our own species. Thus far, no traces have been found in America of extinct human or humanoid species, of Neanderthals, Pithecanthropi, or Australopitheci; nor, moreover, have any traces of great anthropoid primates as yet been found. Everything thus leads us to believe that America was truly the "New Continent" and that man reached it only in very recent times, geologically speaking. He there encountered animals—such as mammoths, certain species of horses, mastodons, a variety of camel—that became extinct at least ten thousand years before the Christian era. There is evidence that even at this early date he possessed a certain artistic sensibility: a cameloid bone carved in the form of a coyote head, found in Tequix-quiac, in central Mexico, proves that these hunters, like our distant European ancestors, enjoyed creating images of the animals among which they lived.

The way of life of ancient peoples who were hunters and gatherers was perpetuated in Mexico, on the margin of agricultural civilizations, up until the Spanish Conquest and even as late as the eighteenth century: it was the typical way of life of the "Chichimecs" (from the Aztec word *chichimeca*, "barbarians") who wandered about the semi-desert mountains of the Sierra Gorda and the vast cactus plains of northern Mexico. They subsisted on game (deer, rabbits, birds), roots, and wild berries; they made a sort of farinaceous bread by crushing the beanlike pods of a spiny tree or shrub, mesquite (*Prosopis juli-flora*). Thus, for many centuries two fundamentally different types of culture coexisted in Mexico—more or less as if, in Europe, the civilized producers of wheat and wine had been able to see troglodyte hunters left over from the Stone Age wandering about beyond the confines of their rich cultivated lands and their cities.

What is called, in the Old World, the "Neolithic Revolution," that is, the invention of agriculture and the domestication of animals around 8000 B.C., took place in Mesoamerica around 4000 B.C.—though with an extremely important restriction: no domesticable animal existed at the time that would have provided man with a source of manure, milk foods, meat, energy. The Amerindian had at his disposal no cows, oxen, horses, donkeys, goats, sheep, or pigs. No pack or draft animals. No manure for the fields. No milk or meat. Only (edible) dogs and turkeys were domesticated, along with bees. Hence man was all the more dependent upon plants for subsistence. For the Indian, maize was, and still remains, both today and five thousand years ago, the staff of life par excellence. But where and when did this precious maize first make its appearance?

There are few problems that have given rise to so much scholarly research and aroused so much controversy as that of the origin of maize. It was long believed that the ancestor of maize was *teosinte* (from the Aztec *teocentli*, "divine maize"), a plant that grows wild, in Guatemala in particular. We know today, however, thanks especially to the work of the botanist Paul Mangelsdorf, that this hypothesis must be rejected. On the other hand, it is now a well-established fact that a variety of wild maize, a cereal grass with miniature ears, existed in Mexico long before man arrived there: pollen discovered by deep probing in the central valley proves that this plant was already growing there eighty thousand years ago!

The archaeologist Richard ("Scotty") MacNeish has devoted more than thirty years of research to the problem of the beginnings of

Mesoamerican agriculture. His brilliantly directed excavations, the first of them in Tamaulipas, and especially those later on in Tehuacán (state of Puebla), enable us to arrive at two conclusions. First of all, contrary to what had been a widely held belief, maize was not the first plant cultivated by the Indians. As early as 6500 B.C. gourds were domesticated, followed by squash, beans and peppers, avocados and cotton. And secondly, it appears that the decisive phase leading to the domestication of maize lasted, in the Tehuacán Valley, from around 5000 to 3500 B.C. (the "Coxcatlán phase"). Maize such as we know it evolved little by little from the meager ears of the wild plant. Man intervened in this evolution by selecting his seeds and by carefully cultivating this plant as a source of food. For centuries, maize remained merely a supplementary item of diet for Indians who led a semi-nomadic life, hunting small game. But from the second half of the fourth millennium B.C. on, agriculture provided enough food, with sufficient regularity, to foster the development of hamlets in the form of groups of circular huts in the valley. Leading a more and more settled life, close to their fields, round about their granaries, these Indians began (circa 2000 B.C.?) to fashion and to fire clay vessels: pottery thus made its appearance. The sequence brought to light by MacNeish at Tehuacán unfolds beneath our eyes from the years 10,000 to 1500 B.C., leading from little wandering bands to villages of peasants.

We may regard it as certain that an analogous evolution took place throughout the Mesoamerican area: analogous, though not necessarily identical. The environment of the high valleys of central Mexico and Oaxaca—*Tierra Fría*, "Cold Land"—and that of the seacoasts and the rivers of tropical regions—*Tierra Caliente*, "Hot Land"—confront man with different problems and suggest different solutions: climate, rainfall, natural resources all vary, depending on altitude. The coastal regions provide an abundance of fish, crustaceans, and shellfish. The jungle in which jaguars and snakes are a danger for man is rich in big game—deer, peccaries, tapirs—and in game birds such as wild pheasant. In the border regions between present-day Mexico and Guatemala, the cultivation of tubers—sweet potatoes, manioc—appears to have preceded that of maize, originally confined to semi-arid zones.

What is quite obvious is that from 1500 B.C. onward, up until the beginning of the Christian era, a certain way of life becomes the general pattern throughout Mesoamerica. It is characterized by a rapid increase in population, the establishment of more and more numerous villages, the diversification of animal and plant resources. Pottery no longer serves utilitarian purposes alone: everywhere, countless figurines representing human beings, most often women, and perhaps related to a cult or magic practices to ensure fecundity and abundance, make their appearance. The attire, the headdresses, the ornaments of these figurines are proof that village society had developed differences in status and indeed become hierarchized: certain of the persons represented might well be shamans, masked priests.

If, therefore, we restricted ourselves to the facts that have been set forth above, we would retrace the social evolution of Mesoamerica in the simple form of a continuous line linking archaic hunter-gatherers and the civilized societies of the classic period: a constant, often imperceptible development, albeit one that accelerates as we approach the beginning of our Christian era, as it passes through the phase of the domestication of plants as a source of food and fixed human settlements. Each phase of this development would thereby have its origins in the preceding phase and lay the foundations for the following phase: the clearest, most rational schema imaginable.

But at this point the Olmecs appear on the scene! A high civilization possessed of an inimitable style, with no discernible roots anywhere, that traverses the pre-classic horizon like a meteor (but can it be categorized as "pre-classic" when its works are as highly perfected, as sophisticated, as those of the great civilizations of the first thousand years A.D.?), that disappears as inexplicably as it springs into being, while at the same time leaving behind it a heritage that will be transmitted from age to age until the very end, until the fall of the Aztecs and the Mayas; a civilization, moreover, contemporaneous with the first archaic, faltering footsteps of others, a civilization whose monumental sculpture soars amid the stifling jungles bordering the Gulf of Mexico at precisely the same time that Mesoamerican peasants are modeling their crude, clumsy figurines. What is more, these Olmecs mingle with the Indians of the plateaus and the remote valleys, leaving their traces alongside those of these humble villagers.

*Olmeca, Uixtotin:* "the people of the rubber country, those on the shores of salt water." That is how the Aztecs, at the beginning of the sixteenth century, described the inhabitants of the Gulf coast. They considered them to be highly civilized, and skillful craftsmen. There is no certain proof, obviously, that the few Indians of this region were the descendants of those who marked with their imprint the prestigious sites of La Venta and San Lorenzo. The very term "Olmecs," hallowed by tradition, is ambiguous: in antiquity, it was also applied to a people that occupied the plateau of Puebla and fought the Toltecs. It is therefore necessary to make a very clear distinction between the "archaeological Olmecs," whose civilization is the subject of the present book, and the "historical Olmecs," who in turn must be divided into two categories, those of the coast and those of the central plateau. It would doubtless have been preferable to find another term to designate the ancient civilization of the coast, but it is too late for that now.

We do not know what name the Olmecs called themselves by, what language they spoke, or where they came from. Half a century ago, we knew absolutely nothing about them. Their sudden appearance on the scene in Mesoamerican antiquity had the same effect as one of those devastating hurricanes that their region sometimes undergoes: the accepted schemas suddenly collapsed, and it was necessary to revise them, to think them through again from the ground up—not without reluctance. The entire familiar panorama, with every detail seemingly in its proper place, was thrown into chaos. It is not surprising that many controversies shook the scholarly world before the facts compelled recognition. Today no one doubts that Olmec civilization reaches far back into antiquity. But there are still a host of unanswered questions: how could it be otherwise when numerous known sites have not yet been the object of thorough excavation, when many other sites remain to be discovered? Perhaps our view of things will undergo other radical changes once monuments as yet completely unknown, stelae buried beneath jungle growth, tombs dating back thousands of years, are brought to light.

But let us go back to the very beginning of the revelation of the existence of the Olmecs: we owe it to a humble Mexican traveler, a jungle explorer, an amateur fascinated by antiquities.

Colossal head, Hueyapan. (Courtesy of Museo Nacional de Antropología, Mexico City.)

# 1

⊠⊠⊠⊠⊠⊠⊠

# The Discovery of
# the Olmecs

The name of this traveler was José María Melgar y Serrano. Finding
himself in 1862 in the region of San Andrés Tuxtla (state of Veracruz),
he learned that an enormous monolith sculpted in the form of a human head had been discovered in a place called Hueyapan. Several
years later, he published a short notice in the bulletin of the Mexican
Geographical and Statistical Society:

> About a league and a half's distance from a sugarcane ha-
> cienda, on the western slopes of the Sierra de San Martín,
> a worker on this hacienda who was clearing jungle noticed
> on the surface of the ground what he took to be the bottom
> of a huge pot lying upside down. He told the owner of the
> hacienda of this discovery, and the latter ordered this object
> to be unearthed. [It was then discovered that it was a colos-
> sal head.]. . . As a work of art, it is, without exaggeration,
> a magnificent sculpture . . . but what most amazed me was
> that the type that it represents is Ethiopian. I concluded
> that there had doubtless been blacks in this region, and from
> the very earliest ages of the world.

Melgar had been so struck by the "negroid" appearance of the
Hueyapan head that two years later he wrote, in the same scientific
review, a second article on the "colossal head of an Ethiopian type

that exists at Hueyapan, in the region of Los Tuxtlas." In this article he developed theories on the "migrations" from the Old World to America which, however unlikely they may seem to us today, nonetheless continue to haunt Mexican archaeology like unsuccessfully exorcised ghosts.[1]

The honor of having been the first to point out the existence of a great Olmec sculpture nevertheless belongs to José María Melgar y Serrano. A quite faithful drawing of it, although it somewhat accentuated its "negroid" features, accompanied his first article. In 1886, the Mexican archaeologist Alfredo Chavero compared the Hueyapan head with a "votive ax" in polished and carved stone representing a supernatural being with the features of a jaguar: this was the first attempt to link two objects together and, consequently, to determine a style. As early as 1890, George F. Kunz, in a book devoted to the precious stones of North America, had the idea of relating the "votive ax" described by Chavero, a jade "ax" belonging to the British Museum, and thirdly the magnificent Kunz ax then in his possession and today in the American Museum of Natural History. The concept was thus dawning that the Hueyapan head and the "votive axes" belonged to one and the same culture; an unknown, and as yet nameless, civilization was beginning to emerge from the shadows.

If, however, one excepts an article by Marshall H. Saville on the Kunz ax (1900) and a visit to Hueyapan by the great German Mexicanist Eduard Seler (1905), silence and oblivion again descend upon these singular sculptures for more than a quarter of a century. Private collections and museums, to be sure, possessed or acquired objects, notably jade pieces, whose style closely resembled that of the Hueyapan head and the axes already described; in 1912, for instance, a wealthy American collector and patron of the arts, Robert Woods Bliss, bought from an antiques dealer on the Boulevard Raspail in Paris a magnificent jade statuette that constitutes one of the most precious treasures of the foundation that Bliss set up at Dumbarton Oaks. But no one had yet undertaken a systematic comparison of these sculpted or carved stones with half-human, half-feline features that were now dispersed over two continents. In most cases their precise provenance remained unknown, and what culture, what era they belonged to was an open question. These witnesses of the art that today goes by the name of "Olmec" were like nameless foundlings.

It was the Danish researcher Frans Blom who opened a new chapter in the annals of discovery. A pioneer of Mesoamerican archaeology who had become a professor at Tulane University in New Orleans, he set out in February 1925 to explore the southeast of Mexico,

[1] See, for instance, R. A. Jairazbhoy.

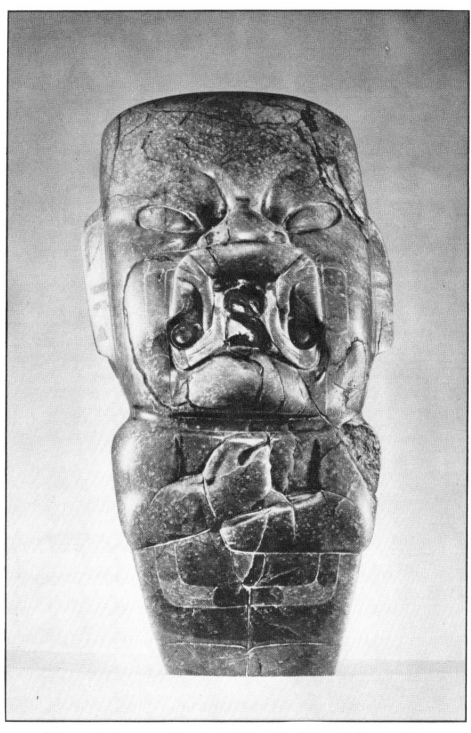

"Kunz ax." (Courtesy of American Museum of Natural History, New York.)

accompanied by the ethnographer Oliver La Farge. In March, the two researchers entered the splendid region of Los Tuxtlas: luxuriant vegetation, volcanic peaks, Lake Catemaco. It was there, on the island of Tenaspi, that they found a carefully polished and engraved stone idol with a human face very similar to that of the Hueyapan head. Farther on, at Piedra Labrada, they were able to observe and sketch a monolithic stela in volcanic stone 2 meters high, covered with inscriptions. Finally, and most importantly, they undertook to ascend the volcano of San Martín Pajapan: at the very top of this mountain, at an altitude of 1211 meters, stood an extraordinary idol, a masterpiece of Olmec statuary (today in the Jalapa Museum). A Mexican engineer, Ismael Loya, had seen it for the first time in 1897 and had made a rather rough sketch of it. This monument represents a seated figure, holding in its two hands a sort of cylindrical bar; the head is surmounted by a mask with slanted eyes and a feline mouth. A small "cache" hollowed out in the ground underneath the statue proved to contain several carved jade pieces, one of them in the form of a rattlesnake.

Continuing on southeast, the two explorers left behind the volcanic region of Los Tuxtlas and entered the half-flooded lowlands, dotted with lagoons and swamps, that extends to the border between the Mexican states of Veracruz and Tabasco, marked by the Tonalá River. In 1518 the Spanish expedition commanded by Juan de Grijalva stopped at its mouth for three days: in his memoirs Bernal Díaz del Castillo mentions that a soldier named Bartolomé Pardo discovered temples and idols farther inland. Was he referring to the site that today is called La Venta? Blom apparently believed so. There is reason to doubt this, however, since according to Bernal Díaz, Bartolomé Pardo found objects made of gold there, a metal not found at any Olmec site. In any event, following directions given them locally, Blom and La Farge went upstream along the Río Blasillo, a tributary of the Tonalá River, till they came to "an island entirely surrounded by swamps": La Venta. They there spied a block of stone 2.25 meters high and 86 centimeters wide, with a carving in relief representing a standing figure, clad in a sort of skirt and wearing a cap. It was what is now known as stela no. 1 of La Venta, lying on the ground and half hidden in the thick vegetation. From there, they caught sight of "a pyramid about 25 meters high," and then spotted four sculpted monoliths, which they referred to as "altars"; one of these monuments, altar no. 4, has a niche carved in it with a figure squatting on its haunches emerging from it, and is thus suggestive of the Maya stelae with niches at Piedras Negras. They also located two other stelae. "After this we came to the most amazing monument of all: a huge bell-shaped boulder. At first it puzzled us very much, but after a little digging, to our amazement we saw that what we had in front of us was the upper part of a colossal head, [which] had sunk deep into the soft ground."[2]

What they had found was the second colossal Olmec head. Blom realized immediately that this monolith resembled the Hueyapan head. We are also indebted to him for having retraced the history of two statues of volcanic stone that at the time were located in the inner courtyard of a school, the Instituto Juárez, at Villahermosa, the capital of Tabasco. These statues had been discovered at the beginning of the century by a certain Policarpo Valenzuela as he was cutting timber in a plot in the forest of La Venta. He had hauled the two statues to the river with the aid of a team of oxen that he used for his work as a woodcutter, and had put them aboard a boat. An attempt to remove altar no. 4 in the same way had failed because of the tremendous weight of the monolith.

In one day—for the two researchers had spent only about ten hours at La Venta—Blom and his colleague had placed on the map the most important site of Olmec civilization. But they did not even suspect that they had done so. They were greatly impressed, to be sure, by the dimensions of the monoliths and by the presence of a pyramidal monument, but they did not realize that they had before them a complex of monuments all marked by a previously unknown and profoundly original style. Their observations are summed up as follows: "La Venta is certainly a place of many puzzles, and further work should be done there in order to ascertain more definitely where this ancient city should be placed in our sequence of cultures."[3] But like most of the archaeologists of the time, they were so fascinated by the Mayas that they made every effort to detect Maya influences in sculptures such as those of stela no. 2 and altar no. 4. "We are inclined to ascribe these ruins to the Maya culture," they concluded. Blom thus missed finding the first known Olmec city, just as later he failed to find the crypt and the man with the jade mask of the Temple of Inscriptions at Palenque: success in archaeology consists of 30 percent science and 70 percent luck.

The results of Blom and La Farge's explorations were published in 1926 under the title of *Tribes and Temples*, an old-fashioned travel book, rich in amusing and colorful details that evoke a Mexico that today has almost completely disappeared. This work naturally attracted the attention of archaeologists: Hermann Beyer, a German scholar who belonged to the school whose guiding light was Eduard Seler, and who lived in Mexico, published a commentary on it in

[2] Blom and La Farge, vol. 1, pp. 84–85.
[3] Ibid., p. 85.

which we note in particular the following passage: "On the volcano of San Martín Pajapan there is an idol that was photographed and sketched by Blom. . . . On the nearly cubical part of the monument (above the mutilated head of the idol itself) there appears the face of a divinity that belongs to the *Olmec* or Totonac civilization. . . . This face bears a close resemblance to that of a stone idol that was in my possession at one time." This text is illustrated by a photograph showing a figure "with slanted eyes, a broad nose, and a monstrous mouth," with a caption that reads: "*Olmec* idol of greenish stone (private collection)."[4]

Thus for the first time the word "Olmec" was applied to representations of faces in a style that appeared both at San Martín Pajapan and at La Venta. Hermann Beyer was a most erudite archaeologist and possessed of a lively sense of intuition. Several of his works are devoted to bringing to light the relations in ancient times between the civilization of Teotihuacán on the high central plateau and that or those of the Gulf coast.[5] He often applied the adjective "Totonac" (Aztec: the Hot Lands people) to the coast cultures. But he was too familiar with the ethnohistory of Mexico not to search for a term less closely linked to a contemporary Indian population occupying a definite region. He knew very well that the ancient Mexicans called the coastal region of the Gulf *Olman*—"rubber country"—and its inhabitants *Olmeca*.

Hence it was Hermann Beyer who first gave the name "Olmec" to the style of the sculptures of southern Veracruz. He was soon followed by Marshall H. Saville, who in 1929 wrote apropos of "votive axes" in this same style, that in spite of the lack of knowledge concerning the origin of the majority of these artifacts, he believed that this particular type of mask could be definitely attributed to the "ancient Olmec civilization" whose center had apparently been in the region of San Andrés Tuxtla, around Lake Catemaco, extending from there along the coast of the Gulf of Mexico in the southern part of the state of Veracruz.

Saville had been fascinated by these strange faces with features that were at once human and feline, for the Olmec style, once one has contemplated a few specimens of it, has an extraordinarily spellbinding effect both on art lovers and on archaeologists. An American researcher, George C. Vaillant, to whom we owe basic works on the past of central Mexico, also fell under this spell. When, in 1932, the American Museum of Natural History received from Mexico a splendid jade jaguar that had come from Necaxa, Vaillant was enchanted

[4] Beyer, 1927, pp. 306, 307. (Italics mine: JS.)
[5] For example: "A Deity Common to Teotihuacán and Totonac Cultures," in *International Congress of Americanists*, pp. 193–99, New York, 1928.

by this object. He kept it for several weeks in a drawer, removing it each day to contemplate and touch it, "for there is a tactile as well as a visual appeal to Olmec jades," as Matthew Stirling, who passes this story on, comments.[6]

Vaillant was the first to clearly establish the existence of an "Olmec complex," characterized by the representation of felines or of men-felines. His excavations in the Valley of Mexico brought the discovery, in the oldest strata, of jade or ceramic artifacts in the "Olmec" style, to which he attributed a southern origin. Around the same date (1932), Albert Weyerstall, of Tulane University, published his observations on the sculptures of southern Veracruz, particularly the Hueyapan head, discovered seventy years earlier by Melgar. Matthew Stirling, at the time a member of the Smithsonian Institution in Washington, intuited that "this head [of Hueyapan] and that of La Venta belonged to the same art style as the jade axes and figures."[7] We might note that Stirling too, at the very beginning of his career, had succumbed to the spell of the Olmec style: as early as 1920, he had studied a little jade mask in the Berlin Museum that had been published by Thomas Wilson in 1898, and had later studied similar ones in Madrid and in Vienna.

And thus, from Melgar to Blom, from Saville to Vaillant, from Beyer to Stirling, the interests of a handful of researchers widely separated in time and space, often unaware of each other's existence, had converged on a single point: the existence of a certain style, common to colossal monoliths and little carved jade pieces. This style, they concluded, must have been the expression of a civilization as yet unknown, whose center was apparently situated in southeastern Mexico, somewhere between Veracruz and Villahermosa, and more precisely in the regions of Los Tuxtlas and La Venta. Beyer first of all, followed by Saville and Vaillant, had given the name "Olmec" to this civilization, the name that it still goes by today.

During the 1930s, more and more comparisons and parallels were drawn between monuments and objects in collections, thus adding substance, so to speak, to this still hypothetical civilization, of whose existence there was as yet no definite proof, only hints: the Tuxtla statuette, a little figurine in green stone representing a man with a bird mask and bearing engraved hieroglyphs, seemed likely to be a product of "Olmec" art; Vaillant had discovered "Olmec" pottery figurines in Gualupita, near Cuernavaca (state of Morelos); in Oaxaca, the leading Mexican archaeologist, Alfonso Caso, had found unquestionable traces of this enigmatic civilization, dating back to earliest

[6] Stirling, 1968, p. 1.
[7] Ibid., p. 4.

"Votive ax," region of Veracruz. (Courtesy of the British Museum, London.)

Jade figurine: jaguar-man, Necaxa, state of Puebla. (Courtesy of American Museum of Natural History, New York.)

antiquity, at Monte Albán. And above all, the "nucleus" in the south-east of Mexico in the states of Veracruz and Tabasco was attracting more and more attention.

It was Matthew Stirling who was to tackle the exploration of this "nucleus" and attain from the very outset the most spectacular re-sults. With the support of the National Geographic Society of Wash-ington and in cooperation with the Instituto Nacional de Antropología e Historia of Mexico City (Alfonso Caso, Ignacio Marquina), he began to excavate the Tres Zapotes site, near the Hueyapan hacienda where the first colossal head had been discovered. During the very first season of excavation (1938–39), Stirling and Clarence Weiant brought to light a broken stela that bore on one of its faces a stylized jaguar mask and on the other an inscription.

This "stela C" had been broken up into two fragments: the larger of the two was discovered by Stirling on January 16, 1939, and is today in the Museo Nacional de Antropología in Mexico City; the smaller one, constituting the top of the stela, was not found until 1969, and has been preserved in the village of Tres Zapotes. As though to confront Stirling with the tortures of Tantalus, the beginning of the inscription had been seriously damaged when the stela was shattered in two. Stirling nonetheless (rightly) interpreted it as a so-called "Long Count" inscription, similar to those that the classic Mayas had en-graved on countless monuments in Mexico and Guatemala.

What is meant by the term "Long Count"? To reduce the subject to its essentials, it is a way of pinpointing a date by enumerating the periods of time that have elapsed between a "zero date" situated very far back in the past (3113 B.C.) and the date in question. In the sys-tem employed by the classic Mayas, there were five such periods, each of them expressed by a number accompanied by a character, or "glyph," that is, the day (kin), the "month" of 20 days (uinal), the tun of 360 days, the katun of 7200 days, and the baktun of 144,000 days.

The oldest known Maya inscription was found on stela 29 at Tikal. It reads 8 baktun, 12 katun, 14 tun, 8 uinal, and 15 kin, and corre-sponds to our date A.D. 292. It has become the custom to transcribe such a date in Arabic numerals as follows: 8.12.14.8.15.

The inscriptions dating from the classic Maya era bear a period glyph alongside each numeral. Other glyphs define the date by situ-ating it in the ritual year of 260 days and in the solar year of 365 days, give the name of the "Lord of Night" ruling over the nocturnal period corresponding to this date, and finally specify the position and the phase of the moon.

Stela C of Tres Zapotes bears a much less complex inscription, though it too has only five numerals, which may be transcribed as

7.16.6.16.18, in other words 31 B.C. according to the Maya computation. The numbers, recorded by means of dots or little disks for each numeral and bars for the figure 5, are not accompanied by any period glyph. In this respect this inscription resembles that engraved on the Tuxtla statuette: 8.6.2.4.17 (that is, A.D. 162).

The discovery of stela C unleashed a veritable storm among specialists in Mesoamerican archaeology. If Stirling's interpretation was adopted, this monument dated from more than three centuries before the beginning of the classic Maya era! But how to explain that an inscription based on the "Long Count" system was definitely pre-Maya? Was it necessary to envisage the possibility that a civilization highly developed enough to conceive of such a sophisticated method of computing time had flowered before the Mayas and outside the region of the Mayas? Controversy immediately arose between "Maya supporters," chief among them J. Eric S. Thompson, who made every effort to prove, with his immense erudition, that Olmec civilization was late—a contemporary of the post-classic cultures—and "Olmec supporters," such as the Mexicans Alfonso Caso and Miguel Covarrubias. Stirling himself argued in favor of a very early date for the civilization of the Olmecs, but came up against the skepticism of a majority of North American archaeologists.

Everyone—both the partisans and the adversaries of the early appearance of Olmec civilization—reasoned as though the "zero" date of the "Long Count" of stela C or of the Tuxtla statuette was necessarily the same as that of the "Long Count" of the classic Mayas. As we shall see, the date of 31 B.C., regarded as much too early at the time of its discovery, today strikes us as being much too late. But let us not get ahead of our story. When Stirling discovered and deciphered stela C in 1939, the reading of the numerical coefficient of the period equivalent to the Maya *baktun* as 7 was doubtful. It was necessary to wait thirty years before the second fragment of the stela, which had finally been discovered, confirmed Stirling's interpretation. And it was not until 1957 that the carbon-14 method of dating pushed the birth and the flowering of Olmec civilization even farther back in the past than anyone had dared to imagine.

It has turned out that the site of Tres Zapotes has been occupied by civilized men for long periods of time: the style of certain monuments is purely Olmec, while others—"monument C," for example, a sort of carved stone chest or coffer decorated with masked figures and motifs in the form of volutes—are suggestive of the style of Izapa, a proto-classic civilization of southern Mexico, on the Pacific side. Izapa, which Stirling visited in 1941, seems to have played the role of an intermediate phase between Olmecs and Mayas.

La Venta, which Matthew Stirling excavated subsequently with

Philip Drucker, appeared to be the real focal point of Olmec civilization. Just after the diggings were begun, four colossal heads were unearthed. Extraordinary monuments soon came to light: altar no. 5, the so-called "altar of the Quintuplets," bears bas-reliefs representing five "babies," at once human and feline, known as "were-jaguar babies," gesticulating in the arms of five adults wearing miters or rigid hats not unlike "bowlers"; one of these figures with a "baby" in its arms is leaning out of the niche carved into the anterior face of the monolith. Stela no. 3, a block of stone 4.26 meters high and weighing probably 50 tons, shows two figures facing each other, one of them relatively short and fat, dressed in a cape and a sort of skirt, and the other one taller, with a bony face and aquiline nose and wearing a goatee—hence the irreverent nickname "Uncle Sam" given him by archaeologists. Both figures are wearing very large, elaborate head ornaments, on which one can make out such motifs as masks, the head of a fish, plumes. Smaller figures, one of which is masked, brandishing unidentified objects (weapons?), seem to be hovering above the two figures facing each other. Both on account of the theme represented and the workmanship of the bas-relief, this stela no. 3 is one of the strangest and most fascinating masterpieces of Olmec art. The fact that vandals at some remote date in the past attacked it with hammers, thus deliberately destroying the face of the fat man and part of the body of "Uncle Sam," constitutes yet another of the many enigmas posed by this monument.

With its pyramid overgrown with luxuriant vegetation that hid its shape so that it was not seen to be a true pyramid until later, with the exquisite jade statuettes contained in caches and the astonishing "massive offerings" of blocks of serpentine buried in deep trenches, with its tombs—one of which has columns of basalt—its magnetite mirrors, its engraved "votive axes," and its stelae sculpted in bas-relief, and above all with its careful layout and orientation as revealed by the disposition of the monuments and the tombs, La Venta was obviously the ceremonial center—and doubtless the center of government and commerce as well—of a population that was fairly large and well enough organized to carry out gigantic work projects. Excavation of the site, conducted by both North American researchers (Drucker) and Mexican specialists (Piña Chan), continued until 1958; unfortunately, however, it lies directly above a petroleum deposit, and the bulldozers and derricks of Pemex, the national oil company, invaded the island of La Venta. The monoliths and all movable objects were hauled off either to the Villahermosa Museum or to the one in Mexico City, but considerable damage was done to the monuments and a "treasure hunt" that became a veritable free-for-all ensued, flooding the antiques market with countless extremely valuable jade pieces.[8] After so many centuries of total oblivion in the jungle and the marshes, the Olmec metropolis was aptly described by Michael Coe (1968b, p. 53) as the theater of "all the horrors of modern industrial civilization. An oil refinery belches fumes, an airstrip bisects the archaeological site. . . . La Venta has fallen victim to the oil under its surface and is dying in its own black blood."

It was not until 1955 that specimens of charred wood were recovered at La Venta. On being subjected to carbon-14 testing in the laboratories of the University of Michigan, these samples proved to date from between 1154 and 604 B.C.! This time it was not only the "Maya hypothesis" of Thompson and Sylvanus Morley that collapsed. Even Stirling and Drucker saw their "modest" estimate, which placed the flowering of Olmec civilization at the beginning of the Christian era, contradicted by the evidence provided by the carbon-14 method of dating. The first Olmecs had settled on the island of La Venta over three thousand years ago!

San Lorenzo, situated on the Río Chiquito, a tributary of the Coatzacoalcos River (state of Veracruz), approximately a hundred kilometers southwest of La Venta, was discovered and excavated by Stirling and Drucker in 1945 and 1946. In reality San Lorenzo consists of three sites: Tenochtitlán (thus named by a local schoolteacher in memory of the Aztec capital); San Lorenzo proper, two or three kilometers farther south; and Potrero Nuevo, approximately the same distance east. Stirling and Drucker brought to light some fifteen sculptures, among them five colossal heads. Michael D. Coe, a scholarly and energetic archaeologist from Yale, who had already directed important excavations in Central America, undertook in 1964 to carry on Stirling's research at San Lorenzo: he was to devote three years to this project, which resulted in a large number of astonishing finds.

The first surprising revelation: San Lorenzo had been a center of civilization *before* La Venta! After carbon-14 testing, the first Olmec remains at this site were assigned the date of 1200 B.C. Even before that date the region had been inhabited, the land cultivated, pottery used. Around 1200 B.C. a highly civilized people took over the plateau of San Lorenzo and sculpted stone there: no fewer than seventy-five monuments were found, among them admirable statues and seven colossal heads, all of purest Olmec style. Moreover, a rapid exploration of the site by magnetometer in 1968 led Michael Coe to estimate that many other monuments—at least thirty-five and perhaps even more—still lay buried in the ground.

A second unexpected discovery: the plateau of San Lorenzo, which

[8] Heizer, 1968, p. 13.

rises approximately 50 meters above the periodically inundated sa-
vanna below, is artificial! It was constructed by the hand of man by
dint of immense labor. The deep ravines that traverse it to the north,
the south, and the west, the twenty *lagunas,* or large ponds, that dot
its surface, the long embankments rising above the ground were all
deliberately built, out of earth and volcanic stone; all of it is man's
handiwork. It is difficult to say *why* it was so constructed. The plateau
is about 1200 meters long from north to south: several hundred
mounds were found, along a north-south axis, grouped together in
such a way as to form rectangular courts surrounded by pyramidal
structures. And finally, a system of underground conduits was discovered in 1967–68, made of stones hollowed out into a "U" and carefully fitted together. The portion unearthed is almost 200 meters long
and at least 30 tons of basalt were used to build it. Are these drainage
canals? Were these conduits connected to the *lagunas* or to one of
them? And for that matter, what were these *lagunas* used for? These
are all questions that we cannot answer. The only thing that is quite
obvious is that an unheard-of amount of ingenuity and human labor
was required to build this entire site of San Lorenzo out of nothing.

And finally, a third surprise: after having flowered for three hundred
years, this civilized center was abandoned. Numerous monuments
found by the archaeologists had been brutally shattered, the statues
decapitated and buried, the altars broken to pieces; the vandals had
even attacked the colossal heads, in which they had laboriously
chiseled out gashes and circular holes. One of the most striking traces
of what must have been an extraordinarily violent revolution is "monument no. 34," a very beautiful statue, representing a kneeling man,
whose head and arms (which must have been jointed and movable)
have been removed; the monumental piece is nonetheless proof of an
exceptional sculptural virtuosity. Coe (1968b, p. 86) explains these
acts of destruction as an explosion of "pent-up hatred and fury" against
the Olmec leaders: in the eyes of a people who had risen up in arms,
the monuments and statues doubtless symbolized the masters who
exacted tremendous physical labor from them.

In any event, the jungle had overgrown the abandoned site when,
around 600 B.C., other Olmecs—who had perhaps come from La
Venta—reoccupied it for three centuries. This recent period of San
Lorenzo, the so-called Palangana phase, ended around 300 B.C., and
it was not until around A.D. 900 that the region was repopulated—
but by that time Olmec civilization had been dead for over a thousand
years.

The list of Olmec sites is today a long one, and growing longer all
the time; all of them are in the southern half of the state of Veracruz
and on the western edge of Tabasco, where monuments, statues, and

carved hard stone pieces have been discovered in the course of the last few years. From El Viejón in the north to La Venta in the southeast, this region which is often described as the "heartland" of Olmec civilization and which Ignacio Bernal calls the Olmec "metropolitan area" covers approximately 18,000 square kilometers. With the exception of the volcanic mountains of Los Tuxtlas, whose average altitude is on the order of 600 meters, the entire region is no more than 100 meters above sea level. It is a vast alluvial plain traversed by the Papaloapán, Coatzacoalcos, and Tonalá rivers as well as their numerous tributaries. There are lagoons and swamps everywhere. Alfonso Caso has compared this region to Mesopotamia. Nowhere else in Mesoamerica has agriculture enjoyed such plentiful water resources, since in addition to the rivers there is abundant rainfall in two seasons (June–November and January–February). The soil along the riverbanks is enriched by deposits left by floodwaters. The vegetation, it is true, is so dense, and grows back so fast, that farmers must constantly clear their land, with implements for that purpose—made of stone in antiquity—and by burning it off. But on the whole the Olmecs had particularly fertile land at their disposal, quite suitable for growing crops even without fertilizer. The same method of cultivation is still used today in the tropical regions of Mexico: cutting down the trees and bushes, burning them, planting maize and beans by means of a simple digging stick, must have given the Olmecs exceptionally high returns. In any event, they were not obliged to confront the problems of arid soil and irregular rainfall that weighed so heavily on the civilizations of the high plateau. Their problem, rather, was the struggle against an excess of water and the creation of drainage systems such as that at San Lorenzo. It is quite likely that the soil and climatic conditions of their habitat enabled them to obtain two harvests a year.

Even today, as was surely true in antiquity as well, the jungle abounds in game of every sort: deer, tapirs, wild pigs, monkeys, pheasants, iguanas. It is probable that the Olmecs kept dogs and turkeys, animals domesticated in very early times on the American continent, but the destruction of any sort of bone remains, both human and animal, by the dampness and the acidity of the soil keeps us from being certain of this. Above all, the sea, the lakes, and the rivers furnished them with an inexhaustible supply of fish, crustaceans, shellfish, all foods rich in proteins and an excellent complement of the vegetable foods in their diet. The Olmec art of carving has left us numerous jade objects: models of boats, shells, aquatic birds. A sculpted stone slab from San Lorenzo (monument no. 58) represents an enormous fish. Certain stones found in excavations of various sites were no doubt weights for fishnets.

In a word, the inhabitants of this region had available to them rich

and diversified sources of food, and hence energy resources that neither their predecessors before the age of agriculture nor the cultiva-
tors of semi-arid lands possessed. Olmec civilization—with the enormous expenditure of physical labor that it required—was no doubt
made possible by the convergence of two modes of subsistence: the
cultivation of maize, invented in the "Cold Lands," on the central
plateau or in high valleys such as that of Tehuacán, and a fishing-
hunting-gathering complex from the "Hot Lands" along the seacoast
and the shores of the rivers. Transplanted to Olmec country, the still
stunted maize of the highlands found fertile soil, water, heat. Man
was able for the first time (around 2000 B.C.?) to combine the benefits
of two different technologies. This obviously does not mean that such
a convergence of agriculture and pre-agricultural patterns of life can
be regarded as the *cause* of Olmec civilization, nor can it be considered to be the origin. But we may regard it as certain that such a
conjunction of sources of energy constituted a *condition* of this origin.
The people, whoever they were, who were about to become the cre-
ators of Olmec civilization, who were about to build San Lorenzo and
La Venta, to sculpt stelae and altars, to carve delicate masterpieces
of green stone, were a people obliged to answer—let us here use a
favorite expression of Arnold Toynbee's—a "challenge" of nature. This
was a people faced with the necessity of felling trees, burning off
jungle, transporting enormous blocks of basalt, journeying far afield
to find jade and serpentine, constructing pyramids and ceremonial
courts—all this amid torrential rains and stifling heat, constantly
struggling against dense vegetation, lianas, insects, snakes. In order
to accomplish their task, it was necessary for them to fight nature
with every means at their disposal and conquer it. And doubtless they
were able to succeed in doing so thanks only to the abundance of food
resources available to them.

Seen from this point of view, the Olmec "metropolitan area," which
in our eyes seems to be so hostile to man, so inauspicious a place for
human settlement—even today it is a region that is only sparsely populated—offered in the past a conjunction of the most favorable conditions for the flowering of a high culture. It was certainly not by
sheer chance that Petén, so similar to the southern part of Veracruz
with its humid and torrid jungle, saw the birth of Maya civilization:
fishing probably did not play a major role in this region, but here too
one notes the conjunction of agriculture and hunting, of maize and
game.

The streams that flow through every part of Olmec territory—the
three rivers mentioned above, and their tributaries and subtributaries
that crisscross the entire region like a capillary network—undoubtedly contributed to the birth of a civilization: first of all because agri-

culture probably spread throughout the coastal "Hot Lands" by descending along these streams and becoming established along their banks; and secondly because in a region covered with vegetation so luxuriant that it is very nearly impenetrable, this network of rivers afforded man an easy means of moving about from place to place and of transporting heavy burdens on boats and rafts. There can be no doubt that the Olmecs used the rivers and the sea along their coasts to transport, for instance, enormous blocks of stone weighing 20 tons and more from the volcanoes of Los Tuxtlas to La Venta. In a region where there are no pack or draft animals or any other source of energy save men's muscle power, transportation by water is the most efficient of all means: more than two thousand years later, the Aztecs were to take advantage in similar fashion of their great lake, plying it in their canoes to conduct their commerce and wage their wars.

In 1942, a "round table" held at Tuxtla Gutiérrez brought together North American and Mexican archaeologists—European ones, alas, were kept from attending by historical circumstance—to try to settle the "Olmec problem." At that juncture, only partial traces of the complex at La Venta had come to light; very little was known about Tres Zapotes and San Lorenzo; and not a single date was available through carbon-14 testing, since the method had not yet been invented. The conference was therefore not able to settle once and for all the question that divided the camp arguing in favor of the priority of Olmec civilization and the camp that insisted that Maya civilization was the older of the two.

Today, however, it has been possible to situate the Olmecs in time as the first civilized people of Mesoamerica.

The Olmecs were the first to construct vast ceremonial centers, to sculpt bas-reliefs and statues in the round, to group together horizontal monoliths or "altars" and stelae, to carve hard stone. They invented symbols that remained in use up until the Spanish Conquest, more than two thousand years after them, and probably a system of writing and a highly perfected calendar as well. Their civilization flourished from Veracruz to Michoacán, from Guerrero to Costa Rica.

"It is no longer necessary to refer to the Olmec as 'little understood' or 'mysterious.' However, one basic mystery does remain to be solved: who were the Olmec and what were their antecedents?" This passage by Matthew Stirling[9] sums up quite well the present state of our knowledge.

Who were the Olmecs? And first of all, what did they look like? Is it possible for us to relate them to a particular ethnic group?

Their art provides us with any number of representations of the

[9] Stirling, 1968, p. 7.

human figure, but these documents must be interpreted with caution: the majority of the faces represented are not purely human, being a mixture, in varying proportions, of human and feline traits. Often the eyes and the nose are human, but the lower part of the face takes on the elongated form of the snout of a jaguar with great fangs. Even though the mouth may not be entirely that of this feline, it is frequently dealt with in such a way as to call a jaguar to mind: a thick upper lip, with the corners drawn downward—the "Olmec mouth," a feature so typical that it suffices to mark the origin of a figurine or a statue.

If we leave aside the humano-feline faces and the faces wearing masks (animal masks in particular), the human representations in Olmec art may be divided into four categories:

I. Faces so realistically rendered that they may be regarded as portraits: this is the case with the colossal heads, which probably represent individuals—dynasts, priests, or champion athletes.

II. Figures, sometimes shown full-length, such as the statue of the "Wrestler" of Uxpanapa, or those of stela no. 3 of La Venta and certain rock reliefs of Chalcatzingo, and those of the cave paintings of Oxtotitlán and Juxtlahuaca. Certain figurines of hard stone, such as the magnificent group that forms offering no. 4 of La Venta, or pottery figurines from Tlatilco or Las Bocas may also be assigned to this same category. Headless statues such as those from San Lorenzo are obviously more difficult to categorize. In any event, these numerous and concordant documents show us quite thickset individuals of average height, with outsize torsos in proportion to their legs. The lines of the body are curved, the figures fat if not downright obese; the neck is short and massive. Those figures that are naked are generally asexual, and representations of females are rare; one man shown in the bas-reliefs of Chalcatzingo is naked, with visible genitals. The male figures are quite often bearded, and sometimes have a mustache as well, as is the case of the Uxpanapa "Wrestler"; but many men are also hairless, with both their skulls and their faces shaved bare. The cheeks are full, the eyes are slanted, and the eyelids have an epicanthic fold (the "Mongoloid eye"), the nose is short and broad, the lips thick, and the mouth "disdainful" or "cruel"—in short, the "Olmec mouth."

III. A much rarer human type is that represented on stela no. 3 of La Venta, the "Uncle Sam" with an aquiline nose and an elongated chin with a goatee. He is notably taller and slimmer than the corpulent figure facing him.

IV. More or less human or more or less feline "babies," a wellnigh obsessive theme of Olmec religious art, borne in the arms of statues, or represented in bas-reliefs, or in the form of figures in hard stone or terra cotta. They are asexual, short and thickset, bald.

No doubt it is best to disregard this last category of human representations: the "babies" have a far too symbolic and mythical air about them to be regarded as realistic depictions of an ethnic type.

What are we to make of category III? Is the bearded figure of La Venta stela no. 3 a stranger, a visitor, as Covarrubias has suggested? It is possible, on the other hand, that a "tall and lanky" physical type with a bony face and an aquiline nose—somewhat resembling the "redskins" of North America or the ancient Indians of Patagonia—coexisted with the ethnic group most widely represented, that with squat, plump, rounded bodies and facial features.

Quite clearly, it is categories I and II that correspond most closely to the characteristic Olmec physical type. It should also be noted that every civilization tends to idealize the fundamental features of human beings in conformity with a certain "canon."

All the Greeks of antiquity did not necessarily resemble the Discus Thrower, all Egyptians of the era of Ikhnaton surely did not have the long, emaciated features so characteristic of the sculptures of Tell el 'Amarna. Since in the case of the Olmecs we lack any trace of bony remains—skeletons, as we have mentioned above, did not withstand the high acidity of the soil—we must look to the present-day Indians (very few in number) who live in the same region as the ancient Olmecs or close by. We know, naturally, that those we see in our day are not direct descendants of the Olmecs known to archaeology. The region has undergone the influence of migrations, of successive colonizations by various peoples, the Nahuas of the central plateau in particular. It is thus all the more remarkable that today, more than three thousand years after the beginnings of San Lorenzo and La Venta, one frequently observes in this zone Indians or even mestizos whose overall body proportions, torsos and faces that tend to be "fleshy," "Mongoloid" eyes, and above all "Olmecoid" mouths with drooping corners, bear a striking resemblance to those of stela figures and figurines of Olmec high antiquity.

Melgar thought he could discern "negroid" features in the colossal head of Hueyapan. In point of fact, neither this head nor the fifteen others known today can seriously be regarded as representing an African black. The eyes of the Hueyapan head are typically "Mongoloid," and the mouth bears only a vague resemblance to African sculptures, whereas it has very close ties to the whole of Olmec art. Jairazbhoy believed that he had been able to breathe new life into the theory of African origins, but his proof is not convincing. Moreover, if, as he claims, the origins of Olmec civilization can be traced back to the landing of a boatload of Egyptians in the region, why would these voyagers, once settled in Mexico, have taken the trouble to perpetuate in stone, at the cost of tremendous physical effort, the faces of their "Ethiopian slaves" rather than their own countenances? And why did they fail to leave a singly typically Egyptian figurine, a single Egyptian hieroglyph, among the thousands of Olmec artifacts that have now been discovered?

The most certain conclusion would seem to be that the Olmecs were American Indians, "Amerindians" belonging for the most part to an ethnic group of which certain physical features have been perpetuated for centuries down to our own day, and one which, perhaps, coexisted with a slightly different Amerindian group.[10]

We naturally do not know what language was spoken by the Olmecs of La Venta or San Lorenzo. However, a glance at the linguistic history and geography of southeastern Mexico allows us to make certain quite interesting hypothetical conjectures.

The Maya linguistic family, such as it exists today, may be seen to be divided into two groups: in the south and east of Mexico, in Guatemala, Belize, and Honduras, the dialects of Maya properly speaking, Tzeltal and Tzotzil, Quiché, Mam, etc.; in the north, Huastec is spoken in the northern part of Veracruz, in Tamaulipas, and in San Luis Potosí.

It is likely that these two languages or groups of languages, or, rather, the common proto-Maya from which they derive, originally covered a continuous area. Mexican traditions known to the Aztecs include a legend concerning the Huastecs, who are said to have been separated from the other tribes in very early times. A new science, still feeling its way along, glottochronology, is attempting to calculate the time that has elapsed between two or more linguistic phenomena, between, for example, the present state of two related languages or series of languages and the moment at which they separated from the common trunk. When history, based on written documents, permits the evolution of a language to be traced, there is no need to call upon the methods of glottochronology: we have, for instance, all the information necessary to follow the steps in the development that led from Latin to the dialect of the Oath of Strasbourg to medieval French to modern French. But if written documents are lacking, the comparison of vocabularies, lexicostatistics, and phonology may allow us to reach certain approximate conclusions. Using such methods, Morris Swadesh has estimated that the separation between Huastec and other Maya languages must have taken place around 3200 years ago.

[10] Andrzej Wiercinski (1972, p. 138) characterizes the type described in our category III above as "Armenoid." This label does not imply a "migration." This same author points to the "heterogeneous" nature of the Olmec population.

With this hypothesis as our point of departure, it would seem as though a non-Maya group had inserted itself like a wedge between the Huastecs and the Mayas, whereupon the Huastecs headed (or were driven) toward the north and the Mayas toward the east and south. This event would seem to have occurred at approximately the same time, around 1200 B.C., that Olmec civilization appeared at San Lorenzo and La Venta—in point of fact, in the center and the south of Veracruz. A coincidence perhaps, but a coincidence worth pondering. We cannot help but think that the people that shattered the unity of the proto-Mayas was also the people that brought Olmec civilization to the region.

Another hypothesis might also be considered, namely, that the Olmecs were themselves part of the Huasteco-Maya family. According to this theory, of all the subdivisions of this great linguistic family, their dialect alone failed to survive. Such a conjecture cannot be dismissed out of hand: who has any idea how many of the world's indigenous languages have totally disappeared! But if we accept this hypothesis, the fragility of proto-Maya Olmec makes it an exceptional case by comparison with the extraordinary resistance of Maya and its related dialects.

The Indians of the state of Veracruz speak either Nahua (in general the so-called *nahuat* variety, without the *tl* characteristic of Aztec) or dialects that are often pejoratively called *popoloca* and that belong to the Mixe-Zoquean linguistic family. The implantation of Nahua in this region is obviously a recent phenomenon. Mixe (the *popoloca* of Sayula and Oluta) and Zoque (the *popoloca* of the Sierra and of Texistepec) are ancient languages, firmly rooted in the states of Veracruz, Oaxaca, and Chiapas since antiquity. In the south of Veracruz, the implantation of these dialects corresponds precisely to the Olmec region from Tres Zapotes to San Lorenzo.

It was on the basis of this observation that Lyle Campbell and Terrence Kaufman put forward the hypothesis that the language of the Olmecs was most likely a proto-Mixe-Zoquean; in support of their argument, they studied in particular the borrowing of Mixe-Zoquean words by other indigenous Mesoamerican languages. According to them, words designating cultivated plants and foods (gourd, cocoa, tomato, bean, maize cake), animals (dog, turkey), ritual elements (copal, incense), techniques (weaving, fishing), etc., were borrowed from Mixe-Zoquean by other languages. These words are tantamount to a "cultural inventory" which would appear to be consonant with that of the Olmecs around the middle or in the second half of the second millennium B.C. Hence the conclusion arrived at by Campbell and Kaufman: "The Olmecs, at least in part, spoke Mixe-Zoque languages." But these two authors add that this is simply a hypothesis

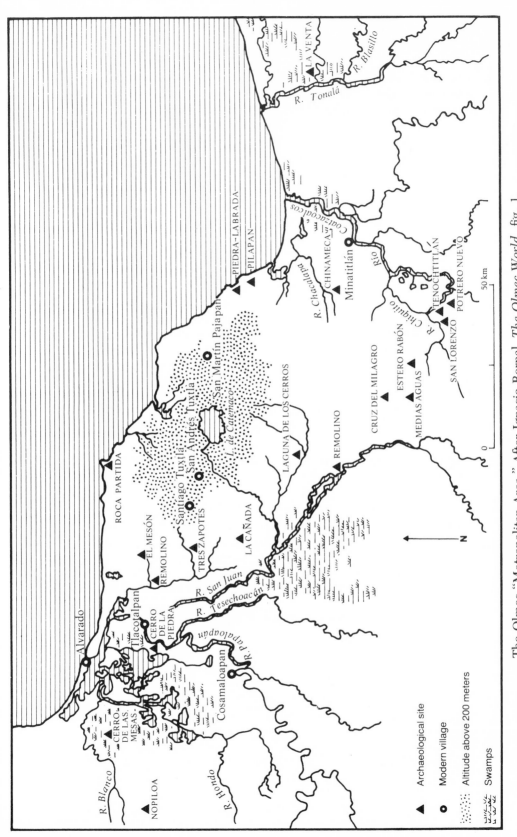

The Olmec "Metropolitan Area." After Ignacio Bernal, *The Olmec World*, fig. 1.

Archaeological site
Modern village
Altitude above 200 meters
Swamps

intended to stimulate further research. It is no doubt wisest to leave the matter there.

Jiménez Moreno, in turn, has suggested that the language of the "archaeological Olmecs" was related to Maya, but that certain among them may have spoken Zapotec. As we shall see, extremely old and profound relations and affinities existed between the Olmec "metropolitan area" and Zapotec country, in the valleys of Oaxaca. In this regard, Ignacio Bernal believes that in the "formative" era in question, around 1500 to 1200 B.C., Zapotec was not yet a separate language, but perhaps, he writes, we must postulate the existence of a "pre-Zapotec."[11]

There is thus no lack of hypotheses. But it is difficult to see how any definitive conclusion could be reached with regard to this problem of the language of the Olmecs.

Half a century after the word "Olmec" had been used for the first time—by Hermann Beyer in connection with a jade statuette and the monument of San Martín Pajapan, what at the time was merely a shadow, a presence hinted at behind a veil, has become a tremendous, fascinating reality. Each day brings a revelation, a sculpture, a mask . . . and we know that a whole world remains to be discovered. But already the fact of the Olmecs' existence dominates all the indigenous past of Mesoamerica, and perhaps in part that of autochthonous civilization in America in general.

Unlike the peoples of the Old World, such as the Sumerians or the Hittites, their civilization cannot be reconstructed from any written record they left behind. There are no cuneiform tablets, no bilingual inscriptions, no dictionaries for the use of scribes. It is through the arrangement of their ceremonial centers, through their exquisite carvings, through their engravings and rock paintings or their fragile pottery that the message of the Olmecs has come down to us.

[11] Bernal, 1969, p. 25, note 43.

# 2

⧮⧮⧮⧮⧮⧮

# The Heart of the Olmec World

At present between thirty and forty Olmec sites have been discovered, four of them in the state of Tabasco and the majority in the state of Veracruz. Of the total of 246 recorded pieces, over 180 are sculptures, stelae, altars, colossal heads found at La Venta, at San Lorenzo (including Tenochtitlán and Potrero Nuevo), and at Laguna de Los Cerros. At certain of these sites, only one object has been found, but of high quality, such as the statue in green stone of Las Limas, the "Prince" of Cruz del Milagro, or the "Wrestler" of Uxpanapa. It is evident that we are still very far from being able to draw up a definitive list of all the Olmec remains that have survived the ravages of time, the elements, and man, Archaeological excavations are difficult and costly. Many masterpieces of the art of sculpture or carving of the first civilized people of Mexico are undoubtedly still buried beneath vegetation and in the soil of the "metropolitan area." La Venta, which—to the best of our knowledge at present—is situated at the eastern limit of this area, was the first great site studied scientifically, though as yet incompletely. Above all others, its name is associated with Olmec civilization. Its principal monument is unique in Mexico. It is there that the civilization of the Olmecs reveals itself to us in all its fascinating originality.[1]

[1] We are here following for the most part the work of Beatriz de la Fuente, though we note that the list of sites mentioned at the beginning of her work (1973, p. 10) does not always correspond exactly to that of the index of monuments found at the end of it. Moreover, while it is true that the monuments of Cerro de Las Mesas date from the classic era, Stirling's excavations in 1960 (Stirling, 1968, p. 5) lead us to agree that this site was occupied by the Olmecs during a late phase of their civilization.

The island of La Venta, surrounded by marshes, is shaped like an elongated oval; its long north-south axis measures around 4.5 kilometers; its average width is 1200 meters, with a maximum of around 2 kilometers. Its surface is dotted with mounds in such a way as to form sets, or "complexes," which archaeologists have designated by letters: "complex A," "complex B," and so on; the one most recently discovered is called the "Stirling complex." Since Blom and La Farge's visit to La Venta in 1925 in the course of their explorations, the monument that towers over the entire site has been referred to as a "pyramid." Up until recently, published plans and diagrams showed this monument as a "classic" Mexican pyramid with a quadrangular base and a flat top. In reality, such dense vegetation covered this structure that no one was able to discern its actual shape until all the jungle growth around it was completely cleared away in 1968. The supposed "pyramid" was then seen to be a sharp-pointed cone, without a platform at the summit, and no ramp or stairway, with ten deep grooves, separated by raised ribs, carved into its sides. This strange monument is 34 meters high and 140 meters in diameter at the base; its volume has been calculated to be 99,000 cubic meters. It is thus a relatively small structure as compared, for example, to the pyramid of the Sun at Teotihuacán (840,000 cubic meters) or to that of the Moon in the same site (210,000 cubic meters).

Since no excavations have been carried out at this "pyramid" (it has become the customary usage to continue to designate it as such), it is impossible for us to say at the present time whether it contains earlier structures or tombs. In any event, it is a vast mound of beaten earth and clay, resting in part on a broad, low platform.

Unlike all other Mexican pyramids, it does not appear to have ever served as the base of a sanctuary. Its summit is not flat and there is no visible trace of any sort of access to this summit. More than the pyramids of the classic era in the center of Mexico or in Maya country, it is suggestive of the *yácatas* of Michoacán and of the circular constructions of the Huastecs, monuments of an archaic stage of architecture in which mounds, tumuli of heaped-up earth, were characteristically built. We could also mention for the sake of comparison the pseudo-pyramid of Cuicuilco, which may be briefly described as a truncated cone built of stones and earth. Nonetheless, the "pyramid" of La Venta is the only known monument with grooves or runs cut down its sides at regular intervals, giving it the appearance of a volcanic cone. This resemblance is quite striking: La Venta is about a hundred kilometers distant from the volcanoes of Los Tuxtlas, and it is in those mountains, at Cerro Cintepec, that the Olmecs quarried the blocks of basalt that they sculpted into altars or colossal heads. Important traces of the Olmecs lay hidden at Lake Catemaco, in the

Altar no. 4, La Venta. Now located in the Parque-Museo de La Venta in Villahermosa, state of Tabasco. (Courtesy of R. Roland–Ziolo, Paris.)

Altar no. 4, La Venta (detail). Now located in the Parque-Museo de La Venta in Villahermosa, state of Tabasco. (Courtesy of R. Roland–Ziolo, Paris.)

middle of the Sierra, and at the volcano of San Martín Pajapan. Could it be possible that the people of La Venta, descending from these mountains and settling on a low island in the middle of swampland, wished to build an imitation, an ersatz, volcano?

To the north of the "pyramid," a vast court, the "ceremonial court" of "complex A," had been constructed; it is a rectangle measuring 40 by 50 meters, surrounded by an enclosure consisting of prismatic columns, each of which weighs between 700 kilograms and 1 ton. It is bounded on the north by what is perhaps the platform of a pyramid, with steps (in a poor state of preservation). If we take careful note of the layout of the monuments (sculptures, colossal heads), the stelae, and the tombs, we perceive that the site was carefully planned, extending north and south of the "pyramid" along an axis oriented just slightly west (8 degrees) of true north. "Complex B," situated south of the "pyramid," has not been completely explored, although among the notable discoveries thus far made are a colossal head and several altars (the two that have been numbered 4 and 5) that figure among the most remarkable works of Olmec sculpture.

The zone situated to the north of the "pyramid" is much better known. The Olmecs executed (around 1000 B.C.?) enormous earthworks there. One of the most extraordinary features of these earthworks is the use of various clays—pink, red, yellow—and different-colored sands, thousands of tons of them, to construct foundations and differentiate various levels. This very original technique was used in particular in the execution of what appear to us to be "massive offerings."

What is a "massive offering" exactly? It consists first of all of an enormous trench (in one case 8 meters deep, 17 meters wide, and 20 meters long) dug in the spongy soil of the island. This trench was then filled up, first with more than 1000 tons of serpentine—that semiprecious stone that appears to have been highly prized by the Olmecs—in the form of juxtaposed slabs, and next with colored clays. The whole was then covered over with earth and completely hidden from men's sight. Three such offerings have been found. The three buried mosaics discovered, one north of the "pyramid" and two beneath the southern platforms of the ceremonial court, are even more surprising, although the technique utilized was similar. Each one of these mosaics is composed of 485 blocks of serpentine, covering a surface that measures approximately 5 by 7 meters; each of the three mosaics represents the stylized mask of a feline, a jaguar, its head crowned by four diamond-shaped ornaments. The greenish color of the serpentine stands out boldly against the yellows of the sand and clay filling the interstices. There is every reason to believe that these mosaics were buried immediately after having been set in place:

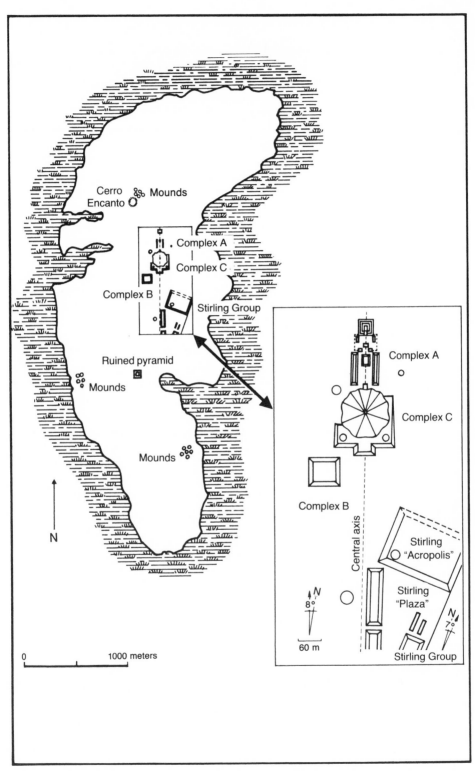

Plan of La Venta. After Ignacio Bernal, *The Olmec World*, fig. 2.

around three thousand years went by before human beings again set eyes on them.

What is the meaning of these interments of green stones, these buried jaguar masks? The only satisfactory hypothesis that has been put forward is that they were offerings to one or more deities—perhaps earth gods, the protectors of agriculture and the masters of plant foods. The jaguar god is undoubtedly an earth divinity.

We are confronted with yet another question: the origin of the materials used. Even the clays of various colors do not come from La Venta. The volcanic stones can scarcely come from anywhere else but the mountains of Los Tuxtlas. Cerro Cintepec appears to have furnished the basalt. As for the serpentine and the hard stones (jadeite, nephrite), we do not know from what place they might have been brought to La Venta; the nearest deposits would appear to have been in the mountains of Oaxaca, or a bit farther away in the Balsas River basin. It is utterly amazing that the Olmecs of La Venta could have devoted so much energy to searching out, extracting from the earth, transporting over long distances, fashioning, and finally burying such tremendous quantities of heavy stones.

An offering of small objects, laid out in the form of a cross, was discovered above the layer of clay covering the jaguar mask of the southeast platform. This offering consisted of twenty small polished axes, carved from jade or serpentine, and a concave mirror made of hematite. Seven of these mirrors in all have been discovered at La Venta. They are made of hematite, magnetite, or ilmenite, and a specialist, J. E. Gullberg, has written (p. 282): "It is impossible to reconstruct the technique used in making these concave mirrors. . . . They have a gracefulness, dignity, and perfection that makes it hard to think of them as . . . only ornamental. The concave side has received a care that would seem to go beyond the standards of even superb lapidaries." What could these mirrors have been used for? All of them except one have perforations in them that seem to indicate that they might have been strung on a necklace. One figurine from La Venta in fact is shown wearing a small mirror as a pectoral. Experiments have demonstrated that these mirrors could be used to focus the sun's rays to light a fire. Perhaps Olmec priests wore these mirrors on their breasts and used them for lighting sacred fires, especially those intended to set the jungle ablaze, the first step in the cultivation of maize.[2]

Nineteen offerings of small objects have been discovered in "caches" in various places within the ceremonial complex to the north of the

[2] Setting the jungle on fire is an important religious act among the (Maya) Lacandones of Chiapas. The fire can be lighted only according to a certain ritual (using a "fire stick").

pseudo-pyramid. The Olmecs were thus the originators of a practice that we find again later in Mesoamerica, among the classic Mayas in particular: that of burying precious objects near monuments, at the foot of walls, under stairways, etc. These offerings at La Venta consist of various categories of objects: small polished axes made of jade, serpentine, diorite, basalt, or schist; figurines, pendants, ear ornaments, necklace pieces in hard stone; models of pirogues, made of jade; miniature jade masks ("maskettes"), representing the face of a jaguar; concave mirrors; earthenware vessels in the form of bowls or basins. The number of objects contained in these caches is often considerable: 895 (necklace pieces) in offering no. 9, for instance, and 1180 (also necklace pieces) in offering no. 11. But even more than the sheer number of objects, it is their extraordinary artistic quality that attracts our attention and calls forth our admiration. Two offerings are deserving of special mention in this respect. The one to which the number 2 has been assigned, found buried along the central axis of the site, contains 51 small polished axes, 14 of which are made of jade. Five of these axes have been decorated with delicately incised designs, one of which is particularly clear and represents a fine Olmec-style head seen in profile, wearing a sort of pointed cap.

But it is above all offering no. 4 that may be regarded as being one of the most extraordinary discoveries ever made at La Venta. Immediately to the west of the platform situated to the northwest of the ceremonial court, just opposite the midpoint of this platform, a strange treasure was found buried at a depth of approximately 60 centimeters in a cache measuring 51 by 35.6 centimeters. In this cavity, standing upright in the sandy soil, were 16 marvelously finished figurines, 2 of them in jade, 13 in serpentine, and one in reddish volcanic stone. This latter figurine was standing with its back to a row of 6 small jade columns set vertically in the back of the cache; the 15 other figures, arranged in a half-circle, were facing it.

All these figurines are of the purest Olmec style. They represent men (though their genitals are not indicated in any way) standing with their legs slightly bent. Their heads, which are very large in proportion to their bodies, are clearly misshapen from having had their skulls bound in infancy. They are bald and beardless; they have the slanting eyes, the mouth with thick lips and downturned corners of the Olmec convention. The little jade columns bear traces of incised designs; it is possible that they were obtained by sawing up a slab of jade incised previously. The figurines themselves were probably carved a fairly long time before being deposited in the cache: they have nicks and cracks in them, and certain of them have lost a foot or part of an arm. Those who assembled this exceptional offering thus would appear to

Tomb A, La Venta. Now located in the Parque-Museo de La Venta in Villahermosa, state of Tabasco. (Courtesy of R. Roland–Ziolo, Paris.)

have gathered together objects that had been fashioned at some earlier time.

The cavity containing this collection of objects had been filled with sand, then hidden beneath several layers of orange, pink, yellow, and white clay. But later on—no one can say when—someone—no one can say who—dug a vertical hole, situated directly above the precise center of the cache, down through the layers of clay. This hole, which no doubt was made in order to verify that the offering was still in the cache below, was then plugged up again; the debris of the upper layers used to fill this "inspection shaft" shows clearly what happened. We may safely conclude that the Olmecs possessed accurate plans or diagrams that enabled them to determine exactly where caches of this quality were located.

But what is the meaning of the scene represented by this offering? The physical type of the figures, their misshapen skulls, their ear ornaments indicate that they were dignitaries of some sort, religious or otherwise; they surround and appear to be listening intently to the only personage not represented by a jade or serpentine figurine. Does this scene commemorate a council in the course of which momentous decisions were made? Or is this group of nobles or priests in the act of performing a rite before the miniature colonnade formed by the vertical pieces of jade? It is perhaps worth pointing out that none of these personages is holding any sort of object in his hands, cradling a "baby" in his arms, or brandishing any sort of weapon; in this respect they are notably different from numerous other Olmec sculptures. This observation would seem to favor the hypothesis that the scene represents a "council" rather than a "rite."

The statuettes constituting this offering had been daubed with bright red pigment. The same custom was observed in the case of burials. "Tomb A," to the north of the "pyramid," is exceptional in that it was built with basalt columns and then covered with a mound of earth, and also because it still contains a few bones, an extremely rare phenomenon at La Venta. Two very young persons, perhaps children, had been interred there beneath a layer of red ocher. When they were buried, a precious collection of funeral offerings was placed alongside them: figurines, among them a female wearing a little hematite mirror on her breast, ear ornaments, two jade hands; two obsidian disks; a concave magnetite mirror; a jade pendant in the form of a shell.

Farther south a sarcophagus 2.81 meters long was found, containing practically no remaining traces of human bodies, but with walls daubed with red ocher. One of the ends of this stone coffer bears a splendid bas-relief representing the face of the feline god, with its eyebrows in the form of flames, its short broad nose, its protruding arched upper lip, its two fangs curving backward. Its forked tongue, however, calls to mind not that of a jaguar but rather that of a serpent. Inside the sarcophagus, ear ornaments and a serpentine figurine had been buried along with the deceased.

Altars, stelae, and colossal heads are characteristic of the art of La Venta.

The term "altar" is no doubt an improper one in this context: there is no indication that any sort of rite was performed round about these aboveground monoliths. Be that as it may, of the seven "altars" discovered at La Venta, five have on one face, which we may consider to be the anterior face, a niche from which a figure is emerging; and in two cases (altars no. 2 and no. 5) this figure is holding a "baby" across its forearms. The principal figure of altar no. 4 is squatting in a niche surmounted by the stylized snout of the jaguar. It is holding in its hands a cord tied to the wrist of another figure shown in bas-relief on the right-hand face of the monument.

Altar no. 3 is badly damaged. It is nonetheless possible to make out a niche on the anterior face from which there emerges a figure sculpted very nearly in the round. Two seated figures and one standing one appear on the lateral faces: one of the seated men has a long pointed beard.

The "baby" motif attains its maximum development, as we have noted above, in the case of altar no. 5, on which five small infants are represented, one lying stretched out across the forearms of the main figure, and four others who appear to be thrashing about in the arms of four adults on the lateral faces.

Despite the erosion that these sculptures have undergone, it is still possible to make out any number of characteristic details: elaborate headdresses, miters, hats, girdles, skirts, and loincloths; ear ornaments, necklaces, pectorals. We can also make out representations of the most common "Olmec" physical type, as well as certain figures with convex noses and thin lips.

Altar no. 5, La Venta. Now located in the Parque-Museo de La Venta in Villahermosa, state of Tabasco. (Courtesy of R. Roland–Ziolo, Paris.)

Of the five stelae of La Venta, the first to have been discovered by Blom and La Farge (stela no. 1) is a basalt monolith 2.50 meters high. On it, shown full-face, is a figure standing in a rigid pose in a niche. It is wearing a sort of round helmet decorated with a medallion on the front, earrings, and a pleated skirt that extends from its waist to its knees. The badly eroded upper edge of the niche resembles the stylized jaguar mask that surmounts the niche of altar no. 4. This stela leaves us with an impression of relative "primitiveness": the rigidity of the figure, the simplicity of the garments, the absence of other iconographic elements.

Stela no. 2, found in "complex C" to the south of the pseudo-pyramid, is altogether different in appearance. In this case, a central figure stands out in high relief, holding obliquely across his torso an object (an ax?) with a fairly long handle. His head is surmounted by a bizarre tri-level headdress. The "Olmec" face, with its almond eyes, its broad nose, its full cheeks, its wide mouth, has a beard—which may well be a false one. The body is short and squat. Around this figure are six other smaller human forms, in bas-relief, brandishing indefinable objects. They are masked, and are wearing head orna-ments, loincloths, and flowing mantles.

Stela no. 3 is no less elaborate: it is the one that depicts the meet-ing, the conversation between an Olmec-type figure and "Uncle Sam." Here too we may note six smaller figures that seem to be flying about the two principal figures.

The other known stelae are so eroded that it is impossible to make out a single detail on them.

Ought we to include among the stelae monument no. 13, a conical block of basalt whose sculpted portion, very nearly circular in shape, measures 80 centimeters in diameter? Despite its overall shape, this bas-relief bears a resemblance to the art of the stelae. Unlike Beatriz de la Fuente, I consider this monument to be Olmec. The face, which is bearded, is suggestive of that of the "Wrestler" of Uxpanapa. The figure is shown in profile, in the attitude of a man walking. He is holding in his left hand an object that could be a paddle or a banner. On his head is a voluminous turban that extends downward in the back to form a sort of flowing scarf. He is wearing a necklace, a nose ornament, a loincloth, and sandals decorated with ribbons or feathers. But the most important feature of this sculpture is the fact that the "Ambassador," as this figure is sometimes called, is surrounded by four characters, or glyphs, that give every appearance of belonging to some system of writing. To the left of him is a glyph clearly repre-senting a footprint. If we venture a comparison of this bas-relief with Mixtec or Aztec codices, the meaning of this sign is: "to advance on foot, to walk along"—which fits exactly the attitude in which the fig-

Altar no. 5, La Venta (detail). Now located in the Parque-Museo de La Venta in Villahermosa, state of Tabasco. (Courtesy of R. Roland–Ziolo, Paris.)

ure is depicted. To his right are three other superposed signs, which unfortunately are worn almost completely away. The second one from the top might be taken, however, to represent a flower, and the third the head of a bird with a hooked beak, seen in profile.

The problem of Olmec writing will be dealt with later (see Chapter 9). It will suffice to note here that at least one other monument of La Venta, no. 15, regarded as being unquestionably Olmec, bears a sculpted glyph. Moreover, we might point out that the "Ambassador" and monument no. 15 were both discovered in the same area ("complex A") of the La Venta site, by Stirling in 1943.

Four colossal heads (monuments nos. 1 to 4) from the La Venta site are housed at present in the Villahermosa Museum. They are enormous basalt monoliths, weighing from 11 to 24 tons each; three of them (nos. 2, 3, and 4) were lined up along an east-west axis to the north of the ceremonial court, while monument no. 1—that is, the head discovered by Blom and La Farge in 1925—was located south of the "pyramid." Two characteristics of these sculptures are immediately evident: in the first place, they are not more or less mythical beings, endowed with feline features or wearing masks, but realistic statues; and secondly, these heads are at one and the same time very much alike and highly individualized. Their similarities are quite obvious and leap to the eye: the same broad faces with full cheeks, the same fleshy protuberances just above the bridge of the nose, the same almond-shaped eyes. The nose is large, the lips full, the mouth generally bow-shaped with downturned corners. These heads are surmounted by helmets that have often been likened to those of football players. The general proportions of these four sculptures are identical, and it is quite probable that the respective dimensions of the helmet and the face and those of the various features correspond to one and the same veritable "canon," thereby leading us to believe that these monuments were all sculpted within a relatively brief period, on the order of two centuries. Yet when we examine these heads more closely, we perceive that each one of them possesses individual characteristics, despite the fact that the erosion or the vandalism that they have undergone has tended to efface them somewhat. We thus note, for example, that head no. 1 and, to an even greater degree, head no. 4 are markedly prognathous, while heads no. 2 and no. 3 have flattened faces. Unlike the others, head no. 2 has a "smiling" mouth; even though the expression of this face has perhaps been exaggerated due to the erosion that has completely worn away its upper lip, it is nonetheless evident that the mouth is horizontal and that its corners do not appear to conform to the most common model. Furthermore, the helmets and the ear ornaments differ from one head to

Monument no. 5, known as "La Abuela," La Venta. Now located in the Parque-Museo de La Venta in Villahermosa, state of Tabasco. (Courtesy of Myriam de la Croix, Paris.)

the other; certain helmets are decorated with a bas-relief motif which (especially in the case of head no. 1) might well be a glyph.

In view of all of the above, it is difficult to escape the conclusion that these heads are portraits, those of persons so powerful and so venerated that—either during their lifetime or after their death—immense effort was expended to quarry these enormous blocks of stone in the Sierra de Los Tuxtlas, transport them to La Venta, and sculpt their effigies in them.

Ninety sculptures have been found strewn about the island, half buried in the ground for the most part, and no doubt there are a great many others still hidden beneath the surface. We shall here limit ourselves to pointing out some of these ninety monuments that, for various reasons, are particularly worthy of note.

We should mention, first of all, the figure known as "La Abuela," "Granny," the nickname given it in 1940 by the workers who were excavating the site under Stirling's direction. (In the official nomenclature of the site it is "monument no. 5.") This monument is a basalt statue 1.42 meters high, discovered in the ceremonial court to the north of the "pyramid." It represents a vaguely female kneeling figure, holding a rectangular receptacle in its hands at chest level. The figure as a whole is squat and heavyset. The face is extremely broad and the mouth is that of a feline. A sort of hood covers its head, widening out to form a cape draped over its shoulders. Worn away by time and the elements, this statue nonetheless gives the striking impression of an unusually powerful, concentrated force.

Several pieces of statuary depict figures seated cross-legged, either holding a bar in their hands (monument no. 8) and thus reminiscent of the San Martín Pajapan statue, or else with their arms hanging down at their sides (no. 9) or resting on their ankles (no. 10). One of these seated statues (no. 11) is leaning backward, its head with jaguar features tilted upward. Quite a few of these statues have been disfigured; their heads, arms, hands are missing (nos. 23, 30, 31, 38, 40), but even today we are struck by the beauty of these mutilated bodies.

Monument no. 44, which was not discovered until 1968, buried nearly a meter beneath the surface, to the east of the "Stirling complex," is merely a fragment of a larger basalt sculpture that was deliberately shattered. What remains of it bears a striking resemblance to the San Martín Pajapan monument; the lower part of this fragment is a human Olmec-type face framed by two large ear pendants in the form of masks; the upper part is a humano-feline face. A fluorescent study of the basalt has proved that the stone came from the same deposit as that of the Pajapan monument.

Rather ironically, one of the most beautiful and most significant of the bas-reliefs of La Venta (monument no. 19) was discovered by accident, in 1944 or 1945, by Pemex workers who were constructing an airstrip northwest of "complex A." Exceptionally well preserved, this piece of light gray basalt represents a human figure seated with his legs stretched out in front of him and framed by a gigantic rattle-snake. His head is surrounded by the gaping jaws of an animal (a feline?). Below his chin is a little goatee. In his right hand he is hold-ing a square object with a handle that may be a pouch (an incense sack?) or the ritual object in the form of a "padlock" or a small buckler that we shall discuss in further detail below (see Chapter 8). Above and in front of his head is a cartouche in the form of a square, which is blank (though the area inside this square may have been painted?), surmounted by two motifs with crisscrossed bands.

As for the serpent, it towers majestically over the entire scene. Its tail shows the characteristic rings of the species. Its head, with its gaping jaws, its eye surmounted by an elongated protuberance, like a crest, prefigures that of all the countless serpents of the pre-Colum-bian art of Mesoamerica. Ought we to interpret this latter feature as a plume and confer on this animal the honor of being the oldest "Plumed Serpent" in Mexico? Let us merely say that it is "beyond a doubt one of the meanest-looking reptiles in Mesoamerican art."[3]

Though the island of La Venta is outstanding because of the num-ber and the quality of its sculptures and carvings, pottery, on the other hand, is rare there. This fact is obviously related to the very nature of the site, a ceremonial center and a center of government, but a place where doubtless only a very small number of people, a religious and administrative or military elite, lived. The majority of the population, which provided La Venta with manpower and food, contributing to this center its labor, its skills, and its harvests, must have been scattered over a wide area surrounding the island, though subject to its authority; perhaps founded on the respect inspired by the gods, this regime maintained its own stability and the cohesion of the autochthonous society over which it ruled for six or seven centu-ries (from approximately 1100 to 400 B.C.).

In a first phase (from circa 1100 to 1000 B.C.), the earliest Olmecs to arrive at La Venta began to build the "pyramid" and lay the ground-work for the ceremonial center. Had the island been inhabited before them? It would appear so: in the fill of the earliest mounds of the ceremonial court what seem to be fragments of several layers of col-ored clays have been found; in all probability these were the rubble of previous constructions destroyed during phase I.

Phase II, which extends from 1000 to 800 B.C., was a period of extraordinary activity. The "massive offerings" begin during this pe-riod and continue during phases III and IV, from 800 to 400 B.C. The

---

[3] Drucker, Heizer, and Squier, p. 199.

Monument no. 19, La Venta (copy). Now located in the Parque-Museo de La Venta in Villahermosa, state of Tabasco. (Courtesy of R. Roland–Ziolo, Paris.)

offerings of jade figurines, the tombs containing precious treasures date from these latter centuries, which saw the apogee of the ceremonial center to the north of the pseudo-pyramid.

What happened four centuries before the Christian era? The end of the civilization of La Venta remains shrouded in mystery. The one thing that we can say for certain is that between 450 and 325 B.C. all activity on the island ceased. No more buildings were erected, no more trenches dug in which to bury the serpentine offerings, no more caches filled with jade figurines. The ruling elite disappeared: driven out, exterminated, or departed into exile of its own accord? Whatever the answer, the island remained unoccupied, and the wind covered it over with drifts of sand; and then, though we do not know exactly by whom, or when, another period of activity began—unfortunately one of destruction and pillage this time. Monuments were shattered, statues decapitated, stelae damaged by hammerblows. The vandals dug shafts, doubtless in the hope of discovering jade treasures. Then they too abandoned the island, whose peace remained undisturbed until our own day, which saw the arrival first of a few Mexican peasants searching for land to cultivate, then that of archaeologists, and finally that of petroleum workers.

The site of San Lorenzo, or rather the series of sites along the Río Chiquito, namely San Lorenzo, Tenochtitlán, and Potrero Nuevo, to the south of Minatitlán, is quite different. The excavations directed by Stirling and Drucker in 1945 and 1946, and those by Michael D. Coe, with Richard Diehl and Francisco Beverido, from 1965 to 1968, revealed the importance of these three localities, along with the ranch known as "Los Idolos," between San Lorenzo and El Mixe, which there is good reason to regard as forming part of this same complex. There are more numerous traces of dwellings than at La Venta, first of all, and thus far no offerings of semiprecious stones or tombs full of treasures have been found. On the other hand, the monumental sculpture of San Lorenzo is of prodigious quality; the number of colossal heads, statues, and bas-reliefs already unearthed is on the order of eighty, and doubtless many others still lie hidden below ground.

Stirling discovered five colossal heads, and Coe unearthed three more, plus one (monument no. 19) almost destroyed by unknown vandals. The other heads are in good condition for the most part, even those that bear the traces of attempts to break them open or shatter them. The individuality of each of these sculptures leaps to the eye. The features, the facial expressions, the elaborate headdresses make each of these monoliths different from all the others, though naturally all of them correspond to a general "canon" resembling that of the colossal heads of La Venta.

At San Lorenzo as at La Venta, there were found quadrangular "altars" with a niche carved in their anterior face, in which a figure in high relief is seated cross-legged; either it is holding an infant in its arms or else its arms are hanging down along its torso with its hands resting on the ground alongside its knees: in other words, we find here, once again, the two conventional attitudes of the figures sculpted in the niches of the La Venta altars. One of the lateral faces of altar no. 14 at San Lorenzo shows a figure sculpted in bas-relief that is a masterpiece of craftsmanship. The face is seen in profile, the torso in three-quarter view, with the left shoulder forward. The details of the headdress and the ornaments, fortunately in quite a good state of preservation, are worthy of note: the figure is wearing a round hat on its head, with a thick brim from which five oval elements (drops of water?) are suspended, and the crown of the hat is surmounted by a bird's claw; its hair falls over its shoulders; hanging from its ears are pendants ending in a sort of hook; around its neck is a necklace consisting of two rows of quadrangular plaques (of jade?); below it is a seven-pointed pectoral which may be interpreted as being a shell in cross section. Strange as it may seem, and even though at the present time we are unable to draw any definite conclusion therefrom, the fact remains that the ear ornament described above and the pectoral in the form of a shell were—more than two thousand years later!—the characteristic adornments of the Plumed Serpent, Quetzalcoatl, worshiped by the Toltecs and the Aztecs.

Another altar (monument no. 2 of Potrero Nuevo) inaugurates what was to become a long tradition, evidence of which we find again at Chichén Itzá, for instance, in the eleventh century A.D.: namely, a stone tablet supported by atlantes. Another monument (no. 18 of San Lorenzo), although badly damaged, appears to be quite similar. In both cases, two short, squat figures, obese dwarfs, serve as supports of the upper part of the monument, in the form of a slab. The figures of monument no. 18 are each holding a polished stone ax in one hand. These figures are of the usual "Olmec" type, with no feline features, however.

Certain statues, on the other hand, represent supernatural beings, whose overall appearance is human (they are standing erect on their lower limbs, they have arms and hands, the upper part of their heads and faces is human) but whose noses and mouths are feline in form. Two magnificent examples of such figures merit special mention: monument no. 52—discovered in 1968 beneath a layer of earth through the use of a magnetometer—is one of the finest specimens of the purest Olmec style; on its chest is a glyph in the form of a St. Andrew's cross. Monument no. 10, of comparable aesthetic quality, has another particularly interesting characteristic as well: this humano-feline being is holding in its hands, against its breast, two of

Monument no. 52, San Lorenzo. Museo Nacional de Antropología,
Mexico City. (Courtesy of J. Garcia-Ruiz, Paris.)

the enigmatic objects in the form of small bucklers or "knuckle-dusters" that we find (see Chapter 8) in a number of representations of Olmec figures.

Although its head is missing, the statue of a kneeling man (monument no. 34) is proof of the extraordinary level of craftsmanship attained by Olmec sculpture in this zone. This statue has one unusual feature: it must have had articulated arms that fitted into a large disk at the shoulder. We find this conception again in the more recent civilizations of Veracruz and Teotihuacán. Another very fine statue has been called the "Scribe." It may be a statue of a woman; in any event, the figure is shown sitting cross-legged, holding in its hands a cylindrical bar resting on its thighs. In this case too the head is missing. The attitude of the figure is at once natural and majestic.

There are many representations of animals: a feline (monument no. 7), known as the "Lion"; a seated jaguar (monument no. 37); a strange fish (monument no. 58) sculpted in bas-relief on a broad slab, with a large St. Andrew's cross incised on the body, and a head, oddly enough, ending in a jaguar's snout; an insect or a spider (monument no. 43) with a disk enclosing five points arranged in a quincunx engraved on its head, a glyph that resembles the Maya one for the sun, *kin*, and the Aztec one for turquoise, *xiuitl*. [4]

In 1945 Stirling discovered a sort of fountain or water reservoir in sculpted and engraved stone (monument no. 9, now in the Jalapa Museum) whose overall shape is that of an aquatic bird, with wings bearing five feathers and with three-toed webbed feet. A hole hollowed out in one of its walls has the same dimensions as the conduits of the San Lorenzo drainage system. On the body of the bird, on the portion corresponding to the breast, three figures are engraved: in the center is a very realistic duck with its wings spread and its bill open; on either side of it are wavy lines obviously meant to represent running water.

At Potrero Nuevo (monument no. 3) and at Tenochtitlán (monument no. 1), Stirling's excavations brought to light two sculptures, unfortunately very badly damaged, which may have a profound mythological meaning. Both of them appear to represent a woman lying on her back with a jaguar on top of her. Stirling (1955, pp. 8 and 19) interprets these two pieces as being the representation of the sexual coupling of the feline and the woman. Such an interpretation seems highly plausible when we think of the obsession with the jaguar in Olmec art and religion. Might the "babies" with jaguar features, the humano-feline figures, have been born of the carnal embrace of the

---

[4] In Aztec culture, turquoise symbolized fire, the light of the sun, and the 365-day year, which was also called *xiuitl*.

jaguar god and a mortal woman? It is regrettable that the two monuments have been so badly disfigured, thus making any interpretation of them extremely problematical. While Stirling is inclined to see them as representing the love of a feline and a woman, Beatriz de la Fuente and C. W. Clewlow, Jr., remain skeptical. The latter notes, however: "All the local men with whom I talked in San Lorenzo rather proudly explained this sculpture as representing a sexual act, doing so in most cases with wry grins on their faces." But this local reaction is obviously of no very great importance.

It has occurred to Clewlow (p. 83) to compare these pieces with another Olmec sculpture found at Laguna de Los Cerros (state of Veracruz) in 1960 by the Mexican archaeologist Alfonso Medallín. But according to the description of this sculpture published by the latter, it represents, not a feline and a human, but rather two human figures, one seated on top of the other; Medellín is of the opinion that this scene shows "the surrender and humiliation of a vanquished enemy." Hence we cannot place this sculpture in the same category as the Potrero Nuevo and the San Lorenzo monuments.

On the other hand, we may well weigh the question of whether or not the bas-reliefs sculpted in the living rock at Chalcatzingo, which we shall analyze below (see Chapter 4), depict scenes comparable to those perhaps represented in the two sculptures just mentioned. In point of fact, bas-relief no. 4 of this site (see Gay, 1971, pp. 54–55) depicts two fearsome-looking jaguars, with fangs and claws bared, in the act of leaping upon two human beings lying on the ground. There are no indications as to the sex of these two figures. Gay regards this scene as a reference to a myth of destruction of the human species by jaguars, analogous to the one whereby the Aztecs explained the end of the first universe, the *Ocelotonatiuh*, "the sun of the jaguar." This hypothesis is not at all unlikely. Nor is it beyond the realm of possibility that the Olmec group that had settled at Chalcatzingo, so far from their homeland, sought to engrave upon the face of the rock cliff the traditional images commemorating one of the most important myths of their mental universe.

But let us return now to San Lorenzo. The Olmecs, who, from around 1200 B.C. on, sculpted stones with such a masterful hand, who shaped their plateau at the cost of such tremendous physical effort and constructed a system of subterranean conduits and artificial ponds whose meaning or function we do not yet understand, seem suddenly to appear on the scene as a people already the masters of their characteristic technique and their characteristic art. We must hence grant the fact that they came from another region, where they had learned to transport and sculpt blocks of stone: perhaps, as Michael Coe suggests, they came from the mountains of Los Tuxtlas. As we have already seen, the form of the pseudo-pyramid of La Venta made us look toward these volcanoes and this mountain range rich in basalt. At San Lorenzo as at La Venta, the problem of how these enormous monoliths were to be transported had to be confronted and resolved.

Certain sculptures that have a "primitive" look about them, monument no. 40, for instance, a fragment of a column on which a face and rudimentary hands are carved in bas-relief, might well have been the work of the very first Olmec occupants of the site, or even of a pre-Olmec people. In any event, the flowering of San Lorenzo took place between 1200 and 900 B.C. To our present knowledge, it is thus the oldest Olmec site. But it was at La Venta, not at San Lorenzo, that some of the most brilliant aspects of this autochthonous civilization, in particular the practice of making offerings of semiprecious stones and the carving of jade, were developed.

Proof of the catastrophe that brought the civilization of San Lorenzo to an end is afforded us by the traces of the fury with which these sculpted monuments were attacked. All of the colossal heads—save one—withstood these furious onslaughts, which nonetheless left their mark on them in the form of circular holes. Other pieces were hammered to bits, completely shattered. It was no doubt necessary to hoist heavy blocks of stone above certain monuments and let them fall from considerable heights to achieve this sledge-hammer effect. This work of destruction must have involved tremendous labor, whereupon the mutilated statues, the fragments of sculptures were buried deep in the ground.

More humble than stone, terra cotta pieces managed to escape this wave of revolt or revenge. San Lorenzo is rich in ceramic pieces, in typically Olmec figurines in particular. Numerous fragments of white pottery have been found in the diggings at San Lorenzo: they are shards of figurines or hollow statuettes comparable to those of Tlatilco and Las Bocas, on the central plateau. "In subject matter, the entire range from human beings to jaguars is covered; figurines depicting the so-called 'one-eyed god' are also found, as well as ball players," Michael Coe (1968a, p. 46) writes.

The pottery discovered at San Lorenzo, belonging to the "Palangana" phase, between 600 and 300 B.C., resembles that of La Venta quite closely. It would therefore seem that it was Olmecs from La Venta who briefly reoccupied the San Lorenzo site, erecting in the center of the plateau a series of mounds forming a ceremonial court modeled after the one at their place of origin, although smaller in size.

La Venta and San Lorenzo have one feature in common: neither of these two great sites was occupied by the Olmecs after the fifth or, at the very latest, the fourth century B.C. Such is not the case at

Terra cotta figurine, Las Bocas. (Courtesy of Museum of the American Indian, New York.)

Tres Zapotes, formerly called "Hueyapan," the site where the first known colossal head was discovered by Melgar; at Tres Zapotes what are unquestionably Olmec remains, clearly contemporary with the flowering of La Venta and San Lorenzo, coexist with more recent monuments. Do they represent a "late Olmec" or an "early classic" phase? Might these "late Olmecs" not have been "pre-Mayas"? These are difficult questions to answer, since our knowledge of this archaeological zone is still quite sketchy. More thorough and more extensive excavations at much deeper levels would be necessary in order for us to have a more definite picture of the history of this site.

The remains found at Tres Zapotes may be roughly divided into two categories: those, firstly, that undoubtedly are those of an Olmec civilization of the La Venta type; and secondly, those that appear to be more recent or of a style related to that of other civilizations. Bernal (1969, p. 107) finds evidence for dividing the chronology of Tres Zapotes into four phases: a very early phase (1500–1200 B.C.); a middle phase (1200–600 B.C.), contemporary with La Venta and San Lorenzo; an "Upper Tres Zapotes I" (600–100 B.C.), contemporary in part with La Venta and the "Palangana" phase of San Lorenzo; and finally, an "Upper Tres Zapotes II," after 100 B.C. and lasting perhaps up to the second century A.D. Influences of civilizations from the central plateau or the Pacific coast then make themselves felt.

Although stone is almost as rare at the Tres Zapotes site as in other Olmec localities, remains of constructions in stone, terraces and stairways, can still be seen there; these may be attributed to the earliest periods. Two of the terraces overlook the banks of the Hueyapan River. Some fifty mounds, either isolated or in groups, are scattered about the site; the largest of these are 55 meters long and 15 meters high. Eight other sites have been located within a radius of 20 to 25 kilometers around Tres Zapotes. This zone was quite obviously one of great activity.

The two colossal heads discovered at Tres Zapotes clearly belong to the first category of remains, those whose relations to Olmec civilization is unquestionable. One of them ("monument A," or "Tres Zapotes I") is the head published by Melgar in 1869. The second one was discovered accidentally by peasants clearing land at the top of a hillock known as Cerro Nestepe. It weighs nearly 8 tons; in 1950 it was transported to the Santiago Tuxtla Museum. It does not seem to bear any traces of attempts to destroy it. The face, with a relatively narrow nose and prominent cheekbones, is more "Mongoloid" and less "negroid" in appearance than other colossal heads, in particular its neighbor, "monument A" or "Tres Zapotes I."

Several sculpted stones, unfortunately very badly damaged, that were found at Tres Zapotes may be linked to the Olmec tradition.

Seated terra cotta figurine, Las Bocas. (Courtesy of Museum of the American Indian, New York.)

This is the case, for example, with monuments "F" and "G"; in both instances, two shoulders, a pair of folded arms, and a face can be made out at the end of a strong tenon approximately 1.5 meters long. The features of the face of monument "G" have been deliberately disfigured; those of monument "F" are still discernible, and bear a certain resemblance to Olmec representations such as colossal heads. It is probable that these sculptures were implanted in the surface of a terrace, at the bottom of a stairway, by means of the tenon to which they are attached.

According to Stirling (1955, p. 23), a screech owl (monument II) in basalt, 74 centimeters high, is executed in a technique reminiscent of that of the so-called Olmec "baby face" figurines from the state of Veracruz. The almond-shaped eyes are slanted, like those of figures carved on "votive axes."

It is more difficult to offer an appreciation of other monuments, which we shall divide into two categories, depending on whether or not they bear numerical inscriptions.

Stela A, discovered and described by Stirling, who published a drawing of it (1955, p. 12), is a slab 5.30 meters high and 2 meters long. It was shattered, doubtless deliberately, so that as a result a fragment of it is missing; it must have corresponded to the head of the central figure. The top of the stela is occupied by a gigantic mask which may represent the stylized face of a feline. Below it are three standing figures, the one in the center seen full-face, the two others in profile. The figure on the left is holding in its hand an unidentifiable object; the one on the right is carrying a human head (a trophy head) that he is holding by the hair. The sides of the stela are so badly mutilated that it is nearly impossible to make out the details of it, with the exception of a bas-relief representing a jaguar.

The jaguar mask, like that of stela C which we shall discuss later, is admittedly reminiscent of other Olmec sculptures, being one of the most frequent motifs of Olmec art. But the trophy head is not, to our knowledge, a theme of Olmec iconography. Joralemon (1971, pp. 18, 19) believes that an example of a trophy head can be found at La Venta, but this interpretation is doubtful: the piece in question is, rather, a pectoral in the form of a human face that the figure known as "Uncle Sam" is wearing suspended from a necklace. A trophy head held by the hair is a quite different motif—as can clearly be seen from stela no. 21 of Izapa. In this latter case it is plain that a decapitated man is lying on the ground and that a sacrificer is holding in one hand the weapon used to behead the victim and in the other the severed head.[5] But Izapa, in far-distant Chiapas, is not an Olmec site.

[5] Garth, pls. 1–34.

To anyone familiar with Olmec art, this stela A at Tres Zapotes calls to mind an alien, non-Olmec culture. Its resemblance to the Izapa stela is perhaps not a coincidence: in any event, it is one of the directions in which further research should be carried out (see Chapter 6).

Stela D, a block of basalt 1.45 meters high and 99 centimeters wide, is basically an enormous jaguar head, highly stylized but perfectly recognizable, seen full-face, with its jaws open very wide so as to form a sort of rectangular frame. Three figures are shown in relief on the plane surface thus enclosed. To the right is a bearded, masked individual leaning on a lance, his head crowned with plumes; in the center is a figure clad in a skirt (a woman?), wearing a very elaborate headdress; to the left is a kneeling man. Above them, beneath the upper lip of the feline, a potbellied dwarf appears to be hovering, in a horizontal position. The omnipresent motif of the jaguar and the hovering figure unquestionably call to mind other Olmec sculptures. Moreover, the ornaments and the garments of the bas-relief figures are not notably different from those that can be seen at La Venta. As for their facial features, they are too badly eroded for us to be able to draw any sort of conclusion. The only details still visible are the beard and the prominent nose of the figure on the right, presumably features of a mask. On the whole, this stela leaves us with the impression—though admittedly it is no more than an impression—that what we have before us is indeed an Olmec monument, but one that does not date from the age when Olmec culture was in full flower: a late, more or less marginal work.

In 1905, the German archaeologist Eduard Seler was able to observe at Tres Zapotes, along with the famous colossal "Hueyapan head," a stone chest covered with bas-reliefs; studied later by Stirling, who labeled it "monument C," this object subsequently was turned over to the Museo Nacional de Antropología in Mexico City. Although damaged, this chest, 1.52 meters long and 1.22 meters wide, is a masterpiece of sculpture and engraving[6]—but an "exotic" masterpiece from the point of view of Olmec tradition. Seven figures stand out in relief, surrounded by very decorative volutes. Their attitudes are both animated and graceful, without the slightest rigidity. Moreover, neither the features of the figures, with their faces (or their masks) with long pointed noses, nor the weapons that they are brandishing, nor their head ornaments are at all suggestive of typical Olmec art. Certain details call to mind, rather, the sculptures of Izapa in Mexico and of Kaminaljuyú and other sites in Guatemala.

[6]"This box constitutes a magnificent art object. The complex design is beautifully balanced and, although very intricate, it is executed with fine taste and feeling. The position of the figures is easy and graceful. The composition indicated deep imagination and symbolic thought. As an object of art, it is thoroughly sophisticated, and represents the work of a master craftsman." (Stirling, 1943b, p. 20.)

Two monuments of Tres Zapotes bear numerical inscriptions: stela C and monument E.

Mention has been made above of stela C and the date inscribed on it: 7.16.6.16.18, which would correspond to our year 31 B.C.—provided that the "zero date" of the classic Maya system used three centuries later was employed here. But we have no evidence that this in fact was the "zero date" employed in this case. Just as identical numerals may designate very different dates, depending on whether they represent the number of years that have elapsed since the birth of Christ or the Moslem Hegira, in like fashion the notation 7.16.6.16.18 does not necessarily have one and only one meaning. There is nothing to prove that we must calculate what date it represents in our system on the basis of the Goodman-Martínez Hernández-Thompson correlation which applies to so-called "Long Count" dates of the classic Mayas. If—and here we enter the realm of mere speculation—the Olmec "zero date" was just one *baktun* (394 years) prior to that of the Mayas, this would suffice to date stela C as belonging to the "Upper Tres Zapotes" phase.

The study of stela C from the stylistic point of view reveals nothing that would argue against our placing it in a relatively recent, purely Olmec phase. The dominant feature of the bas-relief, apart from the numerical inscription and a certain number of other glyphs that have been very badly damaged, is a humano-feline face surmounted by a complicated head ornament on which a human face seen in profile can be made out. The jaguar mask, even though it is somewhat abstract and geometrical, shows all the characteristics of a typical Olmec feline: the delineation of the eyes, the nose, and the mouth, and the eyebrows in the form of flames are well within the Olmec tradition of representation.

Another apparently numerical inscription has been found on a rock at the bottom of the Hueyapan River, which covers it with approximately a meter of water during the rainy season. The engraved area stands out about 25 centimeters from the remainder of the rock, forming a quadrangular raised surface measuring 182 centimeters by 152 centimeters. The inscription consists of three superposed signs: from top to bottom, a disk; a horizontal bar; a second horizontal bar with a rectangular appendage suspended immediately below the middle of it. No other glyph, no iconographic motif accompanies these three signs.

There is little doubt that this inscription is a very early one. The rock on which it is engraved is an extension of a deep stratum of occupation, covered over by a layer of volcanic cinders, corresponding to Ignacio Bernal's "Olmec I," that is, the "early Tres Zapotes" phase, prior to 1200 B.C. This is surprising, but appears to be incontrovertible. We thus find ourselves in the presence of what can only be a numeral represented according to the Mesoamerican convention of dots and bars—and one dating back to a particularly early period. But what numeral is it exactly? The disk and the horizontal bar may be taken to represent the number 6. But can the second bar with its rectangular prolongation in the middle of it be interpreted as a 5? If so, the inscription would stand for a total of 11. But why the different form of the lower bar? This sign is more likely a glyph denoting the number 6, and its form is not unlike that of the Maya sign *ik*. It is clear, in any event, that the inscription is not a Long Count one. It nonetheless leads us to conclude that a system of numerical notation employing dots and bars dates back, in this region, to a very early period.

In the center of the Olmec "metropolitan area," to the south of the Los Tuxtlas Mountains, the site of Laguna de Los Cerros was explored in 1960 by an expedition from the Institute of Anthropology of the University of Veracruz. The archaeologist in charge, Alfonso Medallín, who is the director of the Jalapa Museum, studied the monoliths of this ceremonial center. Ninety-five mounds scattered over 46 hectares[7] lead us to believe that in the development of Olmec civilization, Laguna de Los Cerros occupied a place comparable to that of the great sites previously described. Twenty-eight sculpted stone monuments were found there. The majority of them are mutilated—a wave of vandalism swept through this site too—but the purity of the Olmec style and the plastic beauty of the statuary arouse our admiration. All that remains of monument no. 3 is a torso. The heads of statue no. 11, representing a seated figure, and of statue no. 19, that of a standing man, are missing, but the two works are nonetheless strikingly powerful ones. Two humano-feline heads (nos. 1 and 2) with large quadrangular eyes incised with a St. Andrew's cross, and with a jaguar's snout which may be a half-mask with long fangs, clearly belong to the Olmec tradition. The same is true of an altar (no. 5) with a niche carved into its anterior face inside which is a figure wearing a miter. In 1960, at a place called Llano del Jícaro, 7 kilometers from the center of Laguna de Los Cerros, a probably unfinished statue of an obese seated figure was discovered, notable for its enormous rounded head in which the eyes and ears are represented by mere rectangles. Medallín thinks that Llano del Jícaro was a sculpture workshop.

Monument no. 27 is another interesting piece, a disk of andesite 40 centimeters in diameter, in the center of which a circular bas-relief represents a human face, all of whose features conform to the Olmec

[7]One hectare = 2.47 acres. (Translator's note.)

Headless statue, Laguna de Los Cerros. (Courtesy of Museo de Antropología, Jalapa.)

"canon," particularly the form of the mouth. This piece is very much like a sculpted stone disk today preserved in the Santiago Tuxtla Museum; since it has been less badly damaged, we can make out two hands on either side of the face, holding what are doubtless ritual objects.[8] It is quite possible that the face of monument no. 27 also showed hands and certain objects alongside it before being mutilated.

A great deal still remains to be done before we can determine the place of Laguna de Los Cerros within the whole of Olmec civilization and its relationships with the other principal centers. Judging by the pottery found here, the development of this site would appear to have been parallel to that of Tres Zapotes. But as yet we know too little about this locality to be able to trace its exact chronology.

A certain number of Olmec bas-reliefs and statues found outside the major sites are of sufficient archaeological and aesthetic interest to merit brief mention here.

The "Prince" is the name that has been given to a very beautiful statue, fortunately in an excellent state of preservation, that is now in the Jalapa Museum; it came from Cruz del Milagro, in the commune of Sayula (state of Veracruz). The statue is that of a man sitting cross-legged, with his two hands resting on the ground in a pose frequently represented in Olmec sculpture. The head, which is large in proportion to the rest of the figure, is surmounted by a round helmet decorated with a crest and provided with two earflaps. The face is full, the eyelids slightly swollen, the lips fleshy though not exaggeratedly so. One cannot help thinking that this is a portrait statue. The majestic bearing of the figure may well indicate that this was a man who occupied a very high rank in the civil or religious hierarchy.

Because of the overall form and the position of the figure depicted (seated, legs crossed, hands resting in front of the feet), a statue found at Cuauhtotolapan bears a marked resemblance to the "Prince," though unfortunately it has been badly damaged. The facial features have almost completely disappeared: the statue lay until very recently at the bottom of a river.[9]

The "Wrestler," discovered in 1933 at Uxpanapa,[10] is one of the most famous of all Olmec statues. It is a realistic portrait: the man has a beard and a mustache, though his head is shaved completely bare, and he is clad only in a very simple loincloth. His almond-shaped eyes, with well-delineated eyelids, follow the Olmec "canon," whereas the nose is straight and the mouth delicate. Perhaps this is the portrait of an individual (an athlete?) who belonged to that ethnic minority of which the famous "Uncle Sam" of La Venta is a typical

[8] See Cervantes, 1976, figs. 1 and 2. The nature and meaning of these objects will be discussed in Chapter 8.

[9] It is now in the Jalapa Museum.

[10] It is now in the Museo Nacional de Antropología in Mexico City.

representative. The delicacy of his features, the little pointed goatee, the absence of that thick layer of fat that so often envelops Olmec figures, would lead us to believe so. He is doubtless not a wrestler, however, but a ball player shown in the heat of action. We know, from descriptions of this game (*tlachtli*) in the Aztec period, that the players tried to receive the ball on their elbows so as to bat it back, and were often obliged to hunker down in a squatting position all of a sudden in order to intercept the heavy rubber sphere: is this not precisely the pose that the "Wrestler" has assumed? In any event, the expressive power, the precise delineation, and the naturalness of the position of the figure's limbs and hands reveal an extraordinary mastery of his craft on the part of the artist as well as a profound knowledge of anatomy.

The jadeite statue found at Las Limas is more highly stylized, in conformity with the Olmec tradition, and astonishingly powerful despite its modest size (it is only 55 centimeters tall). Its history reads like an adventure novel. Discovered by accident by two children in 1965, the statue was brought to the village. It was there set up in one of the huts, as though on an altar; people brought flowers, and candles were lighted before it. Thus, after many centuries, this masterpiece of religious art had again become what it was originally meant to be: a figure of worship. The news, however, reached the ears of archaeologists from the University of Veracruz, and the statue was removed to the Jalapa Museum.

Second act: One night persons unknown forced a window open, took the statue, and vanished. Fortunately, the archaeologist Alfonso Medellín sent out a notice of the theft, accompanied by a photograph of the statue, to museums, researchers, and collectors all over the world, thus doubtless making it well-nigh impossible for the "kidnappers" to sell the object.

Third (and, let us hope, last) act: A year and a half later, the sheriff of a little town in Texas received an anonymous phone call advising him to search a certain motel room. The sheriff betook himself there immediately and saw on a table the statue from Las Limas: it is now back again in Jalapa.

Sculpted from a single block of green stone, it consists of two figures: a man sitting cross-legged and a "baby" lying stretched out across his forearms. The man is represented in a realistic manner: his nose is slightly curved; his lips are full. The infant is a typically Olmec humano-feline baby, with a broad short nose and the mouth of a jaguar. In other words, the scene so often represented on the anterior face of the "altars" at La Venta is here removed from its usual setting and shown as a separate piece. It is evident that the myth of the baby with both human and jaguar features must have occupied a central

"The Prince," Cruz del Milagro, Sayula, state of Veracruz. (Courtesy of R. Roland–Ziolo, Paris.)

place in Olmec religion. Here, the priest—if the adult figure is indeed a priest—who is presenting the infant does not have a badly eroded face as do the majority of the other sculptures of this type. Hence we can make out clearly not only his facial features but also the delicate tattoo marks engraved on his forehead, his cheeks, and his nose. There are other engravings on his shoulders and his knees. The predominant motif of these engravings, whose sureness of line is astonishing, is the representation of supernatural beings,[11] the tops of whose heads have a deep indentation hollowed out in them. One of them has eyebrows in the form of flames. These figures all have wide-open mouths and fangs. As for the "baby," it too has an indentation in its forehead; its chest and belly are marked with a St. Andrew's cross—a motif consisting of two bands crossed in an "X"—that turns up so often that it might well be called the "Olmec cross."

The theme of the humano-feline being also appears in other sculptures, the head, for example, found at Estero Rabón,[12] a block of andesite measuring 45 by 40 centimeters, in which the treatment of this motif is exceptionally—almost brutally—powerful. While the rounded head covering with earflaps, the forehead, and the eyes denote a human being, the nose and above all the monstrous snout, with two jaws bristling with enormous fangs, reveal a terrifying bestiality.

Isolated stelae have been discovered in various places in the Olmec region. A stela[13] 3.75 meters high was found at El Viejón, in the commune of Actopan (state of Veracruz); it was quite badly damaged, but on the surface of it two standing figures, sculpted in bas-relief, can be made out. One of them has a sort of rod or scepter in its hand, though this object might also be a maize stalk or a flowering branch. The faces are not discernible, but the heavyset bodies and the attitudes are unquestionably Olmec in style.

El Viejón is a vast site, with many large mounds. The stela was found along with a number of potsherds, among them one decorated with a "mouth with drooping corners, lips painted with cinnabar, of high plastic quality and in the purest Olmec style."[14] The El Viejón monolith is not unlike the one that is still in place at Los Mangos, near Catemaco, a stela that is known locally as the "Moctezuma Stone." Here too, the bas-relief represents two figures standing facing each other; one of them is holding in its hand a cylindrical object, "a sort of scepter," according to Beatriz de la Fuente (1973, p. 160).

We should also mention a colossal head (the one discovered most

[11] Coe (1968b, p. 114) and Joralemon (1971, figs. 10, 106, 126, 206, 232, 249, 253) identify them as divinities (see below, Chapter 9).
[12] Now in the Jalapa Museum.
[13] Now in the Jalapa Museum.
[14] Medellín, 1960, p. 82.

Colossal head, Santiago Tuxtla. (Courtesy of Myriam de la Croix, Paris.)

recently, in 1970) found at the Cobata ranch, Cerro El Vigía (state of Veracruz), and now moved to the main square of Santiago Tuxtla. It is 3.40 meters high and 3 meters in diameter, and differs from other known colossal heads, in particular those of San Lorenzo, only in that its workmanship is more rudimentary. It is more or less cone-shaped, widening at the base. Though badly eroded, the eyes on close examination would appear to be closed: the question thus arises (De la Fuente, 1973, p. 125) whether this might not be a representation of a dead man. At the time that it was discovered, the head lay buried with an offering alongside it, consisting of a bowl in orange-colored terra cotta and an obsidian blade, opposite the mouth.

At the northern limits of the Olmec zone, to the west of Alvarado, lies the region known as Mixtequilla. Here, near the southern bank of the Río Blanco, which is fed by the eternal snows of the peak of Orizaba and which empties into the bay of Alvarado, the mounds of an important and enigmatic site, Cerro de Las Mesas, loom up above the surface of the ground. Visited in 1927 by Herbert Spinden and partially excavated by Stirling in 1941, this extensive complex of mounds, platforms, and sculpted stones is doubtless far from having revealed all its secrets. Fifteen stelae and eight monoliths have been discovered there. The majority of the stelae show, in bas-relief, figures with very elaborate garments and ornaments, whose style is more suggestive of Izapa, in Chiapas, or of Santa Lucía Cozumalhuapa, in Guatemala, than of Olmec sculpture. Two of them bear "Long Count" inscriptions. Stela no. 6 bears the date 9.1.12.14.10, which according to the Maya calendar would stand for a 1-*oc* day: the numeral 1 is quite clear, but the glyph that would correspond to the name of the day *oc* is illegible. The date on stela no. 8 reads 9.4.18.16.8, indicating a 9-*lamat* day, the glyph of which bears a close resemblance to the classic Maya sign. The numerals, however, are not followed by period glyphs as in Maya inscriptions.

Their disposition is thus analogous to that of the numerals engraved on the Tuxtla statuette and the inscription carved on the Tres Zapotes stela C. If we grant—even though these are mere hypotheses for which there is no supporting evidence—firstly, that the zero date of the inscriptions of Cerro de Las Mesas is the same as that of the Maya "Long Count," and secondly, that the dates inscribed on these stelae are contemporary with the period in which they were set in place, we are forced to conclude that the corresponding phase in the history of this site is situated in *baktun* 9, that of the apogee of classic Maya civilization, between the fifth and the ninth century A.D. The striking similarities between the style of Cerro de Las Mesas and that of Izapa, which there is ample reason to situate in the period extending

Stela no. 3, La Venta (detail). Now located in the Parque-Museo de La Venta in Villahermosa, state of Tabasco. (Courtesy of Myriam de la Croix, Paris.)

Massive offering: stylized jaguar mask, La Venta. Now located in the Parque-Museo de La Venta in Villahermosa, state of Tabasco. (Courtesy of Museo Nacional de Antropología, Mexico City.)

from the first century B.C. to the beginning of the Christian era, lead us to wonder whether this date attributed to these Olmec stelae is not too late a one. But let us bear in mind that this is a problem that has not yet been resolved.

On one stela (no. 15), two numerals, 1 and 4, are engraved, each of them accompanied by a glyph; these inscriptions may represent dates in the so-called *tzolkin* system of the Mayas and the *tonalpoualli* of the Nahuas,[15] that is, "1-deer" and "4-water." And lastly, one stela (no. 5) bears traces of numerals denoted by dots and bars.

The figures represented in bas-relief on stelae nos. 3, 4, and 9 are the only ones at Cerro de Las Mesas that can be described as "Olmecoid"; no. 9 above all, which resembles the sculpture of Piedra Parada (Guatemala) and will be dealt with later. As for the monoliths, they bear no apparent similarities to Olmec art. Admittedly, we find among them a "colossal head" (no. 2) 2 meters high, but it is in a style completely different from that at La Venta or Tres Zapotes. Monument no. 5, an enormous spherical block sculpted to represent an adipose individual, whose genitals are clearly indicated, does not appear to justify a comparison with Olmec art.

An offering discovered in 1941 consists of 782 pieces carved in jade and other hard stones. Of this exceptionally rich collection, only a few objects are undoubtedly Olmec: a model of a boat on which two jaguar masks are engraved, a magnificent weeping dwarf (or infant), a hunchback, and perhaps a skull. It is probable that these pieces were preserved for generations and finally included in the treasure buried as an offering. They may well have been acquired through trade between Cerro de Las Mesas and Olmec country.

On the other hand, the lower levels reached in the excavation at Cerro de Las Mesas turned up fragments of black pottery with white edges and figurines similar to those found at Tres Zapotes.

All these observations lead us to conclude, at least tentatively, that even though Cerro de Las Mesas is not an Olmec site, a certain Olmec influence played a role there, and an Olmec tradition makes itself felt there in the form of certain precious objects. For the most part, the site belongs to the classic era.

Not far from there, as Ignacio Bernal (1969, p. 148) points out, a stela found at Cerro de la Piedra is unquestionably Olmecoid.

In fact, the entire zone to the west of Alvarado and in the valleys of the San Juan and the Tecolapan, is literally riddled with mounds, in particular at Lerdo, San Francisco, Cerro de Gallo, and El Mesón. In this last location, Stirling (1943b, pp. 28–29) studied a stela 4 meters high that had fallen to the ground; on it is sculpted the represen-

[15] These terms designate a cycle of 260 dates recorded by a combination of thirteen numbers and twenty signs.

tation of a standing man, with his face seen in profile and his torso facing forward. He is wearing ear ornaments and a tall headdress.

Below him is a carved glyph. This monolith closely resembles the one known as the "Alvarado stela,"[16] though it probably comes from a site farther inland, perhaps Cerro de la Piedra. The standing figure shown on this stela is wearing a complicated headdress; hunched down at his feet is an individual, a captive, with bound hands. His mouth with its thick, bow-shaped upper lip is suggestive of the Olmec style. His feet are resting on a horizontal band engraved with motifs: a small disk (the number 1?) and a bar analogous to the lower bar of the inscription on monument E at Tres Zapotes. Opposite the standing man, above the captive, faint traces of a column of hieroglyphics can still be made out.

The heart of the Olmec region is thus bounded to the north and to the west by the Papaloapán River, but the influence of La Venta, San Lorenzo, Tres Zapotes, Laguna de Los Cerros spread throughout the region that lies between the Papaloapán and the Río Blanco.

To the south and west, the basin of the Tonalá River and that of the Blasillo, along with La Venta and the still unexplored site of San Miguel, constitute the boundary of the Olmec "metropolitan area." Farther to the east, Maya country begins, with the westernmost Maya city, Comalcalco.

The fundamental characteristic of this zone is the primacy of sculpture and engraving. There was not enough solid material, enough stone, available to foster enduring architecture. In such a climate, buildings of sun-dried bricks and beaten earth had few chances of lasting very long. The "pyramid" of La Venta is the only large monument that survived the centuries. Everywhere else, all that remains are earthworks and mounds.

It is probable that the most abundant raw material that the Olmecs had at hand, wood, was widely used. Dwellings and sanctuaries built of wood were no doubt erected on the earthwork platforms, and in all likelihood carved wood panels and lintels adorned the temples and the residences of dignitaries. The rains and the insects have not left a single trace of this art. We know how rare Maya carved wood pieces are, though they date from a much later era than the flowering of Olmec civilization. The only Olmec object made of wood thus far discovered is a mask that was found in the state of Guerrero, miraculously preserved in the more favorable climatic conditions there.

The basalt columns of the ceremonial court at La Venta, and those that were used to build Tomb A of the same site, strongly suggest that wooden pillars and tree trunks were used to build fences (pali-

[16]Now in the Museo Nacional de Antropología in Mexico City.

sades) or tombs. The prismatic basalt of volcanoes furnished natural columns, but doubtless it was not possible to transport sufficient quantities of them to La Venta to build numerous structures.

Because of all of these factors Olmec architecture seems poor, despite the fact that fundamental developments such as the carefully planned layout of ceremonial buildings appear at this site for the first time in Mesoamerica.

As for pottery, so abundant and varied in other Olmec zones, as we shall see, it is relatively rare and monotonous between the Papaloapán and the Tonalá. It is possible that in this case too the extreme humidity and the acidity of the soil were largely responsible for the destruction not only of wood but of terra cotta. Ceramic pieces from La Venta and Tres Zapotes are rare: we possess at most only about forty specimens that are complete or well enough preserved for restoration to be possible. Even potsherds, which are found by the hundreds of thousands in other archaeological zones, are not very abundant here. The Olmecs must have used wooden receptacles, and above all gourds, so handy and so easy to come by in the Hot Lands, in preference to pottery, as is still the case today among the Indians of the tropical zones of Mexico (the Lacandones, for example, use gourds almost exclusively). In any event, what Olmec pottery exists is generally monochrome (light or dark brown, white, black, orange) and has incised decorative motifs. The most characteristic types are black pieces with white edges and entirely white pieces. The forms are simple: slightly flared cylindrical bowls, basins, pots. Receptacles have no feet. It would appear that, unlike most of the other peoples of Mesoamerica, the Olmecs did not fashion and fire terra cotta objects for ceremonial use: ritual vessels, censers, braziers. The magnificent brazier of Cerro de Las Mesas, which undoubtedly represents a fire god, is definitely post-Olmec, dating from the classic era.[17]

It is in sculpture and stone-carving that the Olmecs excelled. And this is true from the very beginning. The most astonishing phenomenon in this regard is that with the exception of a few rare pieces that are doubtless not Olmec, such as monument no. 41 at San Lorenzo, the art of working stone, whether it is a question of monoliths weighing dozens of tons, of delicate figurines or ear ornaments that are so thin as to be nearly transparent, gives the appearance of being a mature art in full possession of its means from the beginning to the end. The same is true of the engravings on "votive axes," on pectorals in hard stone, or on the face and body of the Las Limas statue. The sureness of line, the absence of hesitation or of strokes that are misplaced or scratched out, bear witness to an absolute mastery. The

[17] This object, of exceptionally high quality, is now in the Museo Nacional de Antropología in Mexico City. See Bernal, 1969, pl. 69.

same may be said of the perfection of Olmec hematite mirrors. We may conjecture that Olmec sculptors "trained their hand" on wood before attacking stone. Or might they not have begun to sculpt volcanic stone in the Sierra de Los Tuxtlas before founding their ceremonial centers on the plain? This second hypothesis is intriguing, but the fact remains that all the monuments we know of were discovered outside the mountainous zone. Even though it may have had its origins in the Sierra, Olmec civilization is par excellence a civilization of the swampy plain and the fertile river valleys.

We know where the Olmecs quarried the basalt and the andesite for their stelae, altars, and statues. But where did they get the jadeites, nephrites, serpentines that they fashioned with such incomparable art, probably unequaled and in any case never surpassed anywhere on the American continent? No civilized people of the New World ever reached such a high level in the treatment of hard stone. The Olmecs were to first to value jadeite more highly than any other material, a place on the scale of values that it occupied in all of Mesoamerica, from the Mayas to the Aztecs, even when gold and silver became known, beginning in the tenth century A.D. We know how surprised the Spaniards were to note, at the beginning of the sixteenth century, that a *chalchiuitl*—a piece in green stone—was more valuable in the eyes of the Aztecs than a gold jewel.

The jade deposits that the Olmecs most probably exploited are located a long distance away from their territory: those, doubtless, a hundred or so kilometers west of Taxco in the mountains of metamorphic rock of Guerrero, in the Balsas Basin. As for serpentine, they might well have procured it in the present-day state of Puebla. The magnetite from which they fashioned their extraordinary mirrors no doubt came from deposits located to the south of the Olmec "metropolitan area," in Oaxaca and at the southern end of the Isthmus of Tehuantepec.

The jade that the Mayas carved in the classic era was extracted from deposits in the valley of the Motagua River (Guatemala). It is not identical to that of Olmec pieces, which has a bluish tinge. The Nicoya Peninsula (in Costa Rica) seems to have been rich in jade, however, and certain objects from that region are purely Olmec in style.

Hence we are led to conjecture that the search for these stones to which they attributed a supreme value led the Olmecs to send out expeditions, and even to create colonies, at great distances from their principal center, in two directions: toward the west and north, across the central plateau, to procure the serpentines of Puebla and the jades of Guerrero; and toward the south and east, across Oaxaca and the Isthmus of Tehuantepec, along the coast of Chiapas and Guatemala, and as far as El Salvador and Costa Rica. The moving force behind Olmec expansion may well have been the search for rare stones (see the map established by Coe, 1968b, p. 102).

Whatever the reason for it may have been, this expansion has become more and more evident as new discoveries in the last few years have brought to light unquestionable traces of the influence or of the presence of the Olmecs in a vast area of Mesoamerica. The conventions of Olmec art are so original, its themes so easy to recognize that the archaeologist can scarcely go wrong: an Olmec object is so strikingly "Olmec" that it cannot be anything else. The one remaining question to be answered is whether the presence of certain pieces at a given site is due to the appearance there of Olmecs—colonists or warriors—themselves, or whether they are simply objects that found their way there as a result of trade. It is obvious that bas-reliefs or paintings on rock cliffs or in caves are proof of the physical presence of Olmec artists, whereas this is not the case with a figurine or a pendant. We must concede, however, that even portable objects, when there are a great many of them and when they have a definite place in the stratigraphy of a site, are an argument in favor of the occupation of that site by a given human group.

We must now follow the routes of the Olmecs across the continent.

# 3

⧈ ⧈ ⧈ ⧈ ⧈ ⧈

# The Olmec
# Expansion Toward
## The Central Plateau
## of Mexico

The high valleys of Mexico, Puebla, and Toluca, which lie at an average altitude of 2000 meters, were a region of advanced civilization from the beginning of our era up until the conquest of Mexico by the Spaniards. The prestigious names of Teotihuacán, Tula, Cholula, Tenochtitlán-Mexico stand out as landmarks in their history. For an uninterrupted period of a millennium and a half they were the center of high cultures which more than once extended their influence and even their power as far as Yucatán and Guatemala. However, in the very early era in which the Olmec civilization of Veracruz and Tabasco flourished, between 1500 and 400 B.C., these regions were still marginal. The cultivation of maize had taken hold there beginning about 3500 B.C., and the Indian peasants, having become sedentary, lived grouped together in villages, fashioning clay vessels and weaving agave fibers.

To the Olmecs, this was an alien physical and human world, what with its dry, cool climate, its thin air, its volcanoes crowned with glaciers, and its peasant peoples. By venturing into this world in search of rare stones, by opening up trade routes into it, the Olmecs entered into contact with societies much more rudimentary than their own. We will no doubt never know to what extent the evolution of these societies, the birth of hierarchized structures within them, the appearance of artistic and religious complexes were phenomena determined or accelerated by the intervention, the example, or the influence of the Olmecs. Archaeology brings to light only material remains. What is certain is that these vestiges are witness of an Olmec expansion that at this stage of our investigations still appears to us to be sporadic and relatively restricted, though there is every reason to believe that further research will show that it was both more constant and more widespread. Even today, the very general outlines of it that we can discern are extremely striking.

The first stage, if we may call it that: Las Bocas, in the present-day state of Puebla. To get there, it was easy either to head along what today is called the Valley of Izúcar toward the southwestern slope of Mexico (Morelos, Guerrero) or to cross the Puebla-Tlaxcala plateau, and by skirting the two great volcanoes of Popocatepetl and Iztaccihuatl, reach the central valley and its vast lagoon.

Las Bocas is remarkable above all for the abundance and the quality of its hollow statuettes, in white terra cotta, the majority of which represent "babies" with chubby bodies, in many different attitudes (one of these infants is even sucking its thumb), and typical Olmec faces. These babies are asexual. This type of statuette, known as a "baby face," is found in an identical form in the "metropolitan area," at Cruz del Milagro for instance.[1] Other Las Bocas statuettes represent adults, either nude or lightly clothed (a loincloth or a short skirt). This is an art that is unquestionably related to that of the large sculptured pieces, though much less formal and hieratic. Pottery receptacles and *pintaderas*, a tool used to decorate fabrics or the human body, have also been found at this site, and there are many examples of the use of the stylized jaguar as a motif.

The Tehuacán and Necaxa regions, also in the state of Puebla, likewise underwent Olmec influences. As examples, we may cite the supernatural jaguar of Necaxa, an admirable jade statuette; a very beautiful figurine, now in the Puebla Museum, that is doubtless from Tehuacán; a circular vase decorated with jaguar masks. A most interesting figure in the Bliss collection came from Tepatlaxco (Puebla).[2]

Traces of the presence of the Olmecs in the Mexico Basin first came to light at Tlatilco, a necropolis where a great many tombs were

[1] "Baby face" of Cruz del Milagro, state of Veracruz; cf. Pohorilenko, Anatole: *Small Sculptures, in El arte olmeca*, p. 41, fig. 6.

[2] The Necaxa jaguar is shown by Joralemon, fig. 216. The Puebla Museum figurine: Caso, 1965, fig. 13a. The vase with jaguar masks: Piña Chan, 1964, p. 21. The Tepatlaxco figurine: Joralemon, fig. 20; Cervantes, fig. 4.

accidentally discovered by workers from a brick factory digging for clay. The name of Miguel Covarrubias remains permanently associated with this site, for it was he, with his profound sensibilities as a draftsman and painter, along with his vast fund of knowledge, who devoted himself, with boundless enthusiasm, to the recovery and the interpretation of the objects found in prodigious quantities in these graves.

The Olmec pottery of Tlatilco is related to types of earthenware previously discovered in the Veracruz-Tabasco region. Here too we find, in particular, black terra cotta bowls with white patches or edges and an incised pattern. They show a great variety of motifs: outlines of hands or of birds, feet, serpents, fantastic animals, and naturally the stylized Olmec jaguar, its mask, its claws. There are original forms as well, notably dark-colored ovoid "bottles" with a long cylindrical neck, decorated with incised panels. The vast number of terra cotta figurines found at Tlatilco are not always in the Olmec style: far from it. We must therefore take care not to lump together all the styles of different origins present at Tlatilco. Certain pottery or stone figurines, however, are directly related to the tradition of the "metropolitan area." In this regard we may cite as examples a jadeite statuette (Bernal, 1969, pl. 55) and a white ceramic female figurine of exceptional quality (Piña Chan and Luis Covarrubias, pl. 31). As for representations of the "baby face" type, we find them at Tlatilco as at Las Bocas and at other places on the high plateau.[3] It would appear that even though the Olmecs of the central plateau did not use sculpted stone to render homage to the mythical "baby" so important in the art of the *Tierras Calientes*, they nonetheless often employed this theme in their pottery.

Hematite mirrors and jade ornaments, both clearly Olmec importations, have also been found at Tlatilco. A curious stone object, known as a *yuguito* ("small yoke") because it may be regarded as a reduced model of the large "yokes" of the coastal zone in the classic era, has a typically Olmec humanoid face sculpted on it (Bernal, 1969, pl. 58). In view of the fact that no similar specimen has been discovered, to our knowledge, in the Olmec "metropolitan area," and that the "yokes" of the classic civilization of the Gulf belong to a much later period than Tlatilco, we must grant that for the moment this *yuguito* poses a problem that is difficult to resolve.

Whereas at Atoto, alongside Tlatilco, there are no signs of Olmec influence—this site remained merely a pre-classic peasant community—numerous Olmec features are found at Tlapacoya, to the southeast of the Valley of Mexico: polished white pottery incised with dec-

[3] Bernal, 1969, p. 135, mentions San Martín Texmelucan, Cholula, Huejotzingo (state of Puebla), Ozumba and Chalco (state of México).

orations. The motif of the jaguar, the stylized mask of the feline, the oblique almond-shaped eyes of the Olmec style can be made out on potsherds. Two hematite mirrors have likewise been found at Tlapacoya.

Traces of an Olmec presence are found here and there in other places in the Valley of Mexico. A polished ax engraved with Olmec motifs turned up at Tlaltenco (Federal District). A drawing of it was made by Miguel Covarrubias and published by Joralemon (fig. 34); on it we can make out very clearly a face with typically Olmec features seen in profile, surmounted by a conical headdress and a series of motifs that may be glyphs.

George Vaillant had divided the pre-classic period in the Mexico Basin into two principal phases: the earlier one, the so-called Copilco-Zacatenco, represented in particular by the El Arbolillo site, and a later one, Cuicuilco-Ticomán. Many of Vaillant's conclusions are still valid, but the discoveries made at Tlatilco and Paul Tolstoy's more recent research give us a more subtly shaded picture of this past.

Tlatilco, first of all, turns out to be a far from homogeneous site. We find there "Olmec" tombs, containing hollow ceramic statuettes of the "baby face" type and figurines whose style is unquestionably Olmec; tombs whose burial objects are related to the pre-classic cultures of Zacatenco; and finally, a *teritium quid* in the form of specimens in what, for lack of a better term, is called the "Tlatilco style." It is clear that Tlatilco was used as a necropolis for several centuries and that we find at this site traces of at least three different cultural complexes.

Paul Tolstoy's excavations at Ayotla, near Tlapacoya, in the southeast of the central valley, brought to light, among other objects, a splendid "baby face."[4] The study of the pottery at Ayotla leads us to the conclusion that a so-called Ixtapaluca phase, Olmec in character, preceded the pre-classic culture of Zacatenco by approximately three centuries. In other words, the Olmecs would appear to have settled in at least certain parts of the valley before the pre-classics themselves, around 1200 to 900 B.C. These Olmecs cultivated maize (ears of maize have been found at Ayotla) and hunted deer and rabbits. And they buried their dead, or certain of them, at Tlatilco.

Nonetheless, "the Covarrubias thesis, which would bring the Olmec into contact with a preexisting or equally old local tradition of Zacatenco type, still cannot be discounted completely."[5] It is possible, moreover, to conclude that the Olmecs were the first settlers in certain regions, while in other areas they coexisted with other peoples. The demographic density in the Mexico Basin around 1200 or

[4] Tolstoy and Paradis, frontispiece illustration.
[5] Ibid., p. 348.

1100 B.C. was probably so low that large portions of the territory were not occupied. The Olmecs may well have taken advantage of "gaps" that were not yet inhabited, of stretches of land that were not yet cultivated. But, being possessed of a higher civilization, they also may have taken over as a dominent elite in other localities. They may have lent peasant societies an impetus that later, during the pre-classic Ticomán period, led to their erection of structures in clay and earth such as the pseudo-pyramid of Cuicuilco.

At Tlatilco, the tombs containing Olmec objects date from the Ixtapaluca phase; hence they are earlier than the burial sites of the Zacatenco type. As for the third element, characterized by whistling vessels and by pottery pieces with effigies, it leads us to turn our gaze toward the southeastern slope of Mexico: toward the valleys of Morelos and the sites along the Río Cuautla, and then toward Michoacán and the Pacific coast; and finally perhaps, as Tolstoy suggests, toward the Andean region of South America.

Las Bocas, Ayotla, Tlatilco have in common the fact that they are localities that overlook or permit the control of traffic through natural passageways: from the plateau of Puebla to the Mexico Basin and to Morelos; from the Valley of Mexico to the plateau of Toluca. And on the route from Toluca to the *Tierra Caliente* of Guerrero, to Tenango del Valle, a head of a statue in jadeite[6] with distinctly Olmec features serves as a marker, so to speak, along an important itinerary between the high plateau and the Balsas River region.

It is obvious that it was the requirements of trade between the various regions of Mexico and the necessity, for the most dynamic civilization of the era, to control this trade that led to the formation of these "gateway communities," to adopt Kenneth G. Hirth's expression.

It is still too early to try to understand exactly what the Olmecs were doing when they left their normal habitat and ventured forth into regions so distant and so different from their own. They were seeking, as we have said, raw materials such as jade and serpentine, and perhaps certain varieties of obsidian as well: artifacts made of extremely rare green obsidian, scarcely ever found outside of the region of Pachuca (state of Hidalgo), in the northeast of Mexico, were discovered at Ayotla and at San Lorenzo. If, as we may suppose, Olmec travelers or colonists engaged in trade—like the Aztec *pochteca* many centuries later—they must have brought from their place of origin objects or goods that would pique the interest of the peoples who dwelt on the central plateau: the features of tropical birds, rubber, cocoa, carved jade pieces perhaps. These Olmec traders may thus have initiated a certain current of exchanges between *Tierra Cal-*

[6] See Piña Chan and Covarrubias, pl. 18.

*iente* and *Tierra Fría*—the Hot Lands and the Cold Lands—that, practically speaking, has continued uninterruptedly ever since and that
serves to explain in particular how it happens that precious feathers,
balls of rubber, tropical plants such as cacao trees, and jade pieces
are shown in the fresco paintings on the walls of the palaces and
sanctuaries of Teotihuacán.

These Olmec "colonies" of the central plateau cultivated above all
the art of ceramics, which remained secondary at La Venta and at
San Lorenzo, and did not sculpt monoliths, colossal heads, altars, or
stelae. This is evidence that these "colonies" were peripheral forms
of Olmec culture, outposts with quite small and quite undiversified
populations. There were tillers of the soil, artisans, traders there; and
doubtless Olmec travelers on their way to or from the coast of Veracruz and the Balsas Valley used localities such as Ayotla as a stopping-
off place where they were certain of finding compatriots who spoke
their language and shared their beliefs. It is certain that the "Olmec
colonials" of the central plateau were not simply travelers passing
through the Valley of Mexico, since Tlatilco is in part their necropolis. But these small communities, so far from the living center of
their civilization, doubtless possessed neither the material means nor
the spiritual impetus that would have been necessary to undertake
immense construction projects such as those on the plateau of San
Lorenzo or to sculpt statues and bas-reliefs.

The archaeological excavations thus far conducted in the Valley of
Mexico do not allow us as yet to answer the question whether, at any
period, major Olmec centers analogous to those in the "metropolitan
area" ever existed there. The absence of proof is not in itself a proof.
We should note, however, that there are few regions in Mexico that
have been the object of so many scientific excavations, or the site of
so many works projects (the construction of roads, airports, housing
developments) that have turned up important finds. No one can be
sure that an Olmec stela will not come to light one day beneath the
pickax of an archaeologist or the blade of a bulldozer: all that we can
say is that thus far no such evidence has been found.

In any event, we may be fairly certain of two things. The first is
the very early date at which the Olmecs' presence made itself felt on
the soil of central Mexico, not only by way of travelers, traders, or
pilgrims passing through the region, but also through the establishment of small "colonies." The second would appear to be the "decul-
turation" that must have taken place from the moment that the metropolitan center underwent, for reasons that escape us, a definite
eclipse around 400 B.C. From that time on, the colonies abandoned
to their fate amid larger indigenous populations probably lost their
ethnic and cultural identity and disappeared as distinct entities. Ol-

mec vessels and statuettes no longer turn up in the most recent strata (Ticomán-Cuicuilco) of the pre-classic phase. Even diluted, so to speak, in the new culture of the high plateau that was to begin to flourish soon thereafter, at Cuicuilco first and then at Teotihuacán, Olmec civilization had nonetheless made its contribution to that of the classic era. This contribution was part of the heritage that the final period of the pre-classic phase and the first phase of Teotihuacán—the two centuries on either side of our Christian "zero date," that is, between 100 B.C. and A.D. 100—brought to full flower. The specifically "coastal" features of the civilization of Teotihuacán, despite the fact that its center was located on the semi-arid high plateau, show that close contacts existed between the great theocratic city and the Hot Lands, contacts that simply prolonged a tradition established more than a thousand years before by Olmec colonists and traders.

All things considered, it would no doubt not be straying too far from the facts to conclude that by spreading to the central valleys, even in an attenuated form and in a limited number of places, Olmec civilization played the role of a catalyst. It led to decisive steps forward, or quickened the pace of progress. It no doubt implanted in the highlands religious ideas, rough outlines of social structures, that germinated, flowered, and bore fruit in the classic era, that golden age of pre-Columbian Mesoamerica.

# 4

⚏⚏⚏⚏⚏⚏⚏

# Sculpted Rock Faces and Painted Caves:
## The Olmec Expansion Toward the Pacific

From the high fortress of the central Mexican plateau, the continental slope descends to the Pacific coast in successive steps, amid rough mountainous terrain in which the Balsas River, flowing more or less east to west, has opened up a deep breach. Whereas the valleys of Morelos, verdant and blessed with many rivers, at a moderate altitude of around 1200 meters, had in antiquity—and still have today—the appearance of an immense and fertile garden (the Aztec emperors had a marvelous park at Oaxtepec), south of Iguala and Chilpancingo the western slope suffers from aridity and erosion. It is probable that these two ills were less severe in former times, since deforestation had not yet wreaked its havoc. In any event, it was doubtless not arable land that the Olmecs were seeking in this region, but rather the stones, the jades, buried in the Balsas Basin.

Although the archaeology of Morelos is relatively well known, the

Above, carved stone head, state of Guerrero. (Courtesy of American Museum of National History, New York.) Below, wooden mask, state of Guerrero. (Courtesy of American Museum of National History, New York.)

same is not true of the immense present-day state of Guerrero, cut up by precipitous mountain slopes and deep canyons, while the center of the Balsas Basin is isolated, to the north and to the south, by towering mountain ranges. Hence this region is characterized bv a certain "marginality"[1]; outside influences would appear to have played a role there, without having profoundly altered local cultures, however. It is thus all the more remarkable that a fairly large number of Olmec artifacts have been discovered in Guerrero, and such important discoveries of paintings on rock faces and in caves have been made in this region that the question has arisen whether the original center of Olmec civilization may not have been in Guerrero rather than on the Gulf coast.

This is a problem to which we shall return later. For the moment let us note how little we know about the artifacts from the distant past that have come from Guerrero, for lack of systematic scientific excavations in this region. With a few rare exceptions, no precise

[1] Cf. Paradis, 1973.

Relief no. 1, Chalcatzingo. (From C. T. E. Gay and F. Pratt, *Chalcacingo.* Courtesy of Akademische Druck- u. Verlag, Graz.)

origin can be attributed to the specimens of Olmec art from Guerrero—masks, carved jade pieces—that can be seen in museums or
private collections. We do not know exactly where or how these
pieces, often very beautiful ones, were discovered, or whether other
remains, potsherds for instance, were unearthed with them; hence it
is practically impossible to date them. Stylistic evidence alone enables us to link them immediately with the Olmec tradition.

If there is one case in which the physical presence of a population
in a certain place is not subject to doubt, it is when that population
has left its trace, its signature so to speak, in that place, not by means
of small-sized, readily portable objects, but by sculpting the living
rock or painting the walls of caves. From this point of view, the rock
bas-reliefs at Chalcatzingo (Morelos) and the cave paintings at Juxtlahuaca and at Oxtotitlán (Guerrero), even aside from their aesthetic
and symbolic value, constitute documents of exceptional significance.

Reported as early as 1932 by Eulalia Guzmán, the bas-reliefs at
Chalcatzingo have only recently been recognized as being Olmec.
Their symbolism is often obscure, but in any case it is certain that
the Olmec group that took the time and the trouble to sculpt them
was impelled to do so by a powerful religious motivation.

Chalcatzingo (sometimes spelled Chalcacingo) is approximately 130
kilometers southeast of Mexico City and about 30 kilometers west of
Las Bocas as the crow flies. The bas-reliefs are sculpted on the cliffs
of the Cerro de la Cantera, which affords a panoramic view extending
to Popocatepetl to the north, with its towering summit covered with
eternal snows. There are ten of these bas-reliefs in all, divided into
three distinct groups.[2]

The most complex of these reliefs (no. 1) represents a figure, probably that of a woman with long hair, clad in a skirt and a sort of bodice
or cape, and wearing a tall, complicated headdress. Seen in profile,
though her torso is facing forward, she is sitting on a seat decorated
with a double volute and is holding across her forearms—in somewhat
the same way that the priests of La Venta are holding the jaguar-
baby—a rectangular ceremonial bar on which the same double-volute
motif is engraved. Her ears are decorated with pendants, and ankle
bracelets and bits of a necklace are still visible. This is an imposing
figure, that of a priestess or a divinity dressed in elaborate, luxurious
garments. Her feet and the seat on which she is sitting are resting on
the lower edge of a kind of arch that surrounds her and curves up
over her head like a shelter—a cave or a niche. The theme seems to
be the following: a figure sitting in a niche is holding in its arms a
"baby" with feline features (La Venta) or a ceremonial bar with a

---

[2] Gay, 1971, regards the bas-relief known as "no. 9" as being a monument that is
really separate from the panels sculpted in the living rock, and considers it to be of
different, more careless workmanship.

double volute (Chalcatzingo). We are thus led to wonder whether this bar is not simply the abstract symbol of the jaguar-baby.

If we take a close look at the cavern or niche, we see that it is really the gaping jaws of the gigantic animal. The eye of the monster is represented, above the upper edge of the arch, by an oval in which the "Olmec cross" is inscribed. Extremely decorative volutes issue from the mouth of the monster, in the direction toward which the face of the feminine figure is turned.

Four categories of symbols complete this scene:

I. Three stylized representations of clouds piled one atop the other, oddly suggestive of the cloud platforms of the Indians of the southwestern United States. Each one of these "cloud symbols" is made up of three wavy lines, one above the other, beneath which vertical strokes obviously stand for rain falling.

II. Fourteen signs, each one of which is made up of a rectangular band disposed vertically, from which a round or oval element seems to be hanging, like a medal suspended from a ribbon. These signs form three groups (of seven, three, and four, respectively) beneath the three cloud motifs. This fact alone would suffice to show that they are symbols of drops of rain. But that is not all: we find this very same symbol being used more than two thousand years later by the Aztecs. The sign for rain in the Mexican manuscripts is in fact exactly like it, and is used to stand for the element *quiauitl* (rain) in the hieroglyphs of place names such as Quiauhteopan and Tlachquiauhco.[3]

This "raindrop" glyph, moreover, is repeated six times on the headdress of the female figure, known as the "Lady of the Cavern," and three times on her skirt.

III. Five signs in the shape of a disk or a square with rounded angles, marked with a small circle in the center and another circle closer to the edge. One cannot help remarking the similarity of this glyph and that of the ninth day of the classic Maya calendar, *muluc*, which corresponds to the ninth day of the Aztec *tonalpoualli*, *atl* (water). It represents a jade disk, since rain, the precious gift of heaven, is symbolized by pieces of jade falling from the clouds or, as in the mural paintings of Teotihuacán, sent by the beneficent rain god.

IV. Seven elements that can only be interpreted as being a stylized plant (young maize?). Two of these symbols are engraved below "clouds," three are springing up out of the arch of the monster's cavern-jaws, and two ornament the headdress and the hair of the "Lady."

There can be no doubt that this entire tableau (the dimensions of which are quite large: 2.75 by 3.25 meters) is related to rain. Its

[3] Peñafiel, 1885, vol. 1, pp. 170–208; vol. 2 (album, pls. XXIII, XXX).

theme is rain and vegetation. Is it not quite possible therefore that the female figure seated in the cavern is an Olmec rain goddess? And might the volutes coming out of the monster's mouth not symbolize the magic power of the goddess that brings rain and the germination of plants?

Moreover, if the "ceremonial bar" is in some way or other the symbolic substitute for the humano-feline "baby," as seems likely, then this mythical being is himself a young rain god. Ought we to conclude, then, that the "goddess" is his mother? We should point out, however, that the figures at La Venta, San Lorenzo, or Las Limas who are holding this "baby" in their arms are male beings. What is certain is that we here find ourselves in the presence of a set of symbols linked to the cult of a fecundating rain divinity.

Another almost certain conclusion is that this bas-relief contains a number of elements that are "glyphs," that is, abstract symbols of certain things or certain ideas: the sign "clouds," the sign "raindrop," the sign "jade—water," *muluc*, and the sign "vegetation." Let it suffice for the moment to point out here the presence of these glyphs.

To conclude our study of bas-relief no. 1, we should also mention its outstanding technical and aesthetic quality. The artist or artists who executed this work give proof of an astonishing mastery of their craft. The complexity of the subject, the tightness of the composition, and the diversity of the symbols lead us to presume that the sculptor followed a design doubtless drawn up by priests, who were privy to all its esoteric meanings.

Many centuries have gone by, and we know practically nothing about the beliefs and the dreams of these men: nonetheless, the elegant and serene majesty of the goddess and the harmony of the symbolic tableau of which she is the center bother us deeply.

Bas-relief no. 2 no doubt also reflects an aspect of Olmec religion, but this time one that is sinister and disturbing. Four figures fill a panel that is 3.12 meters long and 1.6 meters high. The (ritual?) scene in which they are participating is strange, its interpretation difficult and problematical. To the left, an individual with a typically Olmec face, wearing a rigid hat decorated with an "Olmec cross," dressed in a loincloth and a long cape, appears to be heading toward the left edge of the panel. He is holding a leafy branch or a maize stalk in his hands. His back is turned to two figures who seem to be heading to the right and who occupy the center of the panel. Brandishing two objects in the form of paddles or clubs, they are wearing hats whose shape is similar to that of the headgear of the first figure, though more elaborate. The headdress of one of these individuals, the one farthest to the right, is decorated with an "Olmec cross," above which are two glyphs. But most importantly, these two figures in the center

Relief no. 2, Chalcatzingo. (From C. T. E. Gay and F. Pratt, *Chalcacingo*. Courtesy of Akademische Druck- u. Verlag, Graz.)

of the panel are both masked. The masks combine the features of a bird with a long curved beak and the fangs of a feline; they give these two figures a terrifying air. The last element in this tableau is stranger still: a man lying on his back, leaning against what appears to be an idol, a masked dwarf wearing a turban (?) with an "Olmec cross." The man lying down is naked. His wrists are bound together in front of him. His genitals are clearly visible. He is bearded and is wearing an ornament in the form of a horn on his head. A similar ornament, though smaller, juts out of the top of the head of the idol against which the captive (let us call him that) is leaning.

An enigmatic scene, executed with extraordinary brio, and one made even more striking because of the dynamic attitudes of the threatening figures. But how to interpret it? Michael Coe (1968b, p. 92) sees it as a scene of conquest: two Olmec warriors confronting a prisoner "humiliated, in typical Mesoamerican style, by having his genitals bared." Román Piña Chan (1955b, p. 25) regards the captive as being destined to serve as a sacrificial victim offered to an agricultural divinity, a hypothesis accepted by Ignacio Bernal (1969, p. 140). Carlo Gay (1971, p. 46) also thinks that this scene has to do with an agrarian rite, particularly in view of the fact that the "sacrificers" are wearing headdresses with ornaments in the form of plants, and he interprets one of the glyphs as a rain symbol. He also notes that an object of excellent workmanship found in 1969 in the state of Puebla, a sort of paddle 36 centimeters long, made of serpentine with an Olmec mask engraved on it, is suggestive of the "weapons" or "ritual clubs" being brandished by the two central figures.

The "religious" interpretation seems more likely than the "military" one. It corresponds more closely, moreover, to the general tendency of the Chalcatzingo bas-reliefs. It should be noted, however, that there are no scenes of human sacrifice represented in the Olmec art of the "metropolitan area" thus far brought to light.

While relief no. 3 may represent a feline, barely recognizable because of its poor state of preservation, relief no. 4 clearly shows two jaguars. These two felines and two human beings are sculpted on a square-shaped rock panel measuring approximately 2.45 meters on a side. One of the jaguars has an "Olmec cross" incised on its head, and the other has a leaf motif on its forehead. Each of them is just about to leap upon an apparently naked human figure, whose genitals are not shown, lying on its back with its arms underneath its head. Should this relief be seen as depicting an attack, a fight? Or, if we compare it with the sculptures from Potrero Nuevo and Tenochtitlán mentioned earlier (Chapter 2), should it not be interpreted, rather, as the story, fixed in stone, of the mythical loves of jaguars and women? In this case too, we necessarily remain within the realm of conjecture. The only thing that we can say is that this latter hypothesis is a plausible one.

Relief no. 5, with its theme of a serpent devouring a man, is just as great an enigma to us. The reptile has enormous fangs, the "Olmec cross" just behind its head, and on its neck a three-pointed motif resembling a short wing. Emerging from the serpent's mouth are the head, the upper torso, and the arms of a human being.

On occasion the art of the Chalcatzingo sculptures abandons mythological themes and strives for a realistic effect: thus we find, rather surprisingly, a representation of a beautiful plant (relief no. 6) or a rabbit (no. 7). The fantastic reasserts its rights with relief no. 8, a strange animal with a reptilian body whose very surrealistic head is reduced to two geometrical volutes with two raindrops falling from them.

Relief no. 10, not discovered until 1969, a long distance away from the others near the peak of the mountain, shows a figure seen from the front: its face, surmounted by a pointed headdress, has the short, broad nose, the thick, bowed lips of the Olmec "canon." Only its eyes, which are round rather than almond-shaped, differ from those of the usual type.

The Chalcatzingo site is not only remarkable for the bas-reliefs that we have just described, although they may be regarded as one of the most extraordinary series of sculptures in Mesoamerica. A small mound or tumulus has been excavated, and stratigraphic probes have been

Relief no. 4, Chalcatzingo. (From C. T. E. Gay and F. Pratt, *Chalcacingo*. Courtesy of Akademische Druck- u. Verlag, Graz.)

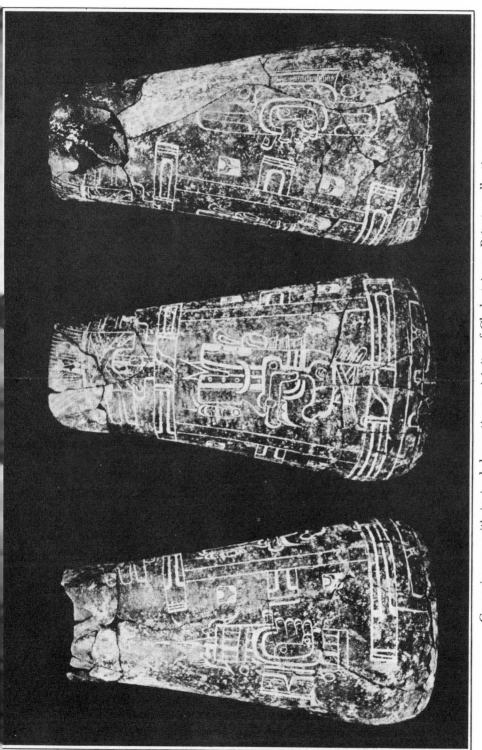

Ceramic vase with incised decorations, vicinity of Chalcatzingo. Private collection. (From C. T. E. Gay and F. Pratt, *Chalcacingo*. Courtesy of Akademische Druck- u. Verlag, Graz.)

Head, "baby face" type, Gualupita, state of Morelos. (Courtesy of Museo Nacional de Antropología, Mexico City.)

made in twleve places. The study of Chalcatzingo pottery shows that the site was occupied as early as the lower pre-classic era, and that an Olmec group settled there around 900 or 800 B.C.[4] Relatively few small Olmec artifacts have been found at Chalcatzingo or its environs: a jade figurine, two or three *sellos,* or seals, in terra cotta, and above all an extraordinary conical vase in terra cotta (Gay, 1971, fig. 43 and pl. XXIII) decorated with a complicated motif comprising a stylized mask with jaguar fangs, "Olmec crosses," and two hands holding objects in the form of "knuckle-dusters," the whole engraved with as great a delicacy and sureness of line as the best Olmec engravings in hard stone.

And finally, a basalt statue with the head missing, now in the Museo Nacional de Antropología in Mexico City, was discovered at Chalcatzingo by Eulalia Guzmán in 1934. It is 53 centimeters high and represents a seated figure with his hands resting on his knees: he is wearing a loincloth, a wide belt, and a rectangular pectoral with crossed bands.

Chalcatzingo is not the only place in Morelos that shows traces of the Olmec expansion. In 1934 Vaillant published the results of his excavations at Gualupita, just outside Cuernavaca, unquestionably an Olmec site: a very fine "baby face," today in the Museo Nacional de Antropología in Mexico City, would be sufficient proof of that by itself.

One of the most remarkable Olmec terra cotta statuettes was discovered by chance in the valley of the Río Yautepec, at Atlihuayán. Twenty-three centimeters high, it is in the shape of a corpulent individual, seated, thrusting its face with a prominent chin forward. The features conform to the usual Olmec convention: a broad nose, thick, bowed lips, "flame" eyebrows. A sort of headdress with a visor covers the head. But most importantly, the figure is enveloped in a great jaguar skin thrown over its back and the back of its head: the feline's paws are fastened to the man's shoulders and thighs.

Two sites in the valley of Cuautla, La Juana and San Pablo, have been the object of excavations. We find there, as at Tlatilco, Olmec ceramics and others in the "Río Cuautla style." San Pablo is a veritable necropolis: a circular mound containing 250 graves was found there.

A "votive ax" of the purest metropolitan Olmec style (Joralemon, fig. 220) comes from the same area. Such an object could obviously have been brought to Morelos by travelers coming from the Veracruz zone. But the abundance of pottery pieces in the valley of Cuautla shows in any event that there was an Olmec population residing in this region as early as the beginning of the first millennium B.C., or

[4] Piña Chan, 1955b, p. 23.

even, at La Juana, the end of the second millennium. The "Río Cuautla style" no doubt dates from a more recent period, in which the
influence of the Pacific coast prevailed, followed by the classic era, in
which the dominant influences from the outside originated in the
highlands, at Teotihuacán. Over the centuries, the Olmec element
gradually dwindled and disappeared.

Caves with painted walls were discovered at Juxtlahuaca (1966) and
Oxtotitlán (1968): both sites are in the state of Guerrero, to the east
of the capital, Chilpancingo.[5] They are the first, and thus far the only,
known Olmec paintings. The faint traces of color still visible on certain monuments from Veracruz and Tabasco lead us to believe that
certain statues and bas-reliefs may have been painted. It is quite possible that wall panels, of painted stucco, decorated buildings made of
pisé and wood, but no trace of them remains. Fortunately, the Guerrero paintings were preserved due to their location within deep caverns.

At Juxtlahuaca, it is necessary to walk more than a kilometer and a
half underground to reach the "Ritual Hall." There a magnificent scene
greets the eye. A painted panel shows a tall, bearded, standing figure, clad in luxurious array and decked with splendid ornaments. He
is wearing a headdress of green plumes, a tunic with polychrome
horizontal stripes, and a light brown cape thrown over his left shoulder. His forearms, his hands, and his legs are covered with jaguar
skin. What appears to be the end of his loincloth (his *maxtlatl*, to use
the Aztec term) is also made of jaguar skin. Or might this figure be a
supernatural being, half man and half jaguar? If we accept this interpretation, what appears to be a *maxtlatl* is in reality the jaguar tail of
this hybrid creature.

In its left hand this figure is holding a cord, the other end of which
is coiled around the second individual depicted on this panel. Of dis-
proportionately small stature, no doubt a deliberate distortion meant
to emphasize by contrast the authority of the jaguar-man, this figure
is shown in a squatting position: seen in profile, he has a face painted
black, a prominent nose, and a little pointed goatee. He is wearing a
red and black headdress and a red tunic. The theme of two figures
facing each other, and that of a cord linking a main figure to a sub-
ordinate one, are frequent in Olmec iconography.

Is this, as Michael Coe (1968b, p. 100) believes, a "secular" scene,
representing a great Olmec chieftain? Coe reminds us that the high-
est Maya dignitaries of the classic Maya era wore jaguar-skin gaunt-
lets. And it is true that at Bonampak, for example, the most important

[5] The paintings at Juxtlahuaca were discovered by Carlo E. T. Gay and Gillett Grif-
fith; the existence of those at Oxtotitlán was reported to the Instituto Nacional de
Antropología e Historia in 1968 by the inhabitants of the village of Acatlán and they
were examined that same year by David C. Grove, of New York University.

warriors are generally shown wearing jaguar-skin ornaments. But let us not forget that the Juxtlahuaca paintings and those at Bonampak are separated by an enormous time gap: a millennium and a half.

If, as has been suggested above, the principal figure is a jaguar-man, then the theme of the painting is religious and mythological. This is undoubtedly true of the second painted panel, in a subterranean gallery just beyond the "Ritual Hall." Here, a huge serpent painted in red is shown facing a feline. The serpent's eye is incised with the motif of bands crossed in an "X" (the "Olmec cross"), and its head is surmounted by a green crest; a sinuous tongue ending in a sort of trident or fleur-de-lis protrudes from its mouth. As for the feline, it too is painted in red, and its back is marked with characteristic jaguar spots.

The jaguar and the serpent: these two creatures haunted the imagination of Mesoamerican Indians for dozens of centuries. Here they are shown together, but appear to be confronting each other.

Whatever the meaning of these paintings—which were no doubt made by the light of torches of resinous wood—we can be certain that caverns hidden so deeply within the heart of mountains[6] were sanctuaries. Rites whose nature we cannot imagine were celebrated in these hypogea by Olmec priests, and pilgrims who had come from the other side of the continent contemplated these paintings that are mysteries to us but to them were charged with the power of myth and were objects of veneration.

The paintings of Oxtotitlán are located about 30 kilometers to the north of Juxtlahuaca, on a cliff face and in two shallow caves. They are more varied, and even more disconcerting, than those of Juxtlahuaca.

On the face of the cliff itself, a figure is shown sitting on the head of a jaguar. While this head is highly stylized, being reduced to its essential features—the outline of the upper lip, two long curved fangs, two oval eyes marked with an "Olmec cross"—the human figure is shown in an asymmetrical and dynamic attitude: his left leg is bent back over the head of the jaguar-monster, and his right leg is dangling in front of the feline's face. His left arm is raised up very high, whereas he is holding his right arm in an oblique position. His body and his face are red, while his ornaments are green (jade). He is wearing very elaborate, complicated attire: a helmet in the shape of the head of a night bird, a mantle edged with feathers, a blue-green pectoral with an "Olmec cross," a green loincloth, a fringed red skirt decorated with two handprints, the palms of which bear a motif in the form of a volute. A red "glyph," on a green background, painted just above

---

[6]The Aztec god called Tepeyollotl, "the heart of mountains," is represented in the form of a jaguar.

the head of this figure, closely resembles the one shown on the head-dress of the "sacrificers" at Chalcatzingo, and may be interpreted as being a sign of "rain" or "flowing water."

Other paintings at Oxtotitlán[7] have been so badly damaged that there is nothing left of them but fragments. Among those in the best state of preservation are a stylized screech owl (painting 1-e), a sort of four-petaled flower with a human face seen in profile in the center (1-a), a very fine Olmec head wearing a serpent half-mask (no. 7), a naked (?) kneeling figure (A-2). Two paintings in a relatively better state of preservation are worthy of mention.

One of them (1-c), in quite good condition, represents a serpent with a bulbous snout and a mouth bristling with long fangs from which there protrudes a forked tongue. The eye is surmounted by a sort of crest. Behind the head, an appendage that resembles a wing can be made out.

The other (1-d) is no doubt the most enigmatic of all these paintings. Two figures are shown in it. To the right, his torso seen frontally and his face in profile, facing left, a man is standing with his right arm upraised. His features are typically Olmec; he is wearing ear ornaments and a diadem. He is painted entirely in black with the exception of the face, the diadem, and an enormous phallus. To the left a jaguar is shown standing upright, turning its back on the man, though its tail is still touching the human figure.

How to interpret this scene? Representations of sex characteristics are extremely rare in Olmec art. It is perhaps significant that the only representations of male genitals are found at Chalcatzingo (relief no. 2) and at Oxtotitlán, in this southwestern area of Olmec expansion. Aside from this, the figure depicted appears to be straight out of a bas-relief at La Venta; it is evident that these paintings are contemporary with the flowering of Olmec civilization on the Gulf coast. The scene doubtless depicts a mythical episode to which the Olmec colonists of Guerrero attached particular importance, for reasons we know nothing of.

Traces of the presence of Olmecs in Guerrero are not limited to cave paintings. A stela discovered at San Miguel Amuco, on the Río San Miguel, a tributary of the Balsas in the western part of the state, was found along with typically Olmec black pottery vessels with white edges. The stela, 85 centimeters high, shows a masked individual in bas-relief, its torso seen in front view and the head and limbs in profile. The mask has a bird's beak and clearly resembles those of the "sacrificers" in relief no. 2 at Chalcatzingo. The figure is wearing a sort of round bonnet with a neck covering at the back, topped by an

[7] The numbers and the letters used below to designate the paintings are those assigned them in David C. Grove's description of them (1970).

ornament in the shape of a fleur-de-lis. A broad cloak hangs from his shoulders. He is holding in the crook of his left arm an object that looks like a bundle of pointed plant stems.

This stela bears a striking resemblance to the bas-relief at Xoc (state of Chiapas), in the Jataté River basin: the same general attitude, the same bird mask, the same way of holding some sort of composite object cradled in the crook of the left arm. We can admittedly note differences in the garments and the headdresses shown on these two monuments, but their inspiration is identical.[8]

Thus, at sites that are more than 900 kilometers apart in a straight line, Olmec colonists sculpted these two stones. The San Miguel Amuco stela is carved of stone found locally and undoubtedly was sculpted *in situ*. As for the Xoc monument, it is a bas-relief carved in the living rock. The presence of Olmecs both at a site close to the border of Guatemala and at another close to the border of Michoacán is thus a proven fact.

The Río San Miguel empties into the Balsas just a short distance away from the place where this river becomes the border between what today are the states of Guerrero and Michoacán. Did the Olmecs make their way into the latter region? Thus far no definite evidence of their presence in Michoacán has been found. A small figurine discovered at El Opeño is sometimes described as "Olmecoid," but it is a rather primitive, badly carved piece that has nothing Olmec about it save for a bow-shaped mouth. It seems almost certain that the Olmecs never went beyond the Balsas, which thus marks the limit of their expansion westward. Perhaps that explains why western Mexico, Michoacán, and the regions in the northwest (the present-day states of Colima, Nayarit, Jalisco) remained outside the area of high Mesoamerican culture, except during the very recent (fifteenth century) phase of the "Tarascan" kingdom of Michoacán. The Olmec catalyst was missing in this part of Mexico.

Numerous artifacts in the Olmec style have been found in the state of Guerrero, either in the center of this state (the Zumpango del Río area) or in sites on the coast such as San Gerónimo or Soledad de Maciel, near Petatlán. Various museums and private collections contain masks, statuettes, etc., of excellent workmanship that are undoubtedly Olmec. We are indebted to Miguel Covarrubias for having been the first to draw our attention to the number and quality of these pieces, and his conclusion that they were fashioned *in situ* is no doubt correct. Certain of these objects are purely Olmec, while others may be described as "Olmecoid." We might, indeed, coin the

---

[8]The San Miguel Amuco stela was described by David C. Grove and Louise I. Paradis in 1970. The rock carving at Xoc (see Chapter 6) was described and sketched by Susanna Ekholm-Miller (1973).

term "Olmec colonial style." Unfortunately, however, the majority of the artifacts from Guerrero preserved in various collections have no documentation as to their precise origin, and at present we lack information based on thorough scientific excavations.

The sole Olmec artifact made of wood that we know of at present comes from Cañon de la Mano, in the state of Guerrero: a very beautiful mask with eyes in the form of two thin slits. The large hole pierced in each of the earlobes was no doubt made for a jade ornament. Tattoo marks are incised on its cheeks. This exceptional piece owes its miraculous survival to the dry climate in this region.

In their 1964 book entitled *El pueblo del jaguar* (*The People of the Jaguar*), Román Piña Chan and Luis Covarrubias published a number of Olmec artifacts from Guerrero: a terra cotta mask with eyebrows in the shape of flames and the mouth of a jaguar; a green serpentine mask that is a human face with Olmec features; a very delicately carved jade mask with a serene expression; an "Olmecoid" mask and a statuette from Mexcala. These latter two objects are perhaps an example of the "Olmec colonial style" or else are the product of a local style influenced by Olmec colonists.

The Dallas Fine Arts Museum possesses a splendid serpentine plaque found at Ahuelicán. It is 23.5 centimeters high and represents a figure in the purest Olmec style, with a V-shaped indentation in the middle of the forehead, slanted eyes, and the mouth of a jaguar. It has very unusual "epaulettes," in the form of masks with feline features. It is holding in its two hands in front of its chest a cylindrical object described as a "torch," and the outline of this same object is incised on its torso. We shall discuss these so-called torches, a quite frequent motif in Olmec representations, later (see Chapter 8).

"Little yokes" resembling those from Tlatilco have been discovered in Guerrero. One of these *yuguitos* comes from Tlacotepec.

A whole series of graceful, realistic terra cotta figurines was discovered, the first of them in 1967, in the vicinity of Xochipala, a village south of Mexcala and northwest of Zumpango del Río. I do not share the opinion of Carlo Gay (1972), who sees in them "the beginnings of Olmec art." There is nothing about these pieces that is Olmec or even "Olmecoid." It is quite obvious that they are examples of a purely local style.

Miguel Covarrubias, along with Carlo Gay, firmly supported the theory according to which the origin of Olmec civilization was to be found in the central region of Guerrero. There are, however, too many converging data pointing to the fact that the focus of this civilization was the "metropolitan area" extending along the coast of the Gulf of Mexico from El Viejón to La Venta. That is quite plainly where it reached its high point in its great ceremonial centers, and it was from there that its travelers, its traders, its priests, its colonists, and perhaps its warriors, crossed the continent, scaled the mountains, reached the high plateaus, and implanted at Tlatilco, at Chalcatzingo, at Juxtlahuaca, certain characteristic cultural features.

Communications between the metropolitan centers and colonial outposts were doubtless neither easy nor rapid.

In its expansion toward the west coast, the Olmec world reached its limits at the Balsas. Toward the southeast, its impetus was to carry it much farther.

# 5

⊠ ⊠ ⊠ ⊠ ⊠ ⊠ ⊠ ⊠

# The Olmec Expansion:
## The Valleys of Oaxaca

It suffices to go through a museum, in Mexico City or in Oaxaca, to visit a site such as Monte Albán, or to glance at photographs of antiquities from Oaxaca, to be struck by the "Olmec" appearance of a great many representations of human or supernatural beings. To cite only this one resemblance: let us observe the famous "Danzantes" (dancers) engraved on the stone slabs of Monte Albán, the Cuilapan "Scribe," the Monte Negro or Yagul braziers, a jadeite mask from Nochistlán.[1] The similarity of the features of these representations (in particular the mouth, more or less resembling a jaguar's) to Olmec pieces that are undoubtedly authentic leaps to the eye. Obviously this is not a coincidence. Moreover, the distances separating the "metropolitan area" from the valleys of Oaxaca are relatively short (it is 350 kilometers as the crow flies from La Venta to Monte Albán, for instance); one can easily cover these distances by going up the rivers that empty into the Gulf.

The major site in Oaxaca is undoubtedly Monte Albán, a sacred city and a necropolis at the top of a mountain entirely remodeled by the hand of man and covered with monuments. This focal point of

[1] Illustrations: "Danzantes," Weaver, 1972, pl. 2. "Scribe," Bernal, 1969, pl. 28. Braziers, Bernal, 1969, pl. 71. Mask, *El arte olmeca*, p. 40.

"Dancer," Monte Albán. (Courtesy of M. Vautier–H. Decool, Paris.)

pre-Columbian civilization was occupied continuously for more than two thousand years, beginning around 900 B.C. The so-called Monte Albán I period corresponds to the five centuries from 900 to 400 B.C. It is contemporary with La Venta and with the second flowering (the "Palangana" phase) at San Lorenzo. During this period, the first occupants of Monte Albán—no traces prior to period I have been found in this locality—constructed stone buildings and built platforms supported by walls on which a sanctuary, reached by a stairway, was erected. This architecture strikes us as being more highly perfected than that of the coastal Olmecs, perhaps for the simple reason that these latter did not have building stone in sufficient quantities at their disposal.

The oldest monument at Monte Albán is entirely surrounded by stone slabs on which the figures commonly known as the "Dancers" are carved. These are naked men, represented in the most diverse attitudes. Some of them are lying or sitting down, others are kneeling, and still others appear to be running or dancing. The faces with full cheeks, thick lips, and drooping mouths irresistibly call to mind the Olmec style. One of the figures, who is bearded, appears to be an old man. Although they are not clothed, the "Dancers" are wearing ear ornaments and in some cases headdresses. Their genitals are sometimes shown in a realistic manner, and sometimes are replaced by curvilinear motifs, tattoos, or body painting.

It is not surprising that these strange figures have given rise to the most diverse interpretations. Could they be prisoners whose status as captives is symbolized by their nakedness? But why these attitudes then, and why aren't they chained or bound? No satisfactory theory has as yet been put forward. Two facts should be stressed in connection with these representations.

Firstly, these are clearly not Olmec works in the same sense as those of the Gulf region or the bas-reliefs of Chalcatzingo. The style of the "Dancers" is nonetheless too close to the Olmec tradition to be merely a chance resemblance. Bernal (1969, pp. 154–55) has pointed out the obvious similarities between the features of the "Dancers" and those of a figure engraved on a pectoral from La Venta. He concludes: "Although it is evident that the danzantes are not characteristic of the Metropolitan Olmec style since they show many different elements, I believe that they bear important analogies and can be placed within the Olmec world." This conclusion should be borne in mind.

Secondly, a very important element makes its appearance here: the majority of the slabs have glyphs engraved alongside the "Dancers," and certain of these glyphs are accompanied by numerals recorded by means of the "dots and bars" system. We are thereby led to de-

"Dancer," Monte Albán. (Courtesy of M. Vautier–H. Decool, Paris.)

duce that the inhabitants of Monte Albán in the period between 900 and 400 B.C. possessed not only a system of writing, or at the very least a set of chronological signs, but also a calendar, no doubt of the same type as the Maya *tzolkin* or the Aztec *tonalpoualli*, in which each glyph is associated with a number.

Caso (1947) notes that certain numbers are less than 13, and hence must correspond to the 260-day (13 × 20) cycle of the *tzolkin*, and that others are between 13 and 20: it is possible that they mark the position of a day in a 20-day "month," in accordance with the typical Mesoamerican calendar.

This is an important observation, first of all because it attests to the fact that certain forms of writing and of time computation appear, in the valley of Oaxaca at least, around the middle of the first millennium B.C.

We see thereby that the civilization of Oaxaca during this period is related to the Olmec world, yet remains original, with its own particular characteristics. While it did not attain the same degree of mastery as the Olmecs in the domain of statuary and bas-reliefs, it developed an important architecture and above all a system of graphic and chronological signs.

Nonetheless, further research must be carried out to determine what may have happened in the valleys of Oaxaca before the beginnings of Monte Albán, that is, before 900 B.C., a date at which San Lorenzo, Tenochtitlán, and Potrero Nuevo were already the center of tremendous artistic activity.

The excavations directed by Kent V. Flannery in one of these valleys, that of Etla, has produced extremely suggestive results. The Etla is a fertile valley, with a temperate climate, where agriculture has enjoyed exceptionally favorable conditions: the ground water level is situated 3 meters below the surface in the alluvial plain, and permanent or nearly permanent streams irrigate the slopes of the valley. Hence the Indians were able very early to master the problem of irrigating their land. We may compare their situation in this respect to that of the Olmecs of Veracruz-Tabasco, who likewise were not obliged to contend with a semi-arid environment.

Another significant feature of the region: numerous deposits of magnetite and other similar minerals are located near two villages, San José Mogote and San Pablo Huitzo.

The pottery discovered at San José Mogote is very much like the Olmec pottery pieces from San Lorenzo, Las Bocas, and Tlatilco. Potsherds show typical incised decorative motifs—a St. Andrew's cross, a jaguar's pawprint—and are mingled with Olmec-style terra cotta figurines whose faces are coated with white slip. Near a platform built of stone on which dwellings in wood and pisé had been constructed, the excavations unearthed fragments of large hollow white figurines, of the same type as those of Las Bocas, and two small heads with humano-feline features.

These dwellings appear to have been occupied by craftsmen. Tools were found in them: burins, perforators, burnishers, and above all, spread over two hectares, innumerable fragments of magnetite, hematite, ilmenite, mica, and quartz, as well as remains of shells from the Gulf coast. Everything seems to point to the fact that there was a workshop here, or rather a series of workshops, where mirrors and ornaments (pectorals, ear ornaments, etc.) were made, using the minerals of the region and mother-of-pearl shells from Olmec country.

Two magnetite mirrors similar to those from San Lorenzo Tenochtitlán were discovered at San Pablo Huitzo.

From all the foregoing there emerges the picture of a double commercial circuit between the Olmec region on the Gulf and the Etla Valley. The importance in the eyes of Olmecs of objects made of magnetite has been mentioned above: artifacts made of this mineral are even more common at San Lorenzo than at La Venta, hence during the earliest phase of Olmec civilization. We must also bear in mind that head or ear ornaments, necklaces and pectorals, and mirrors doubtless possessed a profound meaning in a hierarchized society. They were signs of social status, of prestige, of civil or religious authority, as they were later in all Mesoamerican cultures. Thus the Olmecs most likely were led to establish close relations with Oaxaca, exporting shells to it, and importing from it objects fashioned of magnetite and mother-of-pearl. It is probable that the agricultural population already established in the Etla Valley as early as 1500 B.C. came under the influence of these more sophisticated "clients," copying certain of their decorative motifs, and perhaps adopting certain of their myths or cults. A local aristocracy may well have modeled its way of life on that of Olmec priests and dignitaries.

Hence it would appear that what we find here is not a "colonization," even by small groups of Olmec immigrants, but rather commercial exchanges and neighborly relations between a more refined population and one less highly evolved.

The "San José Mogote" phase prior to 900 B.C. (1000–900?) is contemporary not only with San Lorenzo on the eastern side of Mexico, but also with Las Bocas, with the Ixtapaluca phase (Ayotla, Tlatilco) in the Valley of Mexico, and with Chalcatzingo in Morelos. This was an era of general expansion of Olmec civilization, which appears to have coincided with a rapid increase in population in all those regions where agriculture had been developed.

The following phase, the so-called Guadalupe phase in the Etla Valley, partially coincides with Monte Albán I. We may date it as the period between 900 and 600 B.C. The pottery of this phase is still strongly marked by Olmec connections: we note in particular fragments of hollow statuettes and pottery pieces similar to those from La Venta and Tlatilco. But it is also the era in which the site of Mitla shows the first signs of occupation: we know that this center was to become one of the most important of the classic and post-classic periods. The civilization that we may thus describe as "Zapotec," since it is probable that the same ethnic and linguistic group created and perpetuated it from Monte Albán I until the Aztec era, then arose, characterized by such original features as wall paintings in burial chambers, a complex and majestic architecture, stelae with hieroglyphics, urns bearing effigies of divinities. The memory of Olmec influences lingers on until the Christian era and perhaps even beyond. The magnificent "Scribe" from Cuilapan, that masterpiece of Oaxacan terra cotta sculpture that is so lifelike and so highly individualized, thanks to the glyphs decorating his headdress and incised on his chest, has a face whose mouth and eyes would not detract from the beauty of a statue from Veracruz.[2] Traces of the Olmec style lingered on in Oaxaca even after the civilization of La Venta had disappeared. It is true that Tres Zapotes and Cerro de Las Mesas picked up the torch between 400 B.C. and the beginning of the Christian era, a period that corresponds to the Ticomán-Cuicuilco phase in the Valley of Mexico and to Monte Albán in Oaxaca.

In order to make the duration of this sequence—from San José Mogote through Monte Albán II—that we have just traced more meaningful, let us situate its beginning and end in relation to the history of our own classic antiquity: San José was contemporary with the Trojan War and the Dorian invasion in Greece, and Monte Albán II began at the time of the death of Socrates and ended at the time of the reign of Augustus.

Despite numerous highly competent excavations directed by Alfonso Caso, Ignacio Bernal, and other archaeologists, we still know relatively little about developments in the early periods in Oaxaca outside of its prosperous, populated valleys. The highlands—Mixteca Alta—a rugged country, the habitat of the bellicose and clever Mixtecs, is less well known. Huamelulpan would appear to have been an important site: carved stone slabs bearing glyphs and numerals in the style of Monte Albán II have been discovered there, and even more importantly, a stela-statue whose face unquestionably conforms to the Olmec "canon," while the arms and hands are only very roughly indicated. Bernal is inclined to regard this piece as dating from Monte

[2] See Bernal, 1969, pl. 28. The "Scribe" is now in the Oaxaca Museum. The glyph carved on his headdress and his chest may be read as "13-water": this is the "calendar name" of the person, no doubt the day of his birth.

Albán I, and hence earlier than the stone slabs with hieroglyphics. Its crude workmanship corroborates this view. It may well have been the work of local artisans copying a movable sculpted stone from the coastal region, or working under the direction of Olmec immigrants. It is evident that only the face of the jaguar-man was really meaningful; hence the sculptor concentrated his efforts on it, and on the feline mouth in particular.

All this inclines us to characterize the stela-statue of Huamelulpan as a marginal work, an already dim reflection of the culture of the metropolitan center.

The geographical location of Huamelulpan explains how relations could quite easily have been established between this mountainous area, lying at an altitude of more than 2300 meters in the Cold Lands, and the coastal region of the Gulf. The village is situated along the Río Santo Domingo, which irrigates part of the highlands and empties into the Papaloapan, one of the principal waterways of the Olmec country.

The glyphs and the numbers found at Huamelulpan unquestionably date from a later period than that in which the statue was carved. According to Charles R. Wicke, the style of this sculpture is related to that of certain "votive axes," those that for stylistic reasons are regarded as being the earliest. We may therefore deduce that this monolith is contemporary with the San José Mogote phase of central Oaxaca, and of San Lorenzo in the Veracruz region. Hence it is probably older than Monte Albán I.

There is nothing surprising about this, since the earlier the period considered, the more marked the traces of Olmec influence become in the archaeology of Oaxaca. Hence it is not possible to share the opinion expressed by Wicke (p. 147) that the statue of Huamelulpan enables us to state that "the Olmec style first flowered in the Mixteca Alta." This monument seems, on the contrary, to confirm that the Olmecs of the Gulf region established contact very early (around 1100 B.C.?) with this mountainous area of Oaxaca, as with the Etla Valley. While it is admittedly true that very little is yet known about the archaeology of Mixteca Alta, this in no way justifies the theory that Olmec style originated there before reaching maturity on the Gulf coast, as Wicke suggests. It would appear that Oaxaca has even less reason than Guerrero for claiming the honor of having been the cradle of the first great civilization of Mexico.

On the other hand, there is no doubt that close relations existed between Oaxaca and the Olmec "heartland" from the end of the second millennium B.C. on. It is interesting to note that the influences that had their origin in these contacts continued to exert themselves long after the contacts themselves had ceased. We have offered sev-

eral instances of this above. Flannery (p. 100) notes that the ceremonial architecture of the valley of Oaxaca is not without certain similarities with the tradition of the Gulf coast: "The use of adobe walls
and colored clay in the construction of platforms, and the orienting of
those platforms 8° west of north, are all shared characteristics."

Other sites in Oaxaca also point to a certain spreading of the Olmec
style. At Dainzú, in the Tlacolula Valley, fifty carved stones were
discovered at the foot of a pyramidal platform. Two of them represent
humano-feline beings.

At Monte Negro, to the west of Monte Albán, and at Yagul, fairly
precise dates have been obtained by the carbon-14 method. The date
for Monte Negro is 640 B.C. (plus or minus 170 years), and that of
Yagul between 665 and 615 B.C. The samples that were used to establish the date of Monte Negro came from burned beams of the
temple at this site. No building was constructed on the ruins of this
sanctuary that had burned down, definite proof that the date obtained
is that of the final days of this site, of its disappearance as an inhabited
center, following a civil war or an invasion. In any event, no evi-
dences of culture of the type found at Monte Albán has been discovered at Monte Negro: "Dancers," hieroglyphs, numerals. But vases
or cylindrical urns decorated with an "Olmecoid" mask constitute
typical ceramic pieces from this site. The urns with masks from Yagul
are exactly like those from Monte Negro. In both cases, the humano-
feline face is surmounted by a headdress, a sort of band circling the
forehead, often bearing a "floral" element in the form of a fleur-de-
lis, identical at Monte Negro and at Yagul.

In museums or in private collections we find objects, usually carved
pieces in hard stone, that are unquestionably Olmec and of excellent
quality, but unfortunately their provenance is extremely vague. Joralemon published, for instance, illustrations of six pieces—three "votive axes," a pectoral, a figurine, and a jade plaque—of which the
only thing that can be said regarding their origins is that they come
"from Mixteca" or "from Oaxaca." These are all precious objects that
are easy to transport; they were highly valued in antiquity (and still
are today!) and may therefore have traveled a long distance. Though
they were found in Oaxaca, they may very well have been fashioned
in the "metropolitan area" itself.

The Pacific coast region of the state of Oaxaca has not yet been the
object of scientific excavations. Speaking of a statue from Jamiltepec,
Bernal (1969, p. 160) mentions "vague Olmec reminiscences." The
area lying along the border between the present-day Mexican states
of Oaxaca and Guerrero, which in the historical era was occupied by
Mixtec principalities (Tutotepec) and by Yopi (or Tlappaneca) tribes
that were able to maintain their independence from the Aztec em-

pire, is, archaeologically speaking, *terra incognita*. We do not know whether the Olmecs made their way through the mountains as far as the Pacific, or whether they used only the Isthmus of Tehuantepec route, heading along the Soconusco toward Guatemala and Central America. It is this second hypothesis that seems more likely: from Olmec country, the passageway formed by the Isthmus, the corridor of *Tierra Caliente* separating the Sierras of Oaxaca from those of Chiapas, is a natural route leading toward the Pacific coast. Moreover, it is a region whose climate and vegetation would not make travelers coming from the south of Veracruz or Tabasco feel out of their element. Presumably, the Olmecs would have encountered no serious difficulties in passing from one ocean to the other via this route.

# 6

⊠⊠⊠⊠⊠⊠⊠

# The Olmec Expansion:
## Southeastern Mexico and Central America

If we draw a straight line from north to south, beginning at La Venta, we note that the ancient Olmec capital of Tonalá, near the Pacific coast, is 200 kilometers distant. It is approximately 220 kilometers from Tonalá to the Mexico-Guatemala border (the Río Suchiate). The same distance, more or less, separates the mouth of the Suchiate from the site of Xoc in the Jataté River basin. And finally, La Venta is about 250 kilometers distant in a straight line from Xoc. If we draw a trapezoid connecting these four points on a map of the state of Chiapas, the area within its limits contains an impressive number of Olmec sites, monuments, and remains, even though the exploration of this vast expanse is still very far from complete; it is reasonable to suppose that many discoveries have yet to be made, especially in the humid jungles of the Lacandones' country.

Moreover, this area of Chiapas—which in fact includes almost the entire state—is rich in relics, particularly sculptures, which without being Olmec may be described as "Olmecoid," that is, vestiges of a culture considered to be an intermediate stage between Olmec civilization and that of the Mayas.

Finally—even though here too there have been far too few scientific excavations—this southeastern zone of Olmec expansion extends even farther: to Guatemala, to El Salvador, and even—in the form at least of isolated finds—to Honduras and Costa Rica, that is, to the outermost limits of Mesoamerica, where it comes in contact with the outposts of the South American world. We shall return to the question of defining the border lines between the Olmec influence and that of Mesoamerican civilizations: for the moment we shall merely note that the extraordinary impetus that began to build up more than a thousand years before the Christian era in the region of San Lorenzo and La Venta spread like a shock wave all down the continent to the outer limits of another sphere of influence, that of the Andean countries of South America.

Since our knowledge at present is so fragmentary, stemming as it does either from sporadic diggings or from the study of isolated and sometimes wrongly identified objects, the best approach is doubtless to follow the traces left by the Olmec expansion from the borders of Veracruz, Tabasco, and Chiapas to Central America.

In 1944 Matthew Stirling went on an exploratory field trip to the east of La Venta. At San Miguel he noted the presence of three sculptured Olmec-style stones. Román Piña Chan and Carlos Navarrete proceeded to conduct excavations at San Miguel in 1953. The site, according to them, represents a "small ceremonial center of little importance,"[1] where there is evidence of a strong Olmec influence.

Also in the state of Tabasco and to the west of the Grijalva River, the region of Cárdenas is situated within the orbit of the Olmec style, if we may judge from two pieces found there: a stone mask (Joralemon, 1971, no. 25) and a "scepter" now preserved in the Villahermosa Museum (Navarrete, fig. 16). The mask is of purest La Venta style. As for the "scepter," it is worth dwelling on in more detail. Because of its workmanship first of all, for it was carved, with astonishing virtuosity, from a sort of rod of black stone 25 centimeters long; next, because the head, with the slanted eyes, the broad, short nose, and the typically Olmec mouth that forms one end of it, is surmounted by what looks like some kind of conical headdress, whereas the other end represents a stylized serpent's head; and finally, because this object forms part of a group of similar pieces spread over a vast territory.

In fact, the "scepter" that we have just described comes from the commune of Cárdenas, from the Ejido Ojoshal to be even more precise. A fragment of a "scepter" in green stone, found at Ocozocuautla,

[1] Piña Chan and Navarrete, p. 11.

"Scepter" in black stone, Cárdenas, state of Tabasco. Museo de Villahermosa.

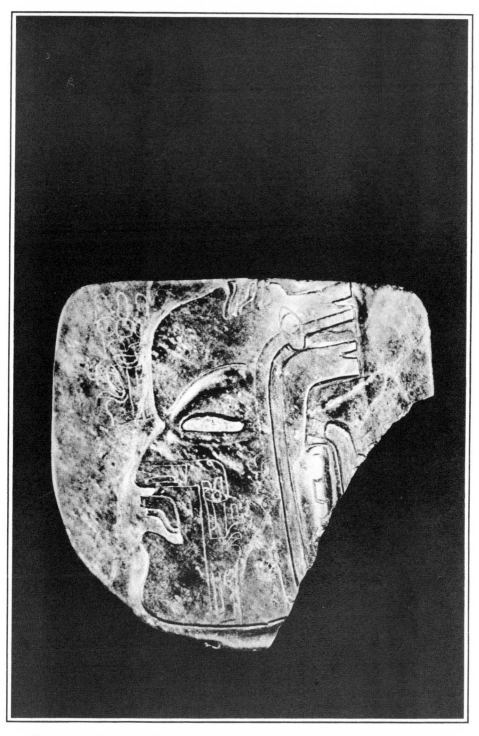

Fragment of engraved serpentine plaque. (Courtesy of Museo Nacional de Antropología, Mexico City.)

a locality in the center of the state of Chiapas, more than 100 kilometers south of Cárdenas, is absolutely identical with the upper end
of the object from Ojoshal: it is an Olmec face surmounted by a conical element. The remainder of the piece has disappeared, but we
may be reasonably certain that the other end was carved in the form
of a serpent's head.

Two other fragments which clearly were once parts of similar
"scepters" have been described by Carlos Navarrete: one of them, a
stylized serpent's head, is from Paso del Toro (state of Veracruz), and
the other, whose precise origin is unknown, is in the Guatemala City
Museum of Archaeology.

And finally, a figurine in serpentine of the most traditional Olmec
type, which belongs to a private collector in Mexico City, is holding
against its chest, in the crook of its left arm, an object that is none
other than the representation in miniature of a "scepter" exactly like
those from Tabasco and Chiapas, including the pointed "headdress."
In this case too, the origin of the piece is not known, but it can only
have come from a region and an era in which the Olmec style was in
full flower.

Hence we begin to see a sort of line of force, or of radiation, that
starts in Veracruz-Tabasco and descends directly southward, toward
the central region of the state of Chiapas.

In point of fact, this central zone, around Ocozocuautla and Chiapa
de Corzo, approximately midway between the two oceans and between La Venta and Tonalá, abounds in relics, certain of which are
purely Olmec. This is true of a splendid jadeite figurine, now in the
Tuxtla Guitiérrez Museum, found at Piedra Parada, not far from Ocozocuautla (Anton, pl. 18). A partially mutilated mask and a jadeite
figurine, described by Navarrete (figs. 13 and 14), were found in the
same region. Not only is the figurine, representing a figure with a
deformed skull and a downturned mouth, the artistic equal of any in
the offerings at La Venta; it also is holding in its hands a conical
object which bears a certain resemblance to the "headdress" forming
the upper ends of the "scepters" described above.

At Chiapa de Corzo, Olmec remains appear in the earliest phases,
but an original culture developed in this central depression of Chiapas. We note "Olmecoid" remains, however, as late as circa 400 B.C.,
as can be seen by studying an engraved pendant fashioned from a
shell that was published by Lee (p. 174, fig. 129c). A stela in a poor
state of preservation discovered at Chiapa in 1961 bears a "Long
Count" inscription that can be read as: 7.16.3.2.13, a date which would
correspond to the year 35 B.C., and hence one four years before that
of the inscription on the famous stela C of Tres Zapotes. This is the
case, naturally, only if we concede that the "zero date" to which this

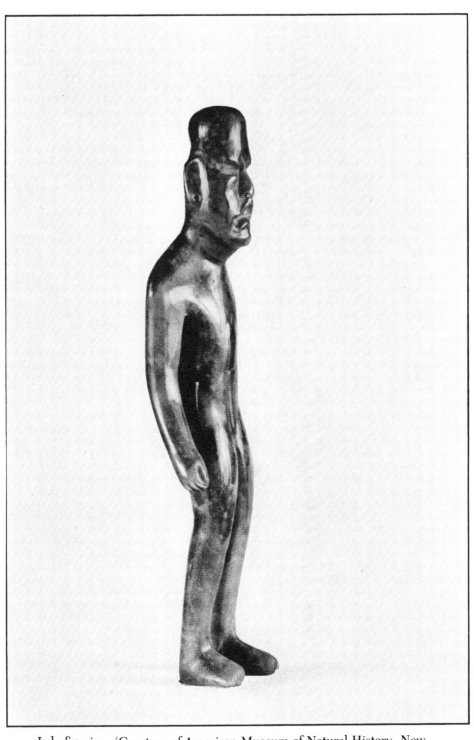

Jade figurine. (Courtesy of American Museum of Natural History, New York.)

Statuette, serpentine. (Courtesy of American Museum of Natural
History, New York.)

inscription refers is that of the classic Maya system, a problem to which we shall return later.

Before following our route farther south, toward the Pacific coast, we should point out a certain number of sites or simply of archaeological objects to the north, east, and southeast of the central region.

From Pichucalco (Chiapas), we have a flat figurine in jade, 12 centimeters high, whose facial features—eyes, nose, mouth—are of the most classic Olmec type. The thickset figure is shown in the same attitude as the statue of San Lorenzo known as monument no. 10: its arms are folded across its chest, and in its hands are two objects in the form of "knuckle-dusters" or small bucklers.[2]

Joralemon (1971, p. 51, fig. 148) has published an engraved ax. The principal motif is an Olmec-type head seen in profile, with very elaborate ornaments and headdress. The delicacy and precision of the design are remarkable; it could only have been executed by an artist thoroughly familiar with the great tradition of La Venta. This artifact is described by Joralemon as coming from Simojovel (Chiapas), a locality situated to the east and slightly south of Pichucalco, at a distance on the order of 60 kilometers in a straight line.

It must be pointed out, however, that in 1947 Alfonso Caso published the same readily recognizable design, with the caption: "Ax from Tapijulapa, Tabasco."[3] The two zones in question are not far apart, but this example shows how regrettable it is that all too often we have only vague or contrary indications of the provenance of archaeological pieces. In any event, such a perfect engraved ax, a precious object par excellence and one easy to transport, may very well have traveled a long distance. It is possible that it was brought to the region by traders from La Venta, or that natives of the southeastern region who had come to La Venta on a pilgrimage or for some other reason took this valuable "souvenir" home with them.

While a piece of carved jade may have traveled great distances, the same is obviously not true of monoliths of considerable size and weight, and any and all conjectures as to possible geographical displacement must be excluded when the monolith in question is a living rock in place in its natural site. This is the case with the Olmec vestige found farthest east in Chiapas, isolated in the valley of the Jataté River, a tributary of the Usumacinta, on the borders of the Lacandone jungle: the bas-relief of Xoc.

First reported by Enrique Juan Palacios in the 1920s, interpreted by Frans Blom as a "Maya tiger-god" and by Basauri as a "Maya tiger-priest," described by Blom and Gertrude Duby in 1957 as a "priest or tiger-god," this bas-relief was published by Wolfgang Cordan in

[2] Cervantes, 1976, fig. 14.
[3] Caso, 1947, p. 91; fig. 58.

Colossal head: monument no. 1, San Lorenzo. Museo de Antropología, Jalapa. (Courtesy of R. Roland–Ziolo, Paris.)

Offering no. 4, La Venta. M.N.A., Mexico City. Now located in the Parque-Museo de La Venta in Villahermosa, state of Tabasco. (Courtesy of R. Roland–Ziolo, Paris.)

The "Wrestler," Uxpanapa. Museo Nacional de Antropologíca, Mexico City. (Courtesy of R. Roland–Ziolo, Paris.)

Monument no. 34, San Lorenzo. Museo Nacional de Antropologíca, Mexico City. (Courtesy of R. Roland–Ziolo, Paris.)

Rock paintings, Oxtotitlán. (After David C. Grove.) (courtesy of
Dumbarton Oaks, Washington, D.C.)

Statuette of the "Scribe," Cuilapan, state of Oaxaca. Museo Regional de Oaxaca. (Courtesy of R. Roland–Ziolo, Paris.)

Monument no. 10, San Lorenzo. Museo de Antropología, Jalapa. (Courtesy of R. Roland–Ziolo, Paris.)

Bas-relief, Xoc, state of Chiapas. (Drawing by Anne Bouvier based on reproduction of work published by Susanna Ekholm-Miller.)

1964 (fig. 14). A rather unusual but perfectly recognizable drawing of it was published by Ignacio Bernal (1969, fig. 34) with a caption situating the monument at "Batehaton" (Bachajón?). In any case, what is certain is that it is a sculpture in the purest Olmec style, closely related to the Chalcatzingo reliefs. Thanks to Susanna Ekholm-Miller and the New World Archaeological Foundation (Brigham Young University), this monument was studied and photographed in 1968. Fortunately; for in 1972 a second expedition reported with bitter regret that vandals had ravaged this monument, removing with chisels the part of the rock in relief and carrying it off, doubtless in several pieces. This is a typical case of the pillaging of antiquities that is rampant in the more isolated regions of Mexico.

The site of Xoc (sometimes spelled Xac or El Xhac) includes several mounds and remains of buildings. The bas-relief was carved on a flat limestone rock face. It represents a figure 2.10 meters high; his trunk and arms are shown in front view, his face and legs in profile. Short and heavyset, the man is wearing a loincloth held up by a wide girdle. His left hip is covered by a sort of square panel (leather, cloth?). His left ear, the only one visible, is decorated with a ring from which a fairly long curved element, perhaps made of cloth, is suspended. His face is concealed by a bird mask, and his feet are bird claws. On his head is a towering, monumental headdress, a round, no doubt rigid hat, decorated with an "Olmec cross" and surmounted by a cone with a rounded peak reminiscent of the "scepters" from Tabasco and Chiapas.

This figure is holding in his right hand a cylindrical rod partially concealed by his leg. In the crook of his left arm is a complex object, perhaps a large bundle of branches and leaves.

Finally, a square cartouche, which might have been meant for a glyph, has been carved between the headdress of the figure and the "bundle," but its surface was not engraved.

This is what the bas-relief looks like, or rather what it looked like before the greed of unscrupulous looters chiseled it away from the rock.

Two observations immediately suggest themselves. First of all, it is evident that this is an Olmec sculpture, and in fact a work of high quality. Susanna Ekholm-Miller goes so far as to ponder the possibility that "a master sculptor from the Gulf Coast region might have been commissioned to carve this outstanding Xoc figure."[4] On one score at least there is no possible doubt: we are not in the presence of a more or less "Olmecoid" sculpture; this is beyond question authentic Olmec art. And since this bas-relief was carved in living rock,

[4] Ekholm-Miller, p. 18.

Carved stone head. (Courtesy of American Museum of Natural History, New York.)

we are forced to conclude that Olmecs resided at Xoc, far to the east of their "heartland."

Secondly, certain similarities would seem to enable us to relate this sculpture to other Olmec reliefs. We are tempted to note a number of iconographic resemblances it shares with the reliefs of Pijijiapan, on the Pacific coast, that will be discussed below. These resemblances, however, are quite vague and superficial. On the other hand, the figures with bird masks and rounded hats shown in bas-relief no. 2 at Chalcatzingo, and above all that on the stela at San Miguel Amuco, in Guerrero, appear to bear a close "family resemblance" to the Chiapas figure.

The individual represented at Amuco admittedly is wearing a less complicated headdress and simpler garments than the Xoc figure, and his feet, as far as we can tell, are human feet. But his face is concealed by a bird mask, his attitude is absolutely identical with that of his Chiapas counterpart, and he is holding in the crook of his left arm an object that appears to be a bundle of plant stems or branches. The similarity in this instance is most striking. And finally, two elements that might be glyphs are represented in front of the Amuco figure, just as a cartouche is placed behind the one at Xoc. We may well wonder in both cases whether these are not religious or secular dignitaries: the mask and the "fasces" may be the insignia of their office, and the glyphs may indicate their function or their name.

The very evident "classic Olmec" nature of these sculptures would appear to be at odds with the fact that these are provincial or colonial works, far distant from the "metropolitan area." But this apparent contradiction can be resolved if we grant that Olmec chieftains possessed of important powers and great prestige were charged with the mission of commanding distant outposts. They would quite naturally have had a vast retinue of servants, warriors, and—why not?—artists, sent out also from the "metropolis" and assigned the task of engraving on the rocks of the provinces the record of the Olmec presence.

Although mutilated, the stela of Padre Piedra, located 150 kilometers southwest of Xoc in the upper basin of the Grijalva, is proof that Olmecs lived there. Two and a half meters high in its present damaged state, this stela represents a scene that occurs frequently in Olmec iconography: two figures facing each other, one of them standing and the other kneeling. Moreover, the man who is standing is holding in his left hand the puzzling object in the form of a "knuckle-duster" or a small buckler that we have encountered more than once before.

The Aztecs gave the name Xoconochco, "the country of bitter prickly pears," to the flat, torrid coast, a narrow corridor between the mountains and the ocean, that descends more or less from northwest to

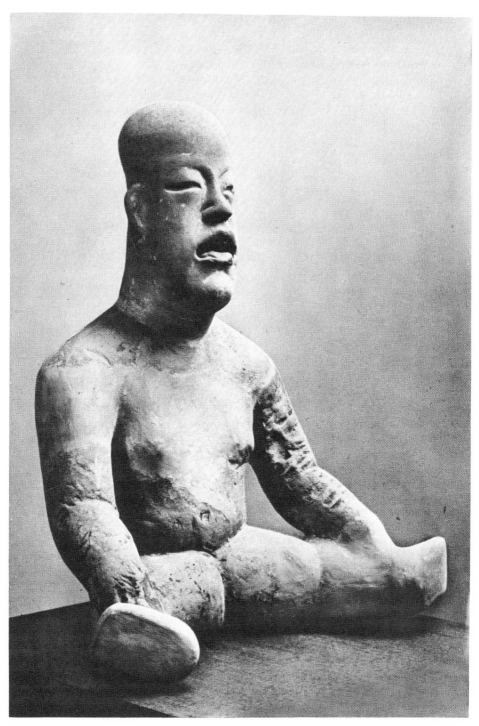

Terra cotta figurine, "baby face" type. (Courtesy of R. Roland–Ziolo, Paris.)

Stela, San Miguel Amuco, state of Guerrero. (Drawing by Anne Bouvier based on reproduction of work published by David C. Grove and Louise I. Paradis.)

Head carved in black stone. (Courtesy of American Museum of Natural History, New York.)

southeast from the Isthmus of Tehuantepec to the Suchiate River. This "Soconusco" country, as it is called today, presented itself as a natural route for traders and soldiers from Tenochtitlán heading toward Guatemala after having crossed the Isthmus. From time immemorial, this was the route along which styles, ideas, and material goods passed, and the Olmecs too undoubtedly made use of it.

The early ceremonial center of Tonalá, with its platforms and its monuments in ruins, stands on a rocky ledge overlooking the coastal plain of Soconusco some 600 meters below: brush country where jaguars abound. The Tonalá site itself is made up of five groups of masonry structures. It has been explored and described, by Edwin Ferdon in 1949 in particular, but no real excavations have been conducted there. There are also stelae, "altars," and carved rocks at Tonalá. The site was unquestionably occupied over a very long period, for Olmec features analogous to the style of La Venta are discernible there, as well as sculptures that are much more recent. As is natural in a place that constituted a key point of passage on the route between the north and the south, certain phases of the culture of Tonalá underwent a northern influence, and others an influence originating in the southeast of Mexico and in Guatemala. The monolith known as "monument no. 5" is sculpted in the likeness of a face with feline features, long fangs, and a sort of crest at the top of the skull, resembling that of certain statues at La Venta. Petroglyph no. 1 is also "Olmecoid." Stela no. 9 bears a close resemblance to that of Padre Piedra. We may even wonder whether the jaguar snout sculpted on altar no. 1 does not derive from the same style. On the other hand, a stela that today may be seen in the railroad station of the small modern town of Tonalá—having been brought there from the ruins or from some other site close by—shows a figure whose legs are protected by thick knee pads (a handball player?) and numerals that would appear to be a 7 and a 9, in the dot-and-bar system of notation. The style of this relief and that of another stela standing in the main square of Tonalá are not suggestive of Olmec art, but rather of that of localities farther south and of more recent phases: Izapa in Mexico, Cozumalhuapa in Guatemala. I am inclined to agree with Bernal (1969, p. 171) that Tonalá was not in fact dominated or "colonized" by the Olmecs, but had contact with them, so that its own style underwent their influence. It is evident that Olmec traders or warriors heading toward Central America along the coast would have had to proceed along the foot of the rocky spurs on which Tonalá was built. Relations—probably peaceful ones—must have been established. Local artists would surely have admired the engraved axes and other typically Olmec pieces that these travelers no doubt showed them, and probably they imitated them. If this hypothesis is correct, systematic excavations at

Standing jaguar, serpentine. (Courtesy of Dumbarton Oaks, Washington, D.C.)

Tonalá would bring to light Olmec artifacts brought there by people from La Venta.

The region around Tonalá must have been densely populated in antiquity. At La Tortuga, a few kilometers north of the present town, are the remains of five platforms, buried beneath vegetation. Sculpted stones have been found there, but none of them seems to be related to the Olmec style. On the other hand, the field research conducted by the New World Archaeological Foundation led to the discovery at Tzutzuculi, a short distance away from Tonalá, of several stone monuments that are proof of Olmec occupation of this site.

The two monuments at Tzutzuculi, a photograph of which was first published in 1977 by Andrew J. McDonald, are roughly cubical blocks of volcanic stone of local origin, measuring approximately 1.5 meters on a side. They were found on either side of a stairway on the southern face of a tumulus ("mound no. 4") that is part of a complex of twenty-five structures and platforms concentrated within an area of 35 hectares lying to the southeast of Tonalá.

Because of its method of construction (beaten earth, clay, and stones) and because of other features such as the platform with rounded corners that supports it, this mound, which is 8 meters high and 62 meters long, is reminiscent of the pseudo-pyramid at La Venta. Moreover, the disposition of the various platforms, grouped as they are to form a ceremonial complex, is highly reminiscent of the main La Venta site. As for monument no. 1, there is no question that it is in the Olmec "metropolitan" style. In fact, engraved on its anterior face is a typical representation of the "were-jaguar," with its characteristic snout. Monument no. 2, more stylized and abstract, is suggestive of a serpent's head or of a dragon-serpent.

When subjected to carbon-14 testing, specimens of charcoal found in the fill materials of the mound gave the two dates 545 and 340 B.C. This dating is confirmed by the study of the local pottery, which can be situated as belonging to a period between the years 550 and 450 B.C.

There are thus well-founded reasons to regard these engraved monuments of Tzutzuculi as yet another proof of the actual presence of Olmecs—or, to be more exact, certain Olmecs: travelers, traders, warriors—in this Pacific coast region that is a passageway leading to Central America.

About 50 kilometers southeast of Tonalá, a little river called the Pijijiapan, which descends from the foothills of the Sierra Madre del Sur and empties into the ocean, flows past the village of the same name. Three large granite rocks, a kilometer away from the river, have been sculpted on one of their faces. The first of them, 2.95 meters high, bears a relief showing three figures known locally as

Jaguar-man, serpentine. (Courtesy of Dumbarton Oaks, Washington, D.C.)

"Los Soldados" ("The Soldiers"). Are they really warriors? It is quite difficult to say for certain, especially since the stone has been badly eroded; moreover, the faces seem to have been intentionally disfigured with hammerblows. The three men have the general bearing, the short, stocky body, of Olmec figures. The torso and the arms are shown in front view, the head and the legs in profile. The figure in the center appears to be the most important one. He is facing left, and is holding in his left hand one of those objects in the form of a small buckler that appear so often in Olmec sculptures. His head is surmounted by a tall headdress with what looks like a wide ribbon reaching to his waist hanging down from one side of it. He is wearing a rectangular pectoral ornament, and a short skirt covers his hips. He is holding his right hand outstretched toward the figure to whom he is speaking, who in turn is represented in an animated attitude, with his left arm raised and his hand pointing upward as though to emphasize a statement. He is wearing a hat or a turban and a long mantle that falls to his ankles. The third member of this trio is standing behind the figure in the center. His hat and mantle are similar to those just described. He is also wearing an oblong pectoral suspended from a necklace.

The composition of the scene, the attitudes of the figures, their garments, the enigmatic object that one of them is holding in his hand are all unquestionably Olmec. And here we are dealing with enormous rocks *in situ*. Hence Olmec sculptors obviously came to Pijijiapan. Perhaps they were members of an Olmec "colony" that was later driven out or overrun, which would explain why the faces of the "Soldiers" were mutilated with hammers.

The second rock has a sculpted area 2 meters high and 6.10 meters wide. This carved surface has been badly damaged, apparently not by men but by the elements, so that the motifs are often indistinct. As well as can be made out, there are five different reliefs: a head whose face is concealed by a mask with a bird's beak reminiscent of those at Xoc, Chalcatzingo, and Amuco; a scene in which three persons forming a compact group seem to be contemplating a tree; a head shown wearing a complicated helmet, ear ornaments, and a feline mask; the bust and the head of a man seen in profile, surmounted by an enormous headdress; and finally, very weather-beaten and almost impossible to make out, a motif, perhaps unfinished, that may possibly represent a seated man.

As for the third rock, damaged by erosion and vegetation, one can make out on it the representation of a reptile (an iguana?).

Leaving aside this latter motif, which has no distinctive features in its present state of preservation, there can be no question that the reliefs on the first two rocks are the work of Olmec sculptors. The

Colossal head: monument no. 4, San Lorenzo. Museo de Antropología, Jalapa. (Courtesy of R. Roland–Ziolo, Paris.)

head ornaments, the hats or helmets, and the masks are quite striking. As for the man without a mask on the second rock, the shape of
his nose and his fat face immediately bring to mind the figures at La
Venta and San Lorenzo.

The pottery found at Pijijiapan—and the remains of pottery pieces
found at Padre Piedra—suggest that these two sites belong to a phase
contemporary with San Lorenzo, between 1000 and 800 B.C.

If we follow the Soconusco corridor farther southward along the
coast, an uninterrupted succession of sites and discoveries, most often
not yet scientifically excavated, leads all the way down to Central
America. Approximately 100 kilometers to the south of Pijijiapan, a
monolith 66 centimeters high and 28 centimeters wide was discovered on land that forms part of the commune of Mazatán, in a place
called Ojo de Agua. This monolith is at present in the Tapachula
Museum. Like other Olmec monuments—the one found at San Martín
Pajapan, for example—it is a composite representation with several
overlapping motifs. The monolith as a whole is in the form of a standing figure, with its arms (partially mutilated) dangling down on either
side of its body, and its head surmounted by a crest; its facial features
have been completely destroyed, no doubt deliberately hammered
away. The figure is shown wearing on its chest a large rectangular
pectoral that can be nothing else but the conventional Olmec jaguar
mask: eyebrows in the form of flames, broad, flat nose, bowed upper
lip. The jaws of the mythical animal are wide open, thus framing a
figure sitting cross-legged on the monster's tongue and lower jaw.
The figure is an Olmec "baby," readily recognizable by the V-shaped
indentation in the middle of its forehead, its slanted eyes, its feline
mouth. Here again we find, in the unmistakable Veracruz-Tabasco
style, the theme of the "baby" with feline features emerging from a
niche that is the gaping mouth of a jaguar, as on altar no. 4 at La
Venta. It is highly unlikely that men hauled a block of stone of this
size by sheer muscle power all the way from La Venta to this site; we
must therefore regard it as convincing proof that Olmec sculptors lived
and worked in this region. Furthermore, this monolith is not the only
trace of the presence of Olmecs in the border region between Mexico
and Guatemala: not far from Ojo de Agua, at Buenavista, peasants
plowing a field unearthed a statue around 90 centimeters high, the
head and face of which suggest a miniature version of the colossal
heads of the metropolitan zone: its features—eyes, nose, mouth—
conform exactly to the "canon" of those sculptures, and the head is
surmounted by a sort of helmet held in place by a chin strap.

On the other side of the Suchiate River, at El Sitio, in Guatemalan
territory, a piece of carved jade poses an interesting problem. On one
of its faces an absolutely typical Olmec countenance is incised. The

eyes, the nostrils, and the mouth were indicated by the sculptor through the use of a bit, a common technique among Olmec stone-workers. On the forehead of the figurine a stylized ear of maize surrounded by leaves is engraved. The other face of the piece bears nine glyphs, incised one above the other in a column. They belong to no known system of writing, such as Maya glyphs, for example, but their general appearance calls to mind the characters carved on the famous Tuxtla statuette.

Certain localities in Guatemala are known for having been places where artifacts that are unquestionably Olmec have been found. This is the case with San Gerónimo, in Baja Verapaz (a stone head, surmounted by a cap with a crest, with a face ending in a long goatee), and Abaj Takalik, in the *departamento* of Retalhuleu (a petroglyph).

The most characteristic Olmec monument in this region is the rock bas-relief at Piedra Parada (San Isidro). The figure shown in it appears to be kneeling or perhaps dancing (Bernal, 1969, pl. 95; Joralemon, 1971, fig. 14), with its two arms upraised. Its very elaborate headdress is held in place by a chin strap, and lines engraved on its arms and legs, at the ankles and wrists, are doubtless meant to indicate jewels, bracelets. The face is as strikingly Olmec as any to be seen anywhere: we may even wonder whether what the artist had in mind was not a feline mask. Extending below the face is what is possibly a short beard. The very nature of this fine bas-relief constitutes irrefutable proof of the presence of Olmecs in this part of Guatemala.

Many other localities in Chiapas and Guatemala confront us with the problem of the "Olmecoid" style or styles and of the transition that led to the rise of Maya civilization: we will deal with this question later on in this chapter.

So far as we know at present, the southernmost Olmec monument is the carved rock at Las Victorias, in the Chalchuapa region of El Salvador. At the same time it is one of the most typically Olmec sculptures imaginable. The four figures shown in bas-relief on the four sides of the rock give the impression of having stepped out of a sculpted panel at La Venta, what with their faces with the characteristic Olmec features, their headdresses—two of them are wearing rigid hats like those of the "priests" of altar no. 5 at La Venta—their pectorals, their mantles. Their attitude calls to mind the figures at Xoc and at San Miguel Amuco: in the crook of their left arm they are holding objects apparently consisting of a cylindrical shaft and a spherical element on which a trilobate motif is incised.[5]

Here, in El Salvador, we come to the end of the path to the southeast traced by the Olmecs, or rather that portion of it that is clearly

[5] Boggs, 1950, pp. 85–92. Joralemon, 1971, fig. 13. Coe, 1968b, fig. 151. Baudez, 1970, fig. 1.

marked by sculptures firmly rooted to the spot. Beyond this point, traces of them do not disappear completely, but we are confronted by the irritating problem and the doubts that arise in the case of small-sized artifacts that are easily transportable and often regarded as precious because of their nature, the material of which they are fashioned, or their style.

The excavations directed by Claude Baudez and Pierre Becquelin at Los Naranjos, near Lake Yojoa, in Honduras, enabled them to distinguish a "Jaral" phase, dating from 800 to 400 B.C., during which Olmec influences came into play: these archaeologists note "similarities in the case of pottery pieces . . . the presence of a head of a figurine in the Olmec style, an ax offering associated with cinnabar" (p. 85).

Several jade figurines in a style that is unquestionably Olmec have been found in Honduras and Costa Rica: a small seated figure with its hands resting on its knees, for instance, from Estado Cortés (Honduras), published by Bernal.[6]

In the southernmost border region of Mesoamerica, in Costa Rica, the jade deposits of the Nicoya Peninsula perhaps served as a pole of attraction drawing to this region Olmec traders or explorers—half traders and half warriors—traveling down the Pacific coast from Tonalá and Pijijiapan by way of Las Victorias. We know of a little jade pendant found at Guanacaste, showing a figure of the very distinctive "Olmec baby" type, which at the same time is ornamented with two wings suggestive of those of bats.[7] This latter motif, which has not been observed elsewhere, may be a reflection of a local style, but the piece is nonetheless Olmec in inspiration: in other words, such an artifact—Michael Coe has pointed out another of the same sort—was probably fashioned on the spot, either by an Olmec artist or by a native of the region who was in contact with Olmec immigrants and strongly influenced by them.

In a recent work (1977), the American archaeologist Doris Stone, whose special field of competence is Costa Rica, draws attention to undeniable Olmec influences in the region of the Nicoya Peninsula. This zone would definitely appear to have been the farthest limit reached by Mesoamerican civilization.

Even when we limit ourselves to noting Olmec remains properly speaking, from the Veracruz-Tabasco area to Costa Rica, the harvest is impressive. But this is only one aspect of an infinitely complex picture, that of the Mexico-Guatemala border region and of the civi-

[6] Bernal, 1969, fig. 102.
[7] Joralemon, 1971, fig. 196. Bernal, 1969, fig. 103.

lizations in that zone that preceded the great classic period dominated by the Mayas.

In this regard, the most important site is that of Izapa, to the east of Tapachula (Chiapas), in Mexican territory at a distance of several kilometers from the Río Suchiate. What is spectacular at Izapa is the stone sculpture: 22 stelae and 19 altars, plus other monuments, all covered with bas-reliefs. The style of these representations is extraordinarily dynamic and "baroque." The scenes depicted refer to a mythology that we know nothing of and that appears to be very different from that of the Olmecs. No more "babies," no hieratic figures in majestic attitudes, but instead lively, often bloody episodes: a man brandishing the head of an individual whom he has just decapitated (stela 21), an animated skeleton—the god of death?—seemingly addressing a living person linked to him by a sort of cord (stela 50), a boatman steering a pirogue along a stream that abounds with fish (stela 67). Birds, plants are represented in quite realistic fashion. The Izapa artist was fond of curved lines, volutes. Everything seems to move, to stir. There is nothing Olmec about this style. Nonetheless, if we look closely at certain details, affinities with Olmec art appear: thus the "Olmec cross" that is very characteristic of stela 11 and above all of monument 2, which shows us a figure kneeling inside the gigantic jaws of a feline—one of the fundamental themes of the art of La Venta and of San Lorenzo. The volutes that appear repeatedly at Izapa are not at all a frequent motif in Olmec country, except at Tres Zapotes, where they date from the very last phase: monument C, a carved stone chest, is an example.

The style of Izapa, symbolic and narrative, is found in other localities on the Pacific side of Central America, at Abaj Takalik for example (Parsons), and even in the highlands of Quiché country, at La Lagunita (cf. Ichon). Moreover, sculpted monoliths representing either heads, often of colossal dimensions, or plump, chubby-cheeked, potbellied individuals, or the stylized snout of a jaguar, have been discovered, usually by chance as people were working the land.

Let us cite, for example, at Monte Alto, a stone head approximately 1.5 meters high, a stylized jaguar mask 1.60 meters high, an obese figure of similar dimensions; at El Baúl, a colossal head; at Bilbao, a corpulent, fat-cheeked statue; and at the Arévalo *finca* (small ranch), a similar figure.[8]

Stanley Boggs and Rafael Girard have unearthed three monolithic statues on land belonging to the Leticia *finca*, in El Salvador. The smallest of them is 1.4 meters high, the largest 2.10 meters. All three belong to the same human physical type: a very large head, without a neck, hunched between the shoulders, exaggeratedly puffy cheeks,

[8]These sculptures are shown in Bernal, 1969, pls. 88–93.

an enormous belly. Is this face "Olmecoid," as Rafael Girard suggests?[9] I for my part think it necessary to limit the domain of the "Olmecoid," insofar as possible. While the features of these statues bear certain vague resemblances to Olmec "baby faces," and while the jaguar mask also bears a resemblance to the La Venta style, the colossal head at El Baúl, on the other hand, with its prominent hooked nose, is not at all Olmec-like. Sculptures of obese figures are frequent in Guatemala, from the Pacific coast to the central plateau: a dozen specimens have been found at Kaminaljuyú, an important site whose rise dates from the classic period.

Still farther distant from the Olmec "metropolitan area," two headless sculptures, 1.20 meters high, were discovered at Copán, on the Atlantic side, in the very heart of classic Maya country. They are very similar to the obese figures found on the Pacific side.

Finally, one cannot help but be struck by the style of the huge mascarons in the form of jaguar heads that decorated the terraces of the earliest monument of the Maya city of Uaxactún, in Petén. This monument, known as "E-VII-sub," in the shape of a pyramid, had been covered over by a more recent construction. It dates from the "Chicanel" phase, that is, from around 700 to 100 B.C.

The tentative conclusion that may be drawn, on the basis of what we know today, is that this border zone between Mexico and Central America saw a period of intense cultural activity in the last centuries of the first millennium B.C. and at the beginning of the pre-classic and proto-classic ēras, between the Olmecs and the Mayas. Various local styles emerged, spread, and changed. Like that of Izapa, like that of the colossal sculptures, they are neither Olmec nor Maya; rather, they sometimes bear traces of the influence and the heritage of the past, and sometimes foreshadow the future.

In this regard, the appearance of chronological inscriptions in certain localities both clarifies and to a certain extent obscures this problem of dating.

If we adopt the classic Maya system and the "G.M.T." (Goodman-Martínez Hernández-Thompson) correlation in order to read these inscriptions, we end up with a table such as the following:

*Chiapas and southern Guatemala*

| | | |
|---|---|---|
| Stela 2, Chiapa de Corzo | 7.16.3.2.13 | 35 B.C. |
| Stela 1, El Baúl | 7.19.15.7.12 | A.D. 36 |

*Olmec "metropolitan area"*

| | | |
|---|---|---|
| Stela C, Tres Zapotes | 7.16.6.16.18 | 31 B.C. |
| Tuxtla statuette | 8.6.2.4.17 | A.D. 162 |

[9]Girard, 1973, p. 200; photographs 7–10.

*Maya, central Guatemala*

| | | |
|---|---|---|
| Stela 29, Tikal | 8.12.4.8.15 | A.D. 292 |
| Leyde plaquette (Tikal) | 8.14.3.1.12 | A.D. 320 |

It is clear that the earliest classic Maya dates (third and fourth centuries A.D.) can be tied in, so to speak, without difficulty with those that follow them during the golden age of the great cities, and that thus a definite chronological continuity can be established from the first Petén inscriptions to the decline of Maya civilization. On the other hand, however, it is immediately evident that the Olmec dates and those of Chiapa and El Baúl are too late.

We have noted (Chapter 2) the similarities in style between Cerro de Las Mesas and Izapa. If the *"baktun* 9" inscriptions of Cerro de Las Mesas are interpreted according to the classic Maya system, and if they are regarded as being contemporary with Izapa, they would lead us to conclude that Izapa was contemporary with the flourishing of the great Maya centers. This seems difficult to accept. We are therefore led to suggest a working hypothesis: the "zero date" of the "Long Count" in the late period of Tres Zapotes and during the proto-classic phase of Chiapas and Guatemala was prior to that of the Maya "Long Count." Hence, the date of stela C of Tres Zapotes, for example, could be situated during what Bernal calls Olmec III, between 600 and 100 B.C. This problem is linked with that of writing, which will be dealt with later (see Chapter 9).

In our search for the traces left by the Olmec expansion, we have arrived at the borders of Maya country. How can we fail to be surprised to note (although it is always possible that future discoveries will cause us to amend the statement) that this expansion, like an irresistible wave proceeding from the center on the shores of the Gulf of Mexico, reached the Mexico Basin, the Balsas River and the Pacific, the valleys of Oaxaca, Chiapas, and Soconusco, and even El Salvador, but left no traces in the region where the great Maya civilization later flowered? This is one of the most intriguing and difficult riddles posed by Olmec civilization.

For the fact is that the area of expansion of this civilization coincides with that of the great cultures of Mesoamerica. The monumental architecture of ceremonial centers, sculpture, an intense religious motivation, and, finally, the calculation of time and hieroglyphic writing are traits common to the evolved societies of the Mesoamerican region. One finds them neither north nor south of the boundary lines marked off very precisely by the traces of the Olmec presence. We may state that, as a general rule, where Olmecs came, Mesoamerican civilization flowered; where they did not come, it did not appear. Despite the artistic quality of their lively and varied pottery pieces, the villagers of northwestern Mexico nonetheless remained very much on the fringes of the classic cultures. The Tarascans of Michoacán did not come to be included within the Mesoamerican cultural area until a very late period. In the southeast, Mesoamerican influences were diluted and never succeeded in penetrating farther south than the middle of Costa Rica, which marks the boundary line of the influence of Chibcha ethnic groups coming up from South America. If the area of Olmec expansion and that of the classic and post-classic civilizations of Mesoamerica coincide, it may well be said that Olmec civilization was the "mother civilization" of this entire portion of the continent.

But . . . there is one exception, constituting an area of enormous size: Maya country. We were, admittedly, able to point out above a number of "Olmecoid" traces in the south of Guatemala. We might mention other objects such as the "Olmecoid" censers found at Ka-minaljuyú (Bernal, 1969, pl. 101). We could also mention, doubtless, the two sculptures discovered at Copán that are (just as vaguely) "Olmecoid," and the Uaxactún jaguar masks. But the fact remains that Olmec civilization seems to have spread neither to Petén, the cradle of high Maya civilization with such cities as Tikal and Uaxactún, nor to Palenque or Piedras Negras in the Usumacinta Valley, nor to Yucatán.

It is true that our knowledge is still extremely fragmentary, and that new discoveries may lead us to less categorical conclusions. By pure chance (the classic case of a peasant clearing a little plot of land) there came to light in March 1978, for instance, what appears to be—judging from the less than clear photograph published in the daily press[10]—an engraved Olmec-style stela. The face that appears on it indeed looks very much like the one engraved on the disk now in the Santiago Tuxtla Museum.[11] Moreover, this stela, 88 centimeters high and weighing around 200 kilograms, was found on the collective land of the Ejido Emiliano Zapata in the commune of Tenosique (state of Tabasco), and thus in the Usumacinta Valley, in what is unquestionably Maya country, east of Comalcalco and Palenque!

It is also true that the almost exclusive attention paid by archaeologists to Maya remains of the classic period (as is quite natural, given the prodigious scientific interest and the incomparable aesthetic value of these remains) has contributed to the fact that remains in Maya territory that might possibly date from the pre-classic period have

---

[10] Article by Zentella P. [Alessio] in the daily *Excélsior*, Mexico City, March 18, 1978. Photograph in the same newspaper, March 29. The stela has been examined by a Mexican archaeologist, Roberto García Moll, who regards it as belonging to the pre-classic period, 500 B.C.

[11] See Cervantes, 1976, fig. 1.

been left in the shadows. Gordon R. Willey[12] does mention an Olmec artifact in jade discovered at Seibal in a cache dating from the middle pre-classic era. But jade objects may, of course, have traveled far, both in time and in space.

Moreover, the excavations recently directed by the French archae-ological mission in the *departamento* of El Quiché, in Guatemala,[13] have brought to light at La Lagunita, among sculptures that are more suggestive of the style of Izapa, a typically "Olmecoid" bas-relief (sculpture no. 12) that Alain Ichon compares most aptly to certain representations at La Venta.

The problem of the relations between Olmecs and Mayas has yet to be resolved. Michael Coe (1968b, p. 103) suggests "a paradoxical solution . . . namely, that the Olmec were the Maya." More pre-cisely, they were pre-Mayas. And at the time of the decline of the Olmec states of San Lorenzo and La Venta, certain groups, he sug-gests (p. 121), began to emigrate eastward, "into the forested lands of the Petén-Yucatán Peninsula, and some up the river valleys into the oak- and pine-covered mountains of Chiapas and Guatemala. What had once been the Olmec civilization eventually transformed itself into the Maya civilization."

Coe situates this transformation as having taken place during the "late formative" period that saw, among other things, the beginnings of the art of Izapa. This latter thus presumably constituted a transition between Olmecs and Mayas.

This reconstruction of Maya proto-history is intriguing, but as Coe himself concedes (p. 122): "Classic Maya art becomes incredibly re-fined and realistic, and it is difficult to believe . . . that the style and its iconography could have had Olmec roots." We are still confronted with three series of unquestionable but nonetheless perplexing facts: first of all, the chronological abyss separating the decline of Olmec civilization, three or four centuries before the Christian era, and the beginning of Maya civilization at the end of the third century A.D.; secondly, the profound discontinuity of styles, which is all the more marked in that, in my view, Izapa cannot be regarded, stylistically, as being an intermediary form between Olmec and Maya sculpture; and finally, the rarity, as we have already mentioned, of definitely Olmec remains in Petén, in the Usumacinta Valley,[14] and in Yucatán. In these Maya localities, where intensive and very carefully con-ducted excavations have been made, including ones that have gone as far down as the lower strata of the Mamom period prior to 400

---

[12] Willey, 1975, pp. 44–45, and 1977, p. 863 (note 6).

[13] Ichon, p. 34, figs. 24 and 25.

[14] Xoc is situated in the Usumacinta Basin, but in a marginal location in relation to important centers such as Palenque, Yaxchilán, Piedras Negras.

B.C., and hence contemporary with the flowering of Olmec culture, there is no evidence of a "formative" phase marking a transition between the civilization of La Venta and that of the Mayas.

While giving due weight to these negative arguments, we must nonetheless note certain classic Maya features that would seem to be more or less a continuation of the Olmec tradition: monolithic altars and stelae, statues of figures that appear to be emerging from niches, caches containing jade offerings, the use of cinnabar in tombs, and, naturally, the very idea of an urban ceremonial center, with its monuments laid out according to a plan whose main axes are determined by cardinal points of the compass. As for the calendar and hieroglyphic writing, it is clear that the Mayas did not suddenly invent them in the third century A.D. We shall have more to say about the origin of glyphs and the computation of time in Chapter 9: the Olmecs undoubtedly were familiar with these two Mesoamerican inventions, and were probably their discoverers. We still must endeavor to determine, however, the point in their history at which they made these discoveries.

If (as the Toltecs were to do much later, at the time of the collapse of Tula in 1168) the Olmecs had emigrated eastward following the decline of La Venta and reached the Yucatán Peninsula, the Usumacinta Valley, and Petén, we would be left with no explanation as to why these three regions show so few traces of their presence during a presumed "formative" pre-classic Maya era. I am therefore of the opinion that we must reject this hypothesis, and shall suggest another that is perhaps more in conformity with our present knowledge.

As we indicated in Chapter 2, the Maya linguistic bloc, which doubtless occupied the coast of the Gulf of Mexico at the beginning of the second millennium B.C., apparently split apart around the middle of this millennium, with the Huastec branch spreading northward and the proto-Maya branch beginning the migration toward the southeast that eventually led it to those regions in which classic Maya civilization was to flourish some 1800 years later. It is likely that these non-Olmec peoples, who remained on the fringes of the great centers, were witnesses of the flowering of the civilization of La Venta. We can imagine them contemplating from afar what at the time were astounding novelties—monumental constructions, sculptures, jade carvings—and we may presume that even though they were neither drawn thereby into the Olmec orbit, nor dominated, nor assimilated, they were inspired by what they saw or by the stories they heard; they most likely adopted, not such strictly Olmec traits as the "baby" with feline features, but, rather, cultural aspects at once more general and more fundamental. In all probability it was not so much a case of imitation as of inspiration. Such a phenomenon is perfectly reconcilable with a stubborn resistance to Olmec penetration into what must have been the heart of Maya country. It is not beyond the realm of possibility to suppose that the proto-Mayas, before entering history with their stone monuments and their hieroglyphic inscriptions, admired the Olmec flowering and retained the memory of it, while at the same time strictly forbidding all incursions into their territory by the Olmecs themselves. This would thus explain why the Maya region shows no signs of Olmec monuments, stelae, sculpted rocks: the Mayas or, rather, those who were to become the classic Mayas we know, in all probability forbade their early neighbors, who were doubtless their adversaries, all access to their country.

These reflections—for here we have left the realm of facts and entered that of theory—lead us to pose the question of the exact nature of this area of Olmec presence that, as we have seen, gradually spread over a great part of Mexico and down into Central America. Was it a state or states? Were there colonies? Was there an "Olmec empire"?

# 7

✠ ✠ ✠ ✠ ✠ ✠

# An "Olmec Empire"?

The vision of a great civilization, covering an immense territory in Mesoamerica, spreading its style, its iconography, and even its obsessions from the Balsas River to Nicoya and from La Venta to Tlapacoya, inevitably calls to mind the image of an empire. We are tempted to speak of an "Olmec empire" as once upon a time it was customary to speak of an "ancient Maya empire." But this latter concept has been abandoned because it has been seen that the classic Mayas, from the third to the tenth century A.D., had cities, leagues, alliances, but not what we could really call an "empire." What can we deduce in this regard from the Olmec vestiges that have been found in a vast portion of Mesoamerica?

First of all, what sort of government did the Olmecs have? And what was the exact role of their cities? Did they form a state or states?

As far as we can determine, the great Olmec centers such as La Venta may be described, to use Alfonso Caso's expression, as "dispersed cities." We must understand by that term that each of the political entities was comprised of a planned center, consisting of earthworks, platforms, pyramidal constructions, with sculptures (stelae, altars), offerings, tombs, the whole oriented along a north-south axis with a deviation of 8 degrees west, and of villages or hamlets, and even isolated dwellings, amid the surrounding fields of maize. Hence the Olmec city was not completely urbanized as Teotihuacán and Tenochtitlán were later to be, but neither was it merely a "ceremonial center." It was the expression of the symbiosis between a population of tillers of the soil, who furnished food and manpower, and an elite of officials, priests, warriors, merchants, craftsmen and artists, sculptors, stone-carvers.

In describing the Olmec city of antiquity in these terms—a description based principally on the ruins at La Venta—we are bearing in mind more recent and better-known facts: the classic Maya city was also a "dispersed city." At Palenque, for example, it is clear that a certain territory subject to a central authority (perhaps, in the seventh century, that of the priest-king with the jade mask buried in the splendor of the crypt beneath the Temple of Inscriptions) contained within its limits the complex of monuments—palaces, sanctuaries, with their marvelous bas-reliefs and their delicately executed stucco panels—plus the dwelling places of a large peasant class whose thatched huts were scattered about on the hillsides.

In short, just as the small Greek cities grouped together their acropolises and their rural "demes," what we sometimes call a Mesoamerican "city" was the result of a synoecism: on the one hand, the center, the residence of the gods and their priests, civic leaders, merchants—a focal point of ritual, administration, and commerce; and on the other, the neolithic villages and hamlets whose daily life—save for their inhabitants' participation in the work projects required by the central authority—had doubtless not changed since the beginnings of agriculture.

Alfonso Caso (1965, pp. 37–38) emphasizes the fact that no trace has been found in the Tabasco-Veracruz region of a great urban concentration that would point to the existence of a real metropolis. The ruins of La Venta cover 550 hectares, those of Tres Zapotes 400 hectares, those of San Lorenzo (including neighboring sites) 2400 hectares. These figures may be compared to the area covered by Mexico-Tenochtitlán at the beginning of the sixteenth century, that is, approximately 1000 hectares. But the Aztec capital, built on islands and sandbars, with its dwellings on pilings lining the edges of canals, was a concentrated city. Olmec cities, by contrast, seem to have constituted a very loosely woven fabric. As in the case of the Mayas, the dwellings in this torrid region were no more than huts built of light materials: wood and leaves, like the huts of the present-day Lacandones. Hence no traces have remained of these flimsy dwellings, save for a few potsherds or grinding stones.

It bears repeating here that our knowledge of Olmec sites is still very sketchy, and many more excavations will have to be conducted before we will be able to see the picture more clearly. Of the Olmec cities of the coastal area as we know them, the one that gives the appearance of being a true capital is La Venta. Not only do we find there the only "pyramid" in the entire region, but also the tombs

Statue, Cuauhtotolapan, state of Veracruz. Museo de Antropología, Jalapa. (Courtesy of R. Roland–Ziolo, Paris.)

with a wealth of precious burial objects give the impression that particularly powerful and illustrious persons were interred there.

Was La Venta the Olmec capital then? There is a very old confederal tradition in Mesoamerica: though Teotihuacán and Tula may have reigned alone, everything seems to point to the fact that the classic Maya cities associated in more or less long-lasting leagues centered on Palenque, Piedras Negras, or Copán. In Yucatán, the post-classic era saw the formation of the league of Mayapán, Uxmal, and Chichén Itzá. And what was the "Aztec empire" if not the tricephalous confederation of Mexico, Texcoco, and Tlacopán, even though the Aztec city was the preponderant power?

Naturally, we have no scientific proof that any inferences we may draw from later phenomena as regards earlier ones, from Maya or Mexican leagues as regards Olmec cities, are valid ones. Let us therefore limit ourselves to the conclusion that it is plausible that centers such as Tres Zapotes, Laguna de Los Cerros, San Lorenzo, etc., were associated, probably under the preponderant influence of La Venta, in a league or federation whose authority extended over the "metropolitan area" (Veracruz-Tabasco).

Within this confederation, who held power?

If we grant that the Olmec city "crowned" villages or hamlets of neolithic peasants, let us turn now to what we know—or can conjecture—about the political structure of these villages. To judge from the figurines from pre-classic sites, certain individuals wore garments, ornaments, masks that set them apart; no doubt these individuals were "shamans," awesome figures, respected and feared, intermediaries between the human world and supernatural forces whose powers lay in a domain somewhere between magic and religion. Such magician-priests still exist today in Indian communities such as those of the (Maya) Mam of Guatemala.

It was doubtless this village "elite" that was the driving force behind the prodigious mutation that took the Olmecs from tiny hamlets to cities, from culture to civilization; and we use the word "mutation" deliberately, for there is no evidence of a "formative" evolution, a gradual maturation over several centuries. This indeed constitutes the very heart of the Olmec mystery. The sudden passage to a superior level thanks to individuals of genius? Innovations suddenly brought in from the outside?—but if so, by whom and from where?

The concept of a "critical mass" with regard to population merits mention here. The island of La Venta might have provided a habitat for 18,000 persons, and the "metropolitan area" might have numbered as many as 350,000 inhabitants. It is possible that an intellectual effervescence, a profound desire for change arose in this human mass, no doubt on occasions such as periodic communal gatherings, markets, or rites.

Was Olmec power essentially based on the waging of war? The Toltec and Aztec states bore the profound imprint of militarism; the art of Tula, Chichén Itzá, and Mexico bear ample witness to this, with their statues of warriors and eagle-knights, their colonnades in the form of armed soldiers standing at attention with their crowns of rigid plumes, their military parades, their animals symbolizing war, eagles and jaguars devouring hearts. In the case of our Olmecs, there is nothing like that. There are admittedly a few flying beings brandishing indistinct objects that may be weapons: but these figures are obviously demons or gods. And admittedly we can see masked men waving clubs, not in the "metropolitan area," but at Chalcatzingo: the scene, however, as I have said, is a religious one, not a military one. And everywhere, more or less, Olmec art represents individuals holding enigmatic objects that resemble small bucklers: we shall have more to say about these later, but there is every reason to believe that they are not weapons.

As is likewise true of Teotihuacán, the vision of itself offered by Olmec civilization is not a warlike one. To compare it with that of the classic Mayas, the closest in time and space: there are no scenes of combat and violence such as those in the frescoes at Bonampak, with their bloody, pleading prisoners, not even any brandished lances, as at Yaxchilán. If the Maya civilization of the first millennium gives us the impression, with a few rare exceptions, of having been a rather peaceful one on the whole (and infinitely less warlike than those of Tula, Yucatán, or Mexico in the following millennium), that of the Olmecs would appear to have been even more so. Its sculptures and its carved objects, its pottery figurines reflect a very strong religious constant. What does this art show us? Priests and gods.

What has just been said is doubtless true, but only as a first overall impression, for while there are indeed many priests and gods (including the jaguar-babies), they are not the only figures. How to interpret, for example, the jade and serpentine figures grouped in offering no. 4 at La Venta, and audience listening attentively to a figure in volcanic stone? Might this not be a representation of a council, of a "place of the spoken word," as the Aztecs called their *Tlatocan* or Supreme Council? These dignitaries are wearing neither the miters nor the ornaments of priests. Could they be "secular" leaders? As for the colossal heads, we are tempted to regard them, as has been said, as the portraits of great chieftains, princes, or kings.

On the other hand, the generally peaceful nature of Olmec civilization did not prevent periods of extreme violence from putting an end to the flowering of San Lorenzo, to cite but one case, nor did it prevent emissaries—armed traders or soldiers—from having practiced the art of war outside the "metropolitan area," in outlying or far-distant regions. It is therefore within the realm of possibility that there were military leaders, at least at certain periods, somewhat in the same way that a Maya city possessed, alongside its priests, a *halach uinic*, a warrior chief.

Another fact must be taken into consideration: the very wide diffusion of what are obviously Olmec objects, carved jade pieces in particular, throughout Mesoamerica. This diffusion suggests a bustling trade, perhaps carried on by agents who, like the Aztec *pochteca*, were at once merchants, spies, and warriors.

Olmec society, as best we can imagine it on the basis of the sparse evidence that we possess, must have been authoritarian and hierarchized: at the bottom, an essentially rural population subject to tribute and forced labor—thus supplying the manpower for the enormous public works projects that were carried out; at the top, probably an elite of magician-priests, observers of the stars, skillful manipulators of their hematite mirrors, worshipers of the jaguar-baby, and city planners and architects as well; alongside this clergy, or dependent upon it, merchants and traders, responsible in great part for the expansion toward the central plateau and the Pacific, and perhaps military dignitaries; and finally, in the centers themselves, in the heart of the "dispersed cities," a host of servants, masons, painters, sculptors, stone-carvers, and craftsmen of all sorts. What is certain is that a very strong and thoroughly accepted authority was necessary to call forth from the people the gigantic efforts that surely were involved in the transportation of monoliths, the construction of ceremonial centers, the building of a pyramid, or the installation of a vast system of underground conduits. Doubtless religion was the basis of this political structure. A theocracy, with marginal mercantile and military aspects: such might be the definition of the Olmec city.

In conclusion, the "metropolitan area" was doubtless, like Petén or the Usumacinta Valley in the case of the classic Mayas, a region of "dispersed cities" sometimes grouped into leagues; La Venta may well have made its authority predominant. These centers and their outlying territories, whether or not they were linked by political structures, had in common a highly original cultural patrimony, a single religion, a single symbology. Military activities do not appear to have played a large part in maintaining their rule. The Olmec expansion may nonetheless have led them to provide themselves with certain means (outposts, garrisons) to protect their trade routes or the little groups of "colonists" who had settled far from the "metropolitan area." The example of Athens in the age of Pericles is sufficient proof that a state may very well be ruled domestically by peaceful means while at the same time it exerts its hegemony beyond its borders by militaristic methods.

It is not difficult to imagine that the native peoples of Mexico who were contemporary with the rise of the Olmecs must have learned of what was springing up in the jungles of the coast with mingled fear and amazement. In the eyes of simple tillers of maize, these strong men who built monuments, who sculpted stone, who celebrated previously unknown rites centered on a god with feline features, must have seemed semi-divine, at once admirable and awesome. News travels fast in Indian country, and in the hamlets of the central plateau this flowering of platforms and altars, of stelae and bas-reliefs down in the low country, far off toward the rising sun and the "divine sea," must have caused a great deal of talk. And when the Olmecs themselves appeared, climbing in caravans up the rough paths that led from the Gulf coast to the Cold Lands, they probably met with very little resistance, and perhaps even settled down here and there in small colonies whose strength lay not so much in their force of arms as in their prestige, in regions which, moreover, were not very densely populated.

Sites such as Las Bocas, Tlatilco, Tlapacoya, Chalcatzingo, and in general all those that have been found in the Federal District and in the states of México, Morelos, Puebla, and Guerrero, suggest a peaceful cohabitation between minority Olmec "nuclei" and more numerous but more primitive peoples. The bas-reliefs on the rock cliffs of Chalcatzingo, the cave paintings of Oxtotitlán and Juxtlahuaca, are admittedly proof of a religious and artistic activity that presupposes the existence of fairly large, organized Olmec groups. But the typical works of the great Olmec art of the "metropolitan area" are not found in these "colonial" regions: there are no colossal heads, and very little statuary. On the other hand, we note a remarkable development of pottery and of stone-carving and engraving, and the bas-reliefs of San Miguel Amuco, of Padre Piedra, and of Xoc are there to demonstrate the unity of a style despite great distances and natural obstacles.

The abundance of artifacts in hard stone (figurines, polished and engraved axes) in Guerrero is such that we may ponder the question whether the Olmec style did not originate in this region. This hypothesis must be rejected, but it is nonetheless true that the density of the finds in the Balsas Valley and environs gives us cause for reflection. If semiprecious stones came from this region, it is likely that Olmec miners settled there permanently, and that craftsmen set up workshops in these same settlements. The population of Olmec origin, come from the distant shores of the Gulf, spread out like an emulsion, in multiple small groups, among native peoples who retained their local culture. But obviously the influence of the newcomers could not help but make itself felt among these indigenous peoples: hence the "Olmecoid" features that can be observed more or less everywhere among the pre-classic peoples from the end of the second millennium B.C. on.

What we know of the valleys of Oaxaca suggests a different picture.

There, a vigorous indigenous culture manifested itself very early, with original features that were to become more and more pronounced with the passage of the centuries, at Monte Albán in particular. It was Zapotec civilization that found itself in contact with Olmecs during its formative phase: a contact of a commercial nature, as we have seen, due to the existence in the region of deposits of magnetite and hematite, but also, naturally, one that involved a stylistic influence as well. Hence the famous "Dancers" and the "Olmecoid" representations that from Monte Negro and Yagul to Cuilapan are proof of a profound and prolonged impact. But as far as we can judge from archaeological research carried out thus far, it would not appear that any great number of Olmecs settled permanently in Oaxaca.

Chiapas, the Soconusco coast, and the Central American sites reveal not only an influence but the actual presence of Olmecs on the borders of Maya country and all along what was apparently the route followed by Olmec traders or warriors (or trader-warriors) whose itinerary passed by way of the Isthmus of Tehuantepec. Those who sculpted the rocks of Pijijiapan in Mexico, of Chalchuapa in El Salvador, were undoubtedly Olmecs who had established permanent settlement in these localities so far distant from their metropolis. Here as elsewhere, their influence, their example had its effect on the non-Olmec peoples surrounding them. Even though the style of Izapa is quite different from that of Olmec works, the very idea of erecting stelae and of sculpting bas-reliefs may well have been a result of the impetus provided by these civilized colonists from the Gulf of Mexico who had relocated on the Pacific coast.

To sum up all the foregoing, can we speak of an "Olmec empire"? No, doubtless, if we wish to preserve the full import of the word "empire," which would imply that vast marginal regions were subjected to the political and military power of the "metropolitan area." We have no proof that there were "governors," permanent garrisons, and an entire structure analogous to that of the empires of the past in the Old World (the satrapies of the Persian Empire, the dioceses and provinces of the Roman Empire) or to that of the Inca state in Peru, with its rigid military, economic, and religious organization.

What we know best in Mexico is the Aztec empire. And while it is true that conquered cities and villages were obliged to pay regular tribute, it is also true that they were left a large measure of autonomy. The *calpixque*, imperial functionaries, were interested only in the payment of taxes; as for the rest, the provinces were permitted to administer themselves as they pleased. Furthermore, Aztec imperialism tolerated not only autonomy but even the independence of states such as Metztitlán, Yopitzinco, Tutotepec, Teotitlán, not to mention Tlaxcala the unconquered. In this case the concept of "empire" becomes more and more elusive as we strive to grasp it.

We might readily speak of an "Olmec empire" if we meant by that term something even less structured and much more haphazard than that of the Aztecs, a sort of loosely organized empire, composed of more or less sporadic settlements, of permanent outposts along certain itineraries, of commercial trading stations, and of spheres of influence. Great overland travelers just as the Phoenicians were great maritime voyagers, the Olmecs do not appear to have integrated their territorial conquests within any sort of overall structure, but rather to have set up networks of "colonies," in the meaning of this term in antiquity, that is, small settlements coexisting with local populations. And as Alfonso Caso writes (1965, p. 42): ". . . it was inevitable that the Olmec should feel himself to be superior, because of his culture, to the neolithic peoples living at the time in Mesoamerica."

Certain portions of this immense zone of diffusion of Olmec civilization were probably administered by individuals (priests? government functionaries? military personnel?) who had come from the "metropolitan area," representing, for example, the leaders of La Venta. Other regions might well have been peopled by Olmecs but allowed to administer themselves. Still others doubtless preserved the basic features of their traditional culture, their language, and their gods, but assimilated, more or less profoundly, certain traits of the more sophisticated civilization that had reached them.

Although we know so little about Olmec religion, it is legitimate to presume that it played a large part in the dynamic expansionist thrust of this people. In world history, proselytism is always a powerful factor in cultural diffusion. Perhaps Olmec "missionaries" journeyed along the long routes of Mesoamerica in order to spread the cult of the jaguar god. The rites related to the "baby" with the feline features do not appear to have taken root outside of the "metropolitan area," but beginning in this very early period and down to the era of the fall of the indigenous civilizations, the jaguar god became one of the dominant divine personalities of the Mesoamerican pantheon.

More cultural and religious than military, more commercial than administrative, the spreading over a wide area of a civilization rather than a power, what we call the "Olmec empire" was chronologically the first, in this part of the world, of those great human edifices, of those groupings of peoples, that successively bore the imprint of Teotihuacán, of the Maya cities, of Tula, of Tenochtitlán. For the first time, a dynamic outpouring of thought and of action, of art and of commerce, a religion, a style transcended the narrow limits of a village. This was the decisive step, the threshold approached but not crossed by other Indians such as the Pueblos: the transition, or rather the mutation, that two thousand years after the first faltering steps in the domain of agriculture, transformed the life of the Mexican peasant by inventing the city, the crucible of new ideas.

# 8

⊠⊠⊠⊠⊠⊠⊠

# Some Features
# of Olmec Life

When we attempt to reconstruct an overall picture of what the life of
the Olmecs must have been like, we are overawed by the immense
depths of our ignorance.

The many centuries and the climate, the ravages of time, and the
torrential rains have left us not a single bone, not a single garment,
not a single dwelling. With the exception of one mask, no artifact
made of wood, either carved or uncarved, no bit of cloth, no piece of
leather has survived. Nothing has remained, save pottery and stone.
Fortunately, the Olmecs modeled clay, sculpted and carved jade and
basalt: all that we know of their life comes solely from this iconography, which is not always easy to interpret.

As for the physical type of the Olmecs, we have dealt with the
subject in some detail earlier. Without question they practiced the
deformation of the skull (compressing it with the aid of a small plank
and strips of cloth while the brain case of the infant was still mallea-
ble) and the mutilation of the front teeth. These two traits are evident
to anyone who looks closely at the figurines, those for example of the
extraordinary offering no. 4 of La Venta. They were doubtless thank
offerings of the upper class, such as we find later among the Mayas of
the classic period. The indentation in the form of a "V," a triangle
pointing downward, marked in the forehead of figures, a feature often
present in representations of humanoids, especially figurines carved

in hard stone, is more difficult to interpret. Many explanations have been suggested: according to some, this slit symbolizes the fontanelle of newborn babies before it has completely closed. To others, it is the depression that can be observed in the skull of a jaguar. But it must be said that these attempts at an explanation are far from satisfactory. What is certain is that the fissured skull is a frequent characteristic of Olmec iconography, and that this surprising representation of the human head occurs again in the art of Teotihuacán, where numerous figurines have a bilobate head with a deep indentation in the middle of the forehead.

Olmec dress: what did it consist of and what material were their garments made of? It appears that for the most part the essential features of Mesoamerican attire were already fixed in this period and did not vary thereafter: the man wore a loincloth, the Aztec *maxtlatl* of the post-classic era, or sometimes a sort of short skirt, and perhaps an ample cloak or mantle; the woman wore a skirt and a bodice, but might leave her breasts bare (as the most tradition-bound Indian women still do today). The climate in Olmec country did not require a more elaborate wardrobe than this. Both sexes might have worn sandals.

It is certain fact that the Olmecs cultivated cotton, a typical textile plant of the Hot Lands. We are not likely to be wrong if we presume that they wove cloth on the sort of Mesoamerican loom still in use today by women of this region.

We have yet to discuss ornaments and headdresses: here, in the very earliest days of Mesoamerican civilization, wrist and ankle bracelets, necklaces and pendants, pectorals, ear and nose ornaments— doubtless the nasal septum was pierced so as to insert jewels in it— already make their appearance. Excavations have unearthed jade necklace pieces, carved obsidian ear ornaments that give proof of extraordinary craftsmanship, being sometimes as thin as a sheet of cigarette paper. The heads of dignitaries are crowned by towering constructions made of feathers and complex ornaments similar to those found—to cite but one example—in the later Maya paintings at Bonampak. But miters and hats are more characteristically Olmec: rigid headdresses, of leather or cloth stretched over wicker armatures, sometimes with quite broad brims, suggestive of the "bowlers" or "homburgs" of our day and age. As for turbans, either relatively simple ones such as those of the colossal heads, or elaborate ones of vast dimensions such as that of the "Ambassador," they cover heads that may have been shaved bare, to judge from the appearance of figurines from La Venta or the statue of the Uxpanapa "Wrestler."

The climate once again explains why there were no dwellings made of stone. But the Olmecs did not construct sanctuaries or palaces in stone or brick either: the relative inferiority of their architecture, compared, for example, to that of the Mayas of Petén living in a similar natural environment, has already been noted. The great earthworks of La Venta or of other sites clearly served as foundations for buildings in light materials such as wood, leafy branches, and vines, which were available in abundance, but which disappeared without a trace. In order to procure them, a polished stone ax sufficed—a tool essential to the survival of a human community in a tropical jungle. This same ax served to clear land, to chop down trees and bushes that were then burned so that maize could be planted.

No traces have been found of missile weapons (bows? spear-throwers?), of agricultural implements such as digging sticks, of musical instruments. As for weapons, Olmec iconography shows us only the paddle-shaped clubs brandished by the threatening figures in the Chalcatzingo rock carving. Nowhere do we see drums, flutes, or horns such as those shown in the paintings at Bonampak. This obviously does not mean that the Olmecs possessed no musical instruments: it merely means that our knowledge is still extremely limited.

Two categories of enigmatic objects appear in the hands of figures shown on bas-reliefs, of statues, and of figurines. The first of these is a sort of cylinder with what might be flames or leaves coming out of the top of it. This is what is often referred to as a "torch." The other object is called a "knuckle-duster" by English-speaking archaeologists and a *manopla* (brass knuckles) by Spanish-speaking specialists.[1] Both objects are sometimes associated with the same person, and sometimes represented separately.

Joralemon mentions the "torch" as motif no. 150 in his dictionary of Olmec motifs and symbols.[2] He cites four examples of it: a figurine from San Cristóbal Tepatlaxco in the state of Puebla (where this motif is associated with a "knuckle-duster"); a figurine of unknown provenance; an engraved ax also of unknown provenance; and an engraved ax in the Museo Nacional de Antropología in Mexico City, the principal motif of which is a figure who is holding a "torch" in one hand and a "knuckle-duster" in the other. María Antonieta Cervantes ("Dos elementos de uso ritual en el arte olmeca," p. 43, fig. 10) has published a more detailed drawing of this latter object.

The third object mentioned by Joralemon represents an individual with his arms crossed over his breast. His hands partially conceal the "torch," which here appears as the bottom half of a sort of bundle of plant stems.

In addition to these specimens we might mention:

[1] Cf., respectively, P. Drucker and M. A. Cervantes.
[2] This dictionary constitutes pp. 7–18 of Joralemon's 1971 *A Study of Olmec Iconography.*

Jadeite figurine with "torch" and "knuckle-duster," San Cristóbal Tepatlaxco, state of Puebla. (Courtesy of Dumbarton Oaks, Washington,
D.C.)

—a jade figurine in the Cleveland Museum of Art, of unknown provenance, with "torch" and "knuckle-duster";

—a stone disk from Santiago Tuxtla, Veracruz, with "knuckle-duster";

—a figurine representing a person whose garment, a sort of short skirt, is ornamented with the "torch" motif;

—a serpentine figurine from Paso de Ovejas (state of Veracruz);

—a plaque of sculpted and engraved serpentine from Ahuelicán (state of Guerrero), belonging to the Dallas Museum of Fine Arts. This impressive piece represents an Olmec figure with a "V" indentation in its forehead, holding a "torch" with both hands; two other "torches" are engraved on its chest.[3]

Are these objects really torches? Naturally, we do not know whether the Olmecs used torches (of resinous wood, no doubt); they must have had something of the sort, however, in order to light their way inside deep caves such as those in Guerrero. If, in the majority of cases, the top of this enigmatic object appears to represent flames, in other cases (Cleveland Museum figurine, figurine from Paso de Ovejas) the cylindrical portion that the individual is holding in his hand ends at the top in what would appear to be a kind of oval paddle. Can the object represented be a bunch of some sort? Shouldn't this object be compared with those that the figures on the stelae of Xoc and of San Miguel Amuco are carrying in the crook of their arm? We must confess that the documents known at present do not permit us to render any definite opinion on the subject.

Does the fact that these "torches" are quite often associated with "knuckle-dusters" contribute in any way to a more precise interpretation of what these "torches" might be?

First of all, however, what exactly is the significance of the "knuckle-dusters"?

This motif is found fairly frequently. Joralemon, who uses this term (no. 73 in his list of motifs), gives five examples of it:

—figurine from San Cristóbal Tepatlaxco, already cited (with "torch");

—engraved ax of unknown provenance;

—engraved ax in the Museo Nacional in Mexico City already mentioned (with "torch");

—engraved ax from La Venta;

—monument no. 10 at San Lorenzo. This last monument is surely one of the most impressive: it is a humano-feline statue with a jaguar

---

[3] The Cleveland Museum figurine is illustrated in fig. 5 of the article by Cervantes cited, and the stone disk from Santiago Tuxtla pl. I; the figurine with the skirt bearing the "torch" motif is reproduced by Piña Chan and Covarrubias (fig. 32); the one from Paso de Ovejas is shown in Cervantes, op. cit., pl. III; and finally, the Dallas serpentine plaque may be found in Gay, 1971, pl. XXIV.

snout, holding in its two hands, in front of its chest, "knuckle-dusters" in the form of half-circles.

Other specimens may be mentioned:

—a stone disk in the Santiago Tuxtla Museum (already mentioned)
represents a humano-feline Olmec face, framed by hands holding a
"torch" and a "knuckle-duster";

—the stela of Padre Piedra (Chiapas), on which the figure represented has a "knuckle-duster" in one of his hands;

—an engraved jade rod of offering no. 4 of La Venta;

—a jade plaque from Pichucalco (Chiapas): on it is an engraved
figure, holding two "knuckle-dusters," whose attitude is very similar
to that of monument no. 10 at San Lorenzo;

—a jadeite plaque, of unknown provenance, now in the Museo Nacional in Mexico City: a stylized "knuckle-duster" is engraved in the
center of this plaque;

—two "knuckle-dusters" forming part of the decoration of a magnificent ceramic vase from Chalcatzingo;

—the central figure of the bas-relief known as "Los Soldados" at
Pijijiapan, in Soconusco, is holding a "knuckle-duster" in his hand.

To complete this list, we should mention two cases in which the
interpretation presents a problem.

The first is that of monument no. 27 at Laguna de Los Cerros. This
is a stone disk that closely resembles the one in the Santiago Tuxtla
Museum: but since it has been badly damaged over the centuries, all
that is left of it is the central portion, the Olmec face. We can only
presume that, as on the Santiago Tuxla disk, this face was framed by
two hands holding objects such as "torches" or "knuckle-dusters"—
but this is merely a hypothesis.

On the other hand, the central figure of monument no. 19 of La
Venta, encircled by serpent coils, is holding in his right hand an object that is usually interpreted as being a sack or pouch, but might
be a variation of the "knuckle-duster," comparable to the stone objects that we shall discuss below.[4]

The geographical distribution of the "knuckle-duster" motif is not
without interest: wider than that of the "torch," it covers the whole
of the "metropolitan area," then extends up onto the central plateau

[4]Illustrations showing these pieces may be found in the following works:
—stone disk, Santiago Tuxtla: Cervantes, pl. I and fig. 1.
—stela, Padre Piedra: Green and Lowe, fig. 42.
—jade rod, La Venta: Cervantes, fig. 7.
—jade plaque, Pichucalco: Cervantes, fig. 14.
—jadeite plaque, Museo Nacional in Mexico City: Cervantes, fig. 15.
—vase, Chalcatzingo: Gay, 1971, fig. 43.
—bas-relief, Pijijiapan: Navarrete, figs. 2–3.
—monument no. 27, Laguna de Los Cerros: De la Fuente, 1973, p. 153.
—monument no. 19, La Venta: ibid., p. 77.

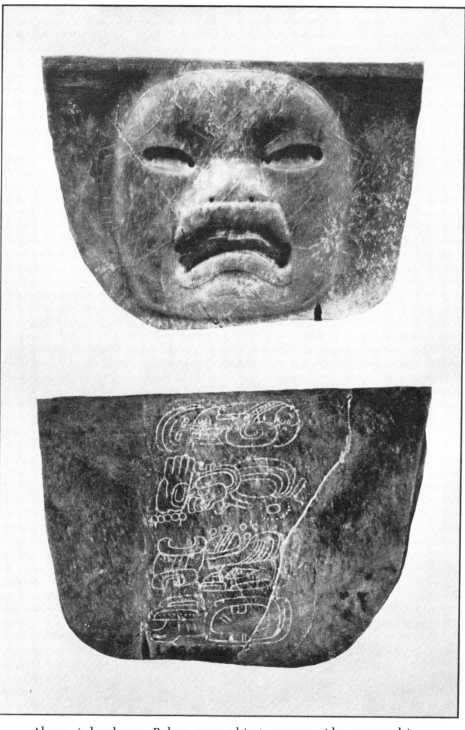

Above, jade plaque. Below, same object, reverse side: engraved inscription. (Both courtesy of American Museum of Natural History, New York.)

in the region of Puebla, and most importantly, to Chiapas and the Pacific coast. It is thus undoubtedly a cultural element that the Olmec expansion diffused, although—at least as far as we know at present—it did not succeed in implanting it in the Valley of Mexico, in Oaxaca, or in Guerrero. Its distribution is clearly limited to the southeast.

How to interpret this object? Was it a weapon, either an offensive one ("knuckle-duster") or a defensive one, such as a small buckler? This seems hardly likely. The best-preserved engravings and sculptures would appear to indicate that the purpose of the "knuckle-duster" was to protect the hand. One cannot help thinking of the stone objects of southwestern Mexico and of Guatemala which have been variously referred to as "sling stones" or "padlock stones," though it now appears that they were part of the equipment of pelota players, or more probably the representation in stone of this equipment, as was the case with the famous "yokes" and "palms" of the classic civilization of Veracruz.[5]

It is evident that "knuckle-dusters" of wood and no doubt of padded leather did not resist the ravages of time, any more than did other pieces of equipment used by pelota players: thickly padded belts, stomach guards, knee pads, etc. The belts are represented by "yokes" and the stomach guards by "palms": this is quite clear from the bas-reliefs of the game of pelota at El Tajín and at Chichén Itzá. At this latter site, six bas-reliefs, each showing fourteen individuals, that is, a total of eighty-four persons, depict a symbolic scene of sacrifice by decapitation—which is reminiscent of the Izapa sculpture dating back to a period of millennium and a half earlier!—and the ball players, shown with all their equipment, from head to foot, have in their right hand a "knuckle-duster" artistically decorated with a jaguar's head. It is clear that this device had a twofold purpose: to protect the player's hand from the extremely violent impact of the ball and to permit the player to fling himself to the ground to bounce the ball off his hip as allowed by the rules of the game.

This "knuckle-duster" could no doubt take a number of different forms. A "palm" described by Tatiana Proskouriakoff (1954, fig. 7) shows a pelota player holding his hand a "knuckle-duster" that very closely resembles the object—generally considered to be a sack or a pouch—that the figure on monument no. 19 of La Venta is holding.

If our interpretation is correct, it follows that the Olmecs were familiar with the game of pelota. There is nothing surprising about this; quite to the contrary, for the "people of the rubber country" may well have invented the ball and the first ways of playing the game. It is true that no enclosed courts such as were built specifically

[5] Cf. Borhegyi.

for pelota playing by the Mayas and other civilized Mesoamericans have been found, but it is possible that during this very early phase the game was played in the open fields. The Uxpanapa statue of the "Wrestler" is much more probably that of a pelota player in one of his characteristic attitudes. The "little yokes" (*yuguitos*) found at non-metropolitan Olmec sites may very well be an indication that the game of pelota was played there.

From La Venta and Chiapas to Chichén Itzá is a long way—in space and especially in time. But the power of tradition in the societies of Mesoamerica is immense, and we know how fraught with meaning the "divine" game, *teotlachtli*, a cosmic symbol, was in the minds of the Indians.

It is not at all unlikely that this tradition arose in the Olmec world before being destroyed, like all the rest, three thousand years later, by the deathblows dealt it by invaders from Europe. It would thus be merely another particular case of the prodigious momentum lent by the Olmecs to the indigenous civilization of this part of the continent.

Is the "torch" often associated with the "knuckle-duster" also related to the game of pelota? For the moment there is no evidence that would enable us either to accept or to reject this possibility. Until we know how pelota was played among the Olmecs, it will be difficult to interpret these objects more precisely.

What appears to be certain, however, is that the fundamental themes, the patterns of life among civilized Mesoamericans developed very early in Olmec society. Whether it be major phenomena such as the way in which land was occupied and used or more limited facts such as the style of dress, the essential features of what were to become the indigenous cultures of Mexico and of Maya country had already made their appearance among the Olmecs, and in their plastic arts as well. We must now determine whether similar observations are possible with regard to the loftiest intellectual and spiritual domains.

# 9

⊠⊠⊠⊠⊠⊠

# Time, the Gods:
## Symbolism and Writing

All the civilized peoples of Mesamerica have shared a common treasure: a certain conception of the universe; an abundant, richly variegated pantheon in which we find similar gods, from Mexico to Nicaragua and from one millennium to the next; a complex system of chronology, at once a method of calculating time and a means of divination; and finally a "hieroglyphic" writing, of which that of the Mayas offers the most sophisticated example, using characters or "glyphs" either as ideograms whose referent is an object or an action, or as phonograms corresponding to a sound, a syllable, or a group of syllables.

Mesoamerican writings are inextricably bound up with chronology, calendars, a vision of the world, religion. A large proportion of Maya inscriptions and manuscripts, as well as of the Codices of central Mexico, consists of dates, references to the movements of the stars, to ritual, and to the gods. The arduous tasks with which scholars who undertook to decipher Maya writing were confronted began with the reading and the interpretation of calendar signs. The great Mexican Codices (*Borgia*, *Borbonicus*, *Cospi*, etc.) are first of all *tonalamatl*, "books of destinies," used by diviners to predict the fate of a newborn child or the success of a war expedition. They are also collections of myths and manuals of rites and ceremonies.

We have long known, of course, that the Aztecs, for example, possessed historical books retracing the events of their past. Less than twenty years ago, it became possible for the first time to interpret certain Maya inscriptions: we find recorded in them the names of dignitaries, the dates of their accession to power, the emblems of cities such as Palenque or Yaxchilán. We may therefore divide these inscriptions into two categories: chronological and non-chronological texts. It is nonetheless true that religion and above all the calculation of time constitute an essential element in any written or engraved text dating from pre-Columbian antiquity.

Did the Olmecs, who were the first civilized people in this America, possess a system of writing? Did this people that invented monumental architecture, sculpture, altars, stelae, hidden offerings, also invent glyphs?

Not a single trace of a book remains to help us answer this question. If the Olmecs had books, which were no doubt kept in the hands of priests, soothsayers, and magicians, these fragile works made of paper, cloth, or animal skins did not withstand the ravages of time. All we have left are bas-reliefs, carved stones, decorated vessels, terra cotta seals.

Before we attempt to interpret these enigmatic and all too rare vestiges, it behooves us to call to mind the general features of the Mesoamerican system of computing time, since the most reasonable hypothesis is to presume that if the Olmecs developed writing, they used it in part for chronological notations.

The system that we find, with certain variants, among all the civilized peoples, both "classic" (Mayas, Teotihuacán, Monte Albán) and "post-classic" (Toltecs, Mixtecs, Aztecs, etc.), is based on the combination of two calendars, which are different yet mesh with each other like the toothed gears of a watch or clock movement.

The first of these calendars (*tzolkin* in Maya, *tonalpoualli* in Nahuatl) is made up of 260 days. Each of these days is designated by a number—from 1 to 13—and by one of the 20 glyphs or signs for the various days. Thus there are 20 of these "13-day periods," making a total of 260 days. If, to take the example of the Maya calendar, one begins to count from the number 1 and from the first sign, *imix*, the second day will be called 2-*ik*, the third 3-*akbal*, etc.; the 259th day will be 12-*cauac*, the 260th 13-*ahau*, and the following cycle will begin, once again, with a 261st day called 1-*imix*.[1]

The second calendar records the solar year of 365 days; it divides it into 18 "months" of 20 days each, to which 5 "empty" or unlucky days are added.

[1] The 20 Maya signs are:
*imix ik akbal kan chicchan*
*cimi manik lamat muluc oc*
*chuen eb ben ix men*
*cib caban eznab cauac ahau/.*

A specific date is defined by four elements: the number and the sign of the 260-day calendar, the number of the day in the month of the solar year, and the name of the month, as for example: 3 *ahau* 3 *zotz*.[2]

In this system the identical date does not appear again for a period of 18,980 days, that is, 73 series of 260 days and 52 solar years. The completion of this cycle of 52 years was marked, among certain peoples, by sad, solemn ceremonies in the course of which rites were performed celebrating the "binding together of the years" and the New Fire was lighted—sometimes on the bloody chest of a human sacrificial victim.

But how to note exactly, in the infinite course of time, a date that came around again every 52 years through the workings of this "eternal return"? The Mayas resolved this problem by what is known as the "Long Count." In the inscriptions of the classic era—between the third and the tenth century A.D.—the date with four elements is preceded by five numbers which, like the dials of an instrument panel, indicate respectively the number of days, of (20-day) months, of years (*tun*) of 360 days, of *katun* (7200 days, a little less than 20 years), and of *baktun* (144,000 days, a little less than 400 years) that have elapsed since a "zero date"—just as we count the years from the year 1 of the Christian era, or Moslems count them from the Hegira. The date 3 *ahau* 3 *zotz*, for example, is preceded by the five figures 9.9.0.0.0, which means that since the zero date exactly 9 *baktun* and 9 *katun* have elapsed, with zeros representing the year, month, and day—in other words, this date marks the end of a *katun*.[3]

The commonly accepted correlation between the Maya calendar and ours allows us to determine that this date corresponds to May 12, A.D. 613.

Finally, we observe that the Mayas, and in general the earliest civilized peoples, indicated numbers by means of a system of dots (or tiny disks) corresponding to the number 1, and dashes or bars corresponding to the number 5. Thus a bar and four disks indicate the number 9.

The preceding admittedly brief and sketchy remarks are merely meant to show that any sculpted or engraved inscription that includes dots and bars, whether associated with glyphs or not, or any series of five numbers, very probably is a notation using the Mesoamerican system of chronology.

It is true that, in the present state of our knowledge, such inscrip-

[2]*Zotz:* fourth month of the Maya year.

[3]The figure of 360 days was chosen arbitrarily, it would appear, because it was divisible by the base number of Maya arithmetic (20). A correction was therefore necessary. It was noted in inscriptions by means of other numbers, the so-called secondary series. Cf. Morley, pp. 244–45.

tions are rare among the Olmecs. But they do exist. And we may note that even a classic site of major importance such as Teotihuacán has relatively few chronological inscriptions.

Altar no. 7 of La Venta, though badly damaged, bears a "crossed bands" or "Olmec cross" glyph, accompanied by three dots. Thus, if we grant that these three dots or little disks correspond to the number 3, this inscription probably indicates a date on the 260-day calendar.

The central figure carved in bas-relief on stela no. 2 of La Venta is wearing a voluminous headdress: its anterior face is in the form of a flat rectangular area on which two symmetrically placed disks, one on either side of a sign that appears to be a stylized plant, stand out clearly. Here again, this is probably a date in the 260-day calendar. Since it is sculpted on the figure's headdress, isn't it likely that it indicates—as was the usage later on in Oaxaca, for example—the birth date and the "calendar name" of the priest or dignitary shown in the bas-relief?

Monument E at Tres Zapotes (described above, Chapter 2) is an engraved rock in the bed of the Hueyapan River. The inscription may be broken down into two parts: at the top, a bar and a disk; below, a bar with a sort of rectangular appendage just underneath it, so that it looks like a capital "T" with a short, broad vertical stroke. The inscription, as we have said, is a very early one, belonging to a very deep stratum of occupation of this site; hence we deduce that the system of noting numbers by means of dots and dashes is likewise very early. A second observation: the glyph that constitutes the lower part of the inscription is probably a day sign in the 260-day calendar. It looks very similar to the glyph, in the form of a capital "T," that corresponds to the second day of the *tzolkin*, *ik* in Maya.[4] It is a sign we find engraved on the eye of one of the dancers in the frescoes at Bonampak, that little Maya center in the Usumacinta Valley where precious mural paintings have been miraculously preserved. The dancers are performing a rite dedicated to water—rain—divinities. Thompson (1950, p. 73) has shown that this glyph is related to wind and rain: the second day of the Nahuatl calendar of central Mexico is called *ehecatl*, wind. The inscription engraved on monument E of Tres Zapotes probably means "6-rain" or "6-wind"—in Maya *uac-ik*, and in Nahuatl *chicace ehecatl*. If so, this is no doubt the oldest known calendar inscription in Mexico.

Blom and La Farge (1926, vol. 1, p. 41) discovered at Piedra Labrada (state of Veracruz) a stela 2 meters high bearing carefully sculpted glyphs. A bar and two dots stand out clearly below a glyph that Hermann Beyer (1927) interpreted as a serpent-eye sign in a

[4] Cf. Thompson, 1962, p. 98.

Stela no. 2, La Venta. Now located in the Parque-Museo de La Venta in Villahermosa, state of Tabasco. (Courtesy of R. Roland–Ziolo, Paris.)

style closely resembling that of Teotihuacán. The site is near great Olmec centers, it is true, yet the glyphs on this stela at Piedra Labrada are not at all suggestive of Olmec reliefs. The only thing we can say is that the system of noting numbers by means of dots and bars—in this case the figure 7—was in use in this locality. This is probably a more recent monument than those dating from the high point of Olmec civilization.

Should certain groups of dots that appear on objects such as four cylindrical ceramic seals from Las Bocas (state of Puebla) or on an engraved stone tablet from Ahuelicán (state of Guerrero) be taken to represent numbers?

Curiously enough, it is the number 3 that is combined with various glyphs: twice with a "star" sign, once with a motif that may symbolize clouds, once with a sort of capital "M" that Carlo Gay interprets as being "a variant of the cave or earth sign,"[5] and finally, once with a very complex set of symbols that are possibly agrarian or telluric, among which an "Olmec cross" is clearly visible.

It is also possible that one of the characters on an Olmec seal from Tlatilco (cf. Gay, op. cit., p. 279) represents the number 4, or even the number 9, if we interpret a quadrangular element situated between four small circles as being a 5.

And finally, one of the cave paintings at Oxtotitlán (Grove, 1970, figs. 14 and 15) represents a fantastic reptilian creature, similar to the Aztec cipactli, accompanied by the number 3, denoted by three small circles above the monster's head.

Three other circles inscribed below it would seem, however, to represent pieces of some sort of necklace. It is probable that the number 6 would have been noted by a disk and a bar rather than by six disks.

To sum up: if we except the stela of Piedra Labrada, we observe that chronological inscriptions relating to the 260-day cycle are found either in the "metropolitan area" (La Venta, Tres Zapotes) or in the sphere of Olmec expansion on the central plateau and the western slope of Mexico.

On the other hand, only two "Long Count" inscriptions can be attributed to Olmec civilization.

The famous Tres Zapotes stela C bears a series of five numbers, denoted by dots and bars, namely, 7.16.6.16.18. On the no less famous Tuxtla statuette we find the series 8.6.2.4.17.

These two inscriptions have features in common. Both are preceded by an "introductory glyph," like those of Maya stelae of the classic era, though these introductory glyphs are very different from those of their Maya counterparts. Moreover, on neither of the two

[5] Gay, 1973, pp. 283 and 286.

stelae are the five numbers corresponding to the five chronological "divisions" of the "Long Count" accompanied by glyphs designating periods such as the *baktun*, the *katun*, etc. And finally, these two chronological inscriptions are associated with other glyphs which are *not* chronological (with one exception, which will be mentioned below).

It is evident, therefore, that these two inscriptions are not Maya. Furthermore, Tres Zapotes and the Sierra de Tuxtla are far from any of the centers in Maya country, but are in the very heart of the Olmec "metropolitan area." As for the dates themselves, they are clearly well before the earliest classic Maya dates.

But can stela C and the Tuxtla statuette be regarded as Olmec?

The posterior face of the Tres Zapotes stela bears, in bas-relief, the stylized face of the feline monster, the Olmec motif par excellence. In fact, there would be no doubt whatsoever as to the Olmec character of this relief if the stela did not bear a chronological inscription. A particularly accentuated "geometrization" of the features of the feline may doubtless be interpreted as proof that this stela belongs to a late phase in the evolution of the sculpture of this site.[6] We may deduce from this that the 260-day calendar, or *tzolkin*, was in use much earlier than the "Long Count," but it would not appear that we can reject the Olmec origin of the stela.

As for the Tuxtla statuette, a mask in the form of a duck's bill conceals the lower half of the face of the figure that it represents. This bird is a fairly frequent motif in Olmec art, and the technique employed in carving this piece in hard stone (nephrite) is in no way different from that of numerous figurines known to be Olmec. In addition to the "Long Count" date, the statuette bears eight columns of incised glyphs, only one of which has a number alongside it in the form of a bar and three disks, that is, the number 8. The sign itself, a rectangle with a small circle marking its center, is somewhat similar to the glyph *muluc*, the ninth sign of the Maya *tzolkin*. The other characters are in no way Maya or "Mayoid."

In short, it is probable that the "Long Count" was invented in the Olmec region in a late period; from there it spread to a vast portion of Mesoamerica, to Chiapas, to Guatemala, before being perfected by the Mayas and reaching the form in which we find it, at Tikal and in Petén in general, at the end of the third century A.D. and the beginning of the fourth.

But should we necessarily grant that the zero date of the "Long Count" is everywhere the same, and identical to that of the classic Maya chronology? If we were to accept this hypothesis, the date on stela C would correspond to the year 31 B.C. and that on the statuette

[6] Joralemon, 1971, p. 43: "late carving."

Statuette, Tuxtla. (Courtesy of the Smithsonian Institution, Washington, D.C.)

to the year 162 A.D., that is, dates that are clearly much too late. With regard to certain "Long Count" inscriptions, Tatiana Proskouriakoff (1968, p. 124) poses the question whether the base point of the chronological notation system is the same in Chiapas, for example, as in Petén. In the case cited by this author, the zero date might well be more recent than that of Maya inscriptions. But as far as Olmec dates are concerned, I am inclined to think that the base point of the "Long Count" lies, on the contrary, farther back in the past. If we hypothesize that this base point is located one *baktun* farther back in time, stela C would then have been sculpted in 425 B.C. And in that case the Tuxtla statuette would date from the third century B.C., a transition period during which or following which, as we shall see, several systems of writing, which might be described as "late Olmec" or "post-Olmec" and at the same time "pre-Maya," made their appearance.

One last remark with regard to calendars: from all indications, the cycle of 260 days, based on the combination of 13 numbers and 20 signs, first appears at a very early period. It played a major role in all the cultures of Mesoamerica, from the Olmecs to the Aztecs, that is, over a period of around three thousand years. And it so happens that certain glyphs—abstract ones in the classic period, and more realistic ones in the case of more recent peoples—correspond to concepts, to beings, that exist only in tropical regions: the crocodile, the monkey, the jaguar. Hence it seems certain that this system of computation and divination, so strikingly original and bearing so little relation to natural phenomena, an intellectual construct typical of Mesoamerica and found nowhere else, originated in the Hot Lands. It is highly likely that its cradle was Olmec country. Hence, glyph-writing, inseparable from the system of chronogical notation, must have originated there also.

While chronological and numerical inscriptions are relatively rare, we have numerous examples of symbolic signs that may be described as glyphs.

At La Venta, monument no. 13 (the "Ambassador" stela) bears four characters grouped about the central figure: to the left, a stylized footprint—a glyph that doubtless signified, and was to signify down through the Aztec period, walking, journeying, traveling—and, to the right, three very badly eroded glyphs, one of which calls to mind a trilobate flower and another the head of a bird with a long beak. These three characters no doubt indicate who the "Ambassador" is, and perhaps also the place to which he is journeying.

The physical type of this person closely resembles that of the

Monument no. 13, La Venta: The "Ambassador." Now located in the
Parque-Museo de La Venta in Villahermosa, state of Tabasco. (Courtesy of R. Roland–Ziolo, Paris.)

Uxpanapa "Wrestler" or athlete. This sculpture is almost certainly of
Olmec origin, and it is difficult to reject the evidence that these four
signs belong to a system of writing.

  Glyph-like characters may be noted on a number of monuments of
the Olmec "metropolitan area":

  —first and foremost, the "Olmec cross," or St. Andrew's cross, inscribed inside a rectangle, which we find more or less everywhere,
for example on altar no. 4 of La Venta, on the body of the jaguar-

baby of Las Limas, on the "jaguar-fish" of San Lorenzo, on the
humano-feline known as "monument no. 52" of the same site, to limit
ourselves to these few instances;

—the "stylized plant" glyph of stela no. 2 of La Venta;

—a character in the form of a square with rounded angles flanked
by three oblong elements, which we find on the helmet of colossal
head no. 1 of La Venta and on a fragment of monument no. 15 of the
same site;

—a "star" sign (a diamond with a circle inscribed inside it) on the
anterior portion of the diadem of the "Prince," a statue at Cruz del
Milagro, Sayula (state of Veracruz);

—a "flowing water" glyph, which appears twice on the stone reservoir (monument no. 9) of San Lorenzo that is decorated with a re-
listic representation of a duck;

—two glyphs on the headdress of the right-hand figure of altar no.
14 of San Lorenzo; the upper glyph is a rectangle in which a circle
divided into two halves by a vertical axis is inscribed; the lower glyph,
a more complex one, is made up of a wavy line and a curved band;

—the person depicted on the left of the same altar is wearing a
pectoral in the form of a sort of star that looks exactly like the shell
cut in two known as the wind-jewel (*ehecacozcatl*) that was the symbol of the god Quetzalcoatl in the post-classic era;

—the "quincunx" glyph—four little circles laid out in a square with
a fifth one in the center—on the head of a fantastic insect or arthro-
pod, a wasp or a spider, on monument no. 43 at San Lorenzo.

This list is admittedly a partial one. A detailed examination of
sculptures that often are very badly eroded would doubtless furnish
many other examples.

The rock sculptures at Chalcatzingo are a veritable treasure trove
of symbolic motifs:

—the sign "rain," "raindrop," represented by a rectangular element with a disk at the lower end of it, like a medal suspended from
a ribbon; this glyph is repeated twenty-three times around the female
figure (a rain or vegetation goddess?) seated in a cavern, on her headdress, and on her garment. The same sign with the same meaning is
found later in Aztec pictographic writing;

—the sign "jade-water plaque," a square with rounded angles surrounding a small disk: this is already the Maya glyph *muluc*, the ninth
day of the *tzolkin;* it is repeated five times;

—the cloud symbol, which appears three times;

—the sign "vegetation," or most likely "maize," in the form of a
stylized plant that is shown growing out of the walls of the cave, that
is, out of the head of the terrestrial monster, in three places; it is
engraved again in two places below the cloud symbol and twice more

on the headdress of the goddess; it also figures as an ornament of the headdresses of the two threatening figures of bas-relief no. 2;

—on the hats of these same two figures are two glyphs resembling the "flowing water" sign at San Lorenzo;

—a double spiral decorates the ceremonial bar that the rain goddess is holding across her forearms; this symbol seems to be the abstract substitute for the jaguar-baby that appears so often in Olmec art, carried in the same fashion by a human adult.

Joralemon (1971) has analyzed Olmec iconography and noted a certain number of symbols that appear again and again: maize (a stylization of the plant); a sign in the form of a capital "U"; a star, a diamond shape that is not unlike the Maya glyph *lamat*, the symbol of the planet Venus; a solar sign in the form of a four-petaled flower, like the glyph *kin*, sun, in Maya writing.

With regard to this last glyph, we also find it in a context that is unquestionable purely Olmec: alongside the humano-feline face of the jaguar god on a cylindrical seal from Tlatilco (Gay, 1973, p. 279)

Another seal of the same provenance (ibid., p. 285) bears eight identifiable symbols: a square with rounded angles divided into two halves by a vertical line, like the glyph, mentioned above, shown on the headdress of the right-hand figure of altar no. 14 at San Lorenzo; a star; the "jade-water" or *muluc* glyph, repeated twice; a "cloud" sign resembling those of the Chalcatzingo reliefs; a cross, surrounded by four points, inscribed within a square; a variant (?) of the sign *muluc*; and finally, two half-circles, each of which enclose a dot.

Olmec axes in hard stone often have an incised decoration: stylized faces, symbols. On an ax carved of green stone from Tlaltenco (Guerrero), various symbols appear above a head with Olmec features surmounted by a pointed cap. One of these symbols is particularly interesting: it is a cross inscribed in a circle, a glyph known as the "*Kan* cross" in Maya writing.[7] To the right of this sign is an appendage in the form of two narrow intertwined bands. It is striking to note that this *Kan*-cross-with-appendage configuration is also found at Monte Albán, where Alfonso Caso has identified it as being the year symbol,[8] in particular on stela no. 12 of the great Zapotec city.

Perhaps this is the proper place to point out that various glyphs found at Monte Albán bear a very close resemblance to those of the Olmecs: the "quincunx" sign, the crossed bands, the capital "U" for instance.[9] And we know that Monte Albán unquestionably had, at a very early date, a well-developed system of writing, at once chronological and non-chronological.

[7] No. 281 of Thompson's *Catalog of Maya Hieroglyphs* (1962, p. 65).

[8] The Tlaltenco ax is reproduced in Gay, 1971, fig. 44a, and 1973, p. 284; and in Caso, 1947, figs. 10 and 65.

[9] Caso, 1947, figs. 22, 61, 62.

Glyphs engraved on a pectoral. Dumbarton Oaks, Washington, D.C. (Drawing by Anne Bouvier based on reproduction of work published by Michael D. Coe.)

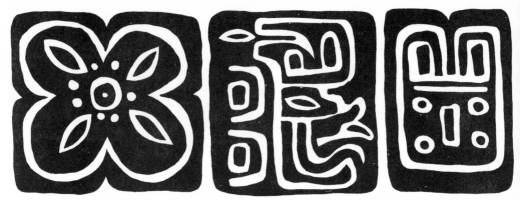

Glyphs: Tlatilco seal. (Drawing by Anne Bouvier based on reproduction of work published by Frederick V. Field.)

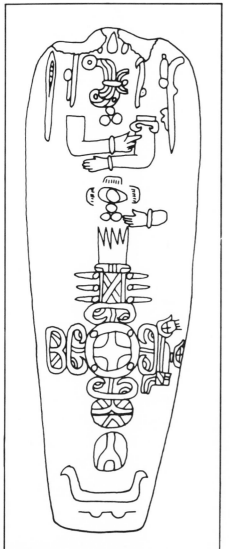

Ax known as the "Humboldt ax." (From Peter D. Joralemon, *A Study of Olmec Iconography*, Studies in Pre-Columbian Art and Archaeology, no. 7. Courtesy of Dumbarton Oaks, Washington, D.C.)

The *Kan* cross is one of the principal motifs of an odd and beautiful piece known as the "Humboldt ax." This artifact, a polished engraved stone ax, was given to Baron Alexander von Humboldt at the beginning of the nineteenth century by a professor at the School of Mines in Mexico City, Andrés del Río. The celebrated German scientist and explorer presented it as a gift to the King of Prussia. From the royal collections, this artifact then passed to those of the Berlin Museum für Völkerkunde but disappeared during the Second World War. Luckily, we possess a drawing of it,[10] and there is a cast of it at the Smithsonian Institution in Washington.

The incised decoration on this ax is both of exceptional quality and extremely complex; it consists of an "Olmec cross" inscribed inside a rectangle, a *Kan* cross, a sign that closely resembles the Maya glyph *ahau,* and a very broad capital "U."

The terra cotta vase with an incised decoration found at Chalcatzingo (Gay, 1971, fig. 43 and pl. XXIII) also bears symbols: "Olmec crosses" and perhaps stylized plants.

There are engraved glyphs found on two particularly interesting pieces in the Robert Woods Bliss Collection at Dumbarton Oaks: a statuette from Arroyo Pesquero (state of Veracruz) which was described and published in Elizabeth P. Benson's 1971 work on this piece, and a jadeite disk, probably a pectoral, shown in the illustrated catalogue of the collection (*Pre-Columbian Art*, pl. X).

The preceding observations are far from constituting a complete list of all the signs or glyphs that can be attributed to Olmec civilization. Certain puzzling artifacts now in the Brooklyn Museum may be glyphs: a piece of jadeite, for instance, in the shape of a trapezoid prolonged by a point and an appendage in the form of a hook, identified as an "Olmec glyph."

Our knowledge is still too rudimentary for us to be able to "read" glyphs or combinations of glyphs as Gay (1973) and Marion Popenoe Hatch (1971) have attempted to do. Agarian images, astral images: it is extremely difficult to interpret a system of thought that is so far removed in time from us and that has come down to us only in the form of obscure graphic symbols. Doubtless prudence dictates that we restrict ourselves to very modest conclusions.

This minimum of conclusions might be summed up as follows:

1. The Olmecs were familiar with the 260-day cycle (13 numbers, 20 glyphs)—either because they invented it or because they borrowed it or inherited it from an earlier culture.

2. They undoubtedly were also familiar with the solar year and

---

[10] Peñafiel, 1890, pl. 119.

Jadeite statuette, Arroyo Pesquero, state of Veracruz. (Courtesy of
Dumbarton Oaks, Washington, D.C.)

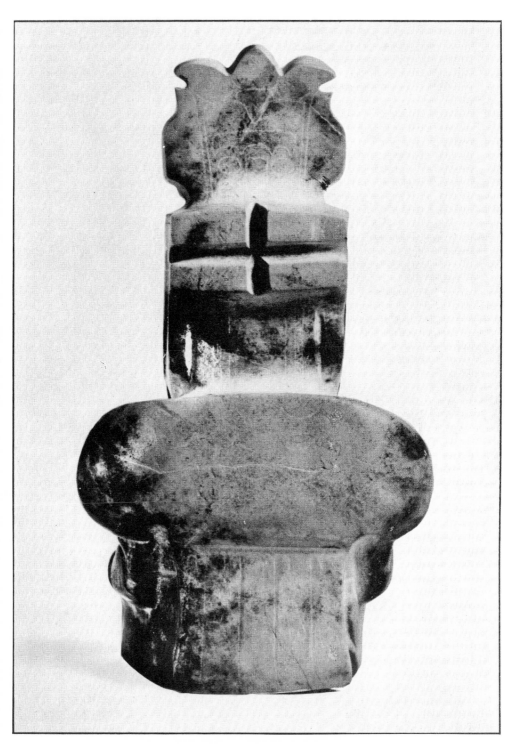

Same object, rear view.

Glyph engraved on the headdress of the figurine from Arroyo Pesquero. (Drawing by Anne Bouvier based on reproduction of work
published by Elizabeth P. Benson.)

probably invented the "Long Count" during the last period in their
history.

3. They used symbolic signs to designate a certain number of concepts, objects, phenomena. Did they organize these symbols into a
coherent system covering the entire range of language, in other words
into a system of writing as the Mayas later did? This is a question
that we are unable to answer definitely at present.

The only thing that we can say for certain is that the Olmecs possessed at least a "proto-writing," advanced enough to have reached

the level where abstract graphic symbols were beginning to be used.

Ignacio Bernal (1969, pp. 96 and 156) arrives at a similar conclusion: "It is undeniable that the Olmecs had discovered at least the length of the year and of the lunar month, and that they also computed time with the system of days that is characteristic of Mesoamerica," he writes. He adds that certain non-chronological inscriptions "do have glyphs, showing the use of a type of writing." And finally, he suggests that the inscriptions at Monte Albán constitute a true system of hieroglyphic writing and that this sacred city of Oaxaca is "the cradle of writing in Mesoamerica." It seems difficult to accept the Mexican scholar's conclusion with regard to this latter point: it would appear, rather, that the writing at Monte Albán derives from Olmec "proto-writing."

There is reason to suppose that between the limit dates of 500 or 400 B.C. (the final period of Olmec civilization) and A.D. 292, the beginning of known Maya inscriptions, the knowledge necessary to establish a calendar and the notion of symbolic glyphs became widespread among the peoples of Mesoamerica, from the central plateau to Guatemala. If the Olmecs were precursors, they were not necessarily the direct initiators of everything that was achieved in this domain. Various experiments, more or less inspired by them, by their example, or by the tradition stemming from their innovations in earlier periods, took place at a number of locations in this part of the continent. Certain of these experiments are known to us only by the rare traces of them that have survived, and they do not appear to have resulted in the creation of coherent hieroglyphic systems, whereas others developed into the "classic" writings of Teotihuacán, Oaxaca, and the Maya cities.

A number of monuments and engraved artifacts from southeastern Mexico and Guatemala bear the traces of certain of these abortive attempts that remained limited to one locality and one period. Let us cite a few examples:

1. Three stelae discovered in Chiapas and in Guatemala bear inscriptions that appear to belong to the "Long Count" system: stela no. 2 of Chiapa de Corzo (Lowe, 1962), stela no. 1 at El Baúl, and stela no. 2 at Abaj Takalik. In all three cases, the inscriptions, though badly damaged, unquestionably bear a reference to a "baktun 7," and their style, like that of the figures shown on the stelae, is neither Maya nor Olmec.

2. Non-chronological glyphic inscriptions are found on three artifacts carved of hard stone (Coe, 1976, figs. 7–9). These glyphs are not related to any known system of writing, though they do bear what we might call a "family resemblance" to Olmec symbols or Maya signs. One of these objects is a green stone pectoral found at Quintana Roo—

and hence in Maya country. It is decorated with an Olmec jaguar face (Coe, 1966). The reverse side bears twenty-four engraved glyphs: among them we find five human profiles and two stylized bird profiles, St. Andrew's crosses in quadrangular cartouches, a flower (?), and geometrical figures. Certain of these characters are accompanied by affixes, as in the Maya system of writing. The inscription as a whole is divided into four paired columns each bearing six glyphs.

Sixteen characters, in two columns of eight signs each, are carved on a statuette in black stone representing a jaguar in the style of Izapa, rather than in the Olmec style. These characters are similar, though not identical, to those of the pectoral mentioned above. The precise origin of this piece is unknown.

Thompson discovered at Hatzcap Ceel, in British Honduras (now Belize), an engraved ax (Thompson, 1931, pl. 33) bearing a dozen partially eroded glyphs, including in particular jaguar heads, a human face, and abstract signs.

Although two of these pieces—those whose origin is known—come from the Maya region, it is clear that the inscriptions on them are very far removed stylistically from classic Maya writing. Perhaps they should be called "pre-Maya."

The same thing may be said of the glyphs engraved on a small jade plaquette in the American Museum of Natural History which bears on one side a typically human Olmec face and on the reverse side an inscription composed of eight characters. The style of these glyphs is reminiscent of that of the Tuxtla statuette and would appear to have some relationship to Maya writing. Two of these characters are accompanied by the number 5, noted by means of five small disks rather than by a bar, hence according to a non-Maya system. Moreover, we cannot definitely reject the hypothesis that these signs were engraved on this piece at some later period. A small carved plaquette such as this was obviously regarded as a precious object that could be handed down from generation to generation. The traces of writing that it bears are hence not necessarily contemporary with the Olmec carving on the front face. And finally, we should note that the provenance of this artifact is unknown.

3. The monument designated as no. 1 found in 1971 at El Portón (Guatemala) is of particular interest (Sharer and Sedat, 1973): in fact, the inscription carved on this stela, though considerably damaged, not only bears chronological glyphs, numbers, and non-chronological signs, certain of which may be regarded as being Olmec or "Olmecoid," but is also highly significant because of the geographical situation of this monument. The site is located in the valley of a tributary of the Chixoy, which in turn empties into the Usumacinta. Furthermore, the region is rich in jadeite deposits, and the archaeological

Monument no. 15, La Venta. (From Peter D. Joralemon, *A Study of Olmec Iconography*, Studies in Pre-Columbian Art and Archaeology, no. 7. Courtesy of Dumbarton Oaks, Washington, D.C.)

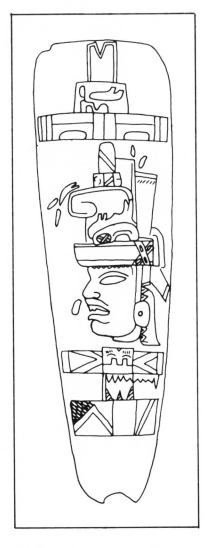

Engraved ax, Simojovel, state of Chiapas. (From Peter D. Joralemon, *A Study of Olmec Iconography*, Studies in Pre-Columbian Art and Archaeology, no. 7. Courtesy of Dumbarton Oaks, Washington, D.C.)

Engraved axes. (From Peter D. Joralemon, *A Study of Olmec Iconography*. Courtesy of Dumbarton Oaks, Washington, D.C.)

research that has been conducted there leads us to think that the local population fashioned objects of green stone and carried on a trade in them. Thus El Portón, in Maya country, possessed one of the raw materials that the Olmecs valued very highly, and could easily communicate with the Gulf coast.

4. Stela no. 10 of Kaminaljuyú, on the outskirts of present-day Guatemala City, is richly carved: figures with elaborate costumes and ornaments, glyphs enclosed within cartouches, whose style is "Mayoid" or perhaps related to that of the characters of Monte Albán, accompanied by numbers denoted by means of bars and dots. One of the figures is shown wearing an ear ornament that is a "quincunx" glyph. Michael Coe (1976, p. 115) is doubtless right when he states that these inscriptions are not Maya, but we cannot rule out the possibility that they should be classified as belonging to pre-Maya and pre-classic systems of writing. After a careful, detailed study of the Kaminaljuyú site, Edwin Shook has gone so far as to declare: "I am almost certain that Maya hieroglyphics originated at Kaminaljuyú or in the neighboring Pacific Coast region."[11]

5. An engraved ax, whose style is undoubtedly Olmec, found at El Sitio (Guatemala) has been mentioned earlier (Chapter 6). It bears nine delicately engraved characters, arranged in a column. They bear obvious resemblances to those on the Tuxtla statuette and to those that figure on objects described above in paragraph 2. It is interesting to note that these various specimens of writings come from a series of sites stretching all the way from the mountains of Los Tuxtlas and the Gulf coast to the Pacific slope of Guatemala, passing by way of the Usumacinta Valley and Yucatán. Many links in this chain have yet to be discovered. What we seem to be able to glimpse, in our present state of knowledge, is a vast Mesoamerican area under the influence or within the orbit of Olmec civilization, where, in the space of four or five centuries, several symbolic systems were invented and perfected, reaching their high point in the Maya writing of the great classic era.

All the vestiges of Olmec civilization that have survived and are known to us—compass-oriented courtyards and earthworks, stelae and sculptured altars, offerings, etc.—are proof that, as in all the civilizations that followed it in Mesoamerica, a driving force behind it was an intense religiosity that found expression in art, which in turn was a reflection of the beliefs, the rites, the ceremonies of the Olmecs. In their eyes, this was the one justification for the unbelievable human effort invested in the search for stones and their transportation, the preparation of the sites, the sculptures and the carvings, the practice

[11] Lafay, 1975, p. 201.

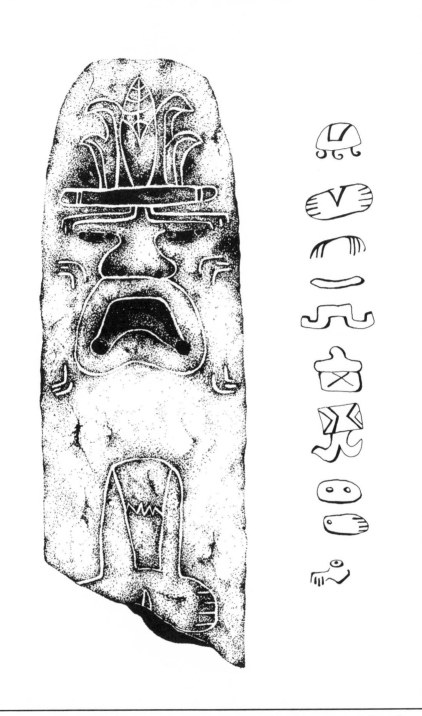

Engraved ax, El Sitio, Guatemala. (Drawing by Anne Bouvier based on reproduction of work published by Carlos Navarrete.)

of massive offerings, the execution of bas-reliefs and paintings on the rock faces of cliffs or in caves. And for us this religious impulse is the key enabling us to understand these accomplishments. This was a people that lived its myths, that projected the image of them in stone. Hence it is only natural that we should seek, among Olmec symbols, those which may designate divinities.

This is a domain where we must take the utmost care not to fall victim to arbitrary classifications. Anthropomorphic or fantastic representations are not all necessarily gods. Another temptation to be avoided is that of shutting our eyes to all contrary evidence and leaping to the conclusion that we find among the Olmecs, a thousand years before the Christian era, the gods of high cultures such as the deities of Teotihuacán or the Aztecs. It therefore behooves us to advance very cautiously and step by step in this terrain laid with a multitude of traps.

A first point on which all authors agree is the primordial importance of the jaguar, or rather of the hybrid, humano-feline being whose characteristic features are tirelessly represented by Olmec sculptors and stone-carvers. What appears almost certain is that this "were-jaguar," as this figure is called by English-speaking archaeologists, was a great divinity, perhaps the principal one, of the Olmec pantheon. The identification of a god in human form or of a man with an animal called in Aztec his *nahualli*, or "disguise," is a very old idea that survives in our day in "nahualism," a belief still very widespread in numerous Indian communities. The Olmec jaguar is perhaps the animal or semi-animal form of a god.

The Indians of tropical regions have always been at once fascinated and terrified by the jaguar, as we note today among the Lacandones of the Chiapas jungles, for example.

This feline must have haunted the humid tropical forests of Olmec country in great numbers. The man of this period, possessed of only the feeblest of weapons, was in no position to defend himself against this powerful and cruel animal who might take him by surprise at any point along a jungle path or at the edge of a maize field.

But what did this animal represent? With his vast store of knowledge as an archaeologist and his immense talent as a draftsman and painter, Miguel Covarrubias (1946b, pl. 4) sought to demonstrate, by means of a table comparing twenty representations from Olmec art and from art of other civilizations ranging from Teotihuacán and Oaxaca to the Aztecs, that the jaguar mask was transformed little by little until it became that of Tlaloc, the great rain god of the central plateau. The one objection to this demonstration that could be raised is that it was the sheer talent of Miguel Covarrubias that enabled him to put before us a sort of tour de force, a dazzling magic trick, admit-

tedly a brilliant one but not entirely convincing. The Tlaloc mask is
ophidian: the mythological animal it represents is not the jaguar, but
the serpent. Moreover, the importance of a rain god is primordial on
the high central plateau, where the climate is a subdesert one, or in
Yucatán with its dry soil: in these regions Tlaloc or Chac was invoked
to obtain rain, an absolutely vital necessity. But the problem of Olmec tillers of the soil was certainly not one involving rain, or if it was,
it was the problem of imploring their god not to send them so much
of it!

Doesn't the jaguar symbolize, rather, vegetative and telluric forces,
those that spring forth from the land as the feline leaps forth from the
thickets or the caves that are its hiding places? In the Aztec period,
a secondary god was called Tepeyollotl, "the heart of the mountain."
He was reputed to dwell within caves, and was portrayed in the form
of a jaguar. Could he be the distant descendant of the Olmec jaguar?

Michael Coe (1968b, pp. 111–14) has adopted Covarrubias' hypothesis and regards the jaguar god as being a "rain god." He is of the opinion that the representations of feline monsters bearing maize symbols
correspond to a god of maize, of agriculture. He also believes that he
has been able to identify the four representations (stylized faces seen
in profile) engraved on the shoulders and knees of the Las Limas
jadeite figure.[12] According to him, these four profiles correspond to
the following divinities:

—on the right shoulder, the god called in the post-classic period
Xipe Totec, the god of spring and of the rebirth of nature;

—on the left shoulder, a god of celestial fire, of the sun, or of
volcanoes;

—on the right knee, Quetzalcoatl, the Plumed Serpent;

—on the left knee, a death divinity.

Along with the jaguar god of rain (a variant of which represents the
god of maize), these four divinities constituted, in Coe's view, the
principal deities of the Olmec pantheon.

Peter David Joralemon, Michael Coe's collaborator and disciple (to
the point that we might speak of them as representing a "Yale school"),
attempted to go even further. In his work on Olmec iconography
published in 1971, he identifies ten divinities, which he designates
by Roman numerals.

I. The jaguar-monster, one variant of which is Michael Coe's "fire
god" and another the maize god.

II. A god bearing on his head a maize symbol.

III. A bird god.

IV. The "jaguar-baby."

[12] Cf. De la Fuente, 1973, pp. 155–58. Coe 1968b, p. 114.

V. A being with a humano-feline face, with two long fangs protruding from its mouth. Joralemon mentions ten specimens of it, but admits (p. 77) that "aside from that the specimens seem to have little in common. Some figures have features which are characteristic of God I, while others have attributes of God IV."

VI. A figure that Michael Coe interprets as representing Xipe Totec.

VII. The Plumed Serpent. Our author lists ten examples, which we shall discuss below.

VIII. The profile engraved on the left knee of the Las Limas statuette, which Michael Coe interprets as a death god. There are no other known representations.

IX. A bearded figure, only two examples of which have been reported: a small jade artifact from Mixtec country in Oaxaca and a figurine of unknown provenance. That this is a divinity appears extremely doubtful.

X. According to Joralemon (p. 86), "God X usually appears as subsidiary or secondary incising on representations of the major deities." The examples mentioned and reproduced by this author do not appear to justify its being classified as a separate divinity.

Of the interpretations by Michael Coe summarized earlier, there seems to be sufficient justification for accepting his feline god—without,however, regarding it as a rain god; the maize god with its vegetation symbols; and perhaps the death god, a face whose upper jaw calls to mind that of a skeleton. This latter representation, however, may not be an evocation of a divinity but rather of the idea of death, or of a "death" day in the calendar, such as the sixth day—*cimi* in Maya, *miquiztli* in Nahuatl—of the 260-day cycle.

I do not believe it possible to identify a Xipe Totec figure in the Olmec era. The argument set forth by Coe and Joralemon in support of their thesis—the presence of a sort of band crossing the eye of the figure—is not an entirely persuasive one. Xipe Totec is a divinity whose appearance is much more recent and whose origin is to be found on the western slope of Mexico. Many other proofs would be necessary before including it among the Olmec gods. It does not seem likely that the Las Limas profile B can be interpreted as being a god of either celestial or terrestrial fire merely because it has eyebrows in the form of flames. Such eyebrows are characteristic of almost all the representations of Olmec mythical beings, of "jaguar-babies" in particular. Bernal suggests that they are not flames but plumes: the Olmecs were fond of combining jaguar traits not only with those of man but also with certain features of other animals such as birds or serpents. As an example we may cite the face sculpted on the sarcophagus known as "monument no. 6" of La Venta (De la Fuente, 1973, p. 61), which has eyebrows in the form of flames (or plumes) and a snake's forked tongue.

And the Plumed Serpent? How tempting it would be to find this beneficent god, the inventor of writing and the calendar, of the arts, of everything that makes life beautiful, at the dawn of high Meso-american civilization! But do the facts in our possession allow us to make this great leap into the past?

We are obliged, first of all, to exclude the figure incised on the right knee of the Las Limas statuette. Michael Coe (1968b, p. 114) sees it as being a Quetzalcoatl because the eye of the figure repre-sented is incised with a St. Andrew's cross, the "Olmec cross" that we find in the eye of reptilian monsters such as the one at Chalca-tzingo, and also because the nose has a vaguely tubular appearance, "indicating his avatar as wind god." But the "Olmec cross" also ap-pears in the eye of humano-feline representations such as monument no. 1 of Laguna de Los Cerros (De la Fuente, 1973, p. 136) and therefore cannot be said to be a symbol associated only with reptiles or ophidians. As for the "wind god" personality assumed by the Plumed Serpent, we have every reason to believe that this was a late phenomenon, for we find no trace of it when the Plumed Serpent makes its appearance at Teotihuacán at the beginning of our era.

The ten specimens of "Plumed Serpents" listed and shown by Jor-alemon (figs. 243–52) may be divided into three categories.

1. The Las Limas profile which has just been mentioned and which is not conclusive proof.

2. Three stylized representations of serpents on ceramic objects whose respective origins are Tabasco, Las Bocas, and an unspecified location on the Gulf coast. These figurations have one feature in com-mon in any event: while they seem indeed to represent serpents, they bear no visible trace whatsoever of plumes.

3. There remain six other representations of reptiles, the most im-portant of which are: a wall painting at Oxtotitlán, another at Juxtla-huaca, a rock relief at Chalcatzingo, and monument no. 19 of La Venta; there is in addition a jade figurine of unknown provenance, and a terra cotta bowl from Tlatilco. In all these cases, the mythical reptiles represented are *not* plumed serpents. Admittedly we see, on the head or rather behind the head, more or less clearly depending on the specimen, an element in the form of a leaf or a crest that with a certain amount of imagination may just possibly be taken for a tuft of feathers. But in any case it will readily be granted that it is a long way from this representation to reptiles whose head and entire body are covered with long plumes, as in the arts of the classic and post-classic eras.

That there was a serpent god seems probable, if only because of the proof offered by the magnificent La Venta bas-relief (monument no. 19) where the majestic reptile, awesome and menacing, dominates the man around whom its sinuous body is coiled. But nothing allows us to state with certainty that the Olmecs adored a plumed serpent, a divine personality that was to acquire a primordial importance well after the disappearance of Olmec civilization.

If we limit ourselves to the most explicit sculpted or painted representations, the most likely Olmec divinities may be listed as follows:

I. The more or less humanized jaguar god. The fact that he is represented as the opening of a cave from which figures are emerging (altars with a niche, at La Venta and at San Lorenzo) or as the cave in which a rain divinity is seated, at Chalcatzingo, would tend to corroborate the hypothesis that this jaguar god, like his late counterpart Tepeyollotl, incarnates telluric forces. Hence, he is a god of vegetation, of maize, the symbol of which decorates his head at Chalcatzingo and in various other representations.[13]

II. The jaguar god in his form as a "baby" with mixed humano-feline features. He is borne on the forearms of human adults, for example at La Venta (altar no. 5, anterior face) or at San Lorenzo (monument no. 20), or yet again, we need scarcely point out, in the case of the splendid Las Limas statuette. A variant of this same mythical being represents it not as an inert small infant, but as a very young child standing gesticulating in the arms of men wearing miters and rigid hats, on the sides of altar no. 5 of La Venta. It is likely that these reliefs refer to episodes in a myth cycle whose point of departure may have been the sexual union of jaguars and women, as we have seen in an earlier chapter. No doubt legendary tales told of the birth and growth of a god or hero from the time that he was merely a "baby" to his adulthood as a great jaguar god.

III. The female figure seated in a cave amid symbols of clouds, rain, and vegetation may well have been a goddess. She is most likely a divinity of abundant vegetation and of beneficial rains, the prefiguration of the Chalchiuhtlicues and Chicomecoatls of the Nahuatl pantheon. It is perhaps significant that this goddess is not represented in the art of the "metropolitan area," where rain was superabundant, but at Chalcatzingo, where drought could threaten the harvests.

IV. Stela no. 2 and stela no. 3 of La Venta show, respectively, one and two figures in bas-relief, surrounded in each case by six figures of smaller dimensions that seem to be flying around and above the central motif, brandishing objects in the form of bars or axes. Are these flying beings minor divinities, something like the little demons

[13] Joralemon, 1971, figs. 170–72: engravings on polished axes representing an anthropomorphic head, the forehead of which is surmounted by a stylized maize plant.

that today are called *chaneques*, fearsome dwarfs that haunt the tropical forest?

V. The frequent representations of figures that are at once humans and birds, of men with bird masks (Chalcatzingo bas-relief, San Miguel Amuco stela, Xoc monolith) should be compared with the symbols reproduced by Joralemon (1971, p. 67). The latter deduces from them the existence, in the Olmec pantheon, of a "God III," combining traits characteristic of birds and certain features of the feline god. It is likely that the custom, widespread in Mesoamerica in the historical era, whereby priests or officiants wore vestments and the mask of the god that they were worshiping, already existed among the Olmecs. According to this hypothesis, the threatening figures of Chalcatzingo are performing rites related to the worship of a god with a bird's head. This god is probably linked with agriculture, in view of the symbols of maize and streaming water ornamenting the headdresses of these officiants.

VI. Serpents, though not plumed ones, do appear in fact to have a place in the Olmec pantheon. But what was the role of the serpent god? We simply do not know.

VII. Hermann Beyer (1928) drew attention to "a Deity common to the Teotihuacán and Totonac cultures," an obese god (*Dios Gordo*), a chubby-cheeked, fat being, representations of whom have been found at Teotihuacán and also in the state of Veracruz. Those from this latter region were automatically designated as "Totonac" at the time when Beyer described them. The German archaeologist mentions a figurine of this type found at Toniná, in the highlands of Chiapas, not very far from Xoc and Pichucalco. At La Venta itself, monument no. 5, which goes by the popular name of "La Abuela" ("Granny"), might well be a statue representing a man with puffy features and thick arms. The physical characteristics of the Olmec ethnic group such as they are represented in its iconography are an argument in favor of the Olmec origin of this *Dios Gordo*, who according to Beyer may have been a god of fertility, well-being, happiness.

VII. If we accept Michael Coe's theory with regard to the subject of profile D of the Las Limas statuette, a god of death, who—like the Ah Puch of the Mayas and the Mictlantecuhtli of the Aztecs—has certain features that are skeleton-like, figured in the Olmec pantheon.

Such is—in the light of what we know or think we know today—our harvest in the field of divinities—*teomilco*, as the Aztecs would say—of the Olmec religion. It is not a very abundant harvest, and it is probable that the pantheon of La Venta or of San Lorenzo included many more gods than we have listed.

Finally, what was the nature of their rites and ceremonies? We

have neither documents nor remains that would enable us to answer
this question. If rock bas-relief no. 2 at Chalcatzingo depicts a rite, it
might be a representation of the preparatory phase of a human sacrifice. Certain stone monuments of the "metropolitan area" that have
cavities hollowed out in them may mean that living beings, either
animal or human, were sacrificed there and that their blood flowed
into these receptacles as into the Aztec *quauhxicalli*.[14] But that is a
far from certain deduction.

In the face of the astonishing spectacle of a civilization that gives
the impression of suddenly springing up in all its originality from an
undifferentiated background of peasant culture, we naturally are led
to ponder the question whether this leap was not due to an exterior
influence, to the arrival of a high civilization come from elsewhere
which took root in the soil of Mesoamerica.

By dint of attempting to prove too much, the ultra-diffusionism of
R. A. Jairazbhoy arouses our skepticism and in the end proves nothing. Egyptians, blacks, Semites, Babylonians, Sumerians, Chinese,
practically all the peoples of Asia Minor and the Far East, met, according to his theory, on the shores of the Gulf of Mexico. Can we
really believe that they did not leave a single Egyptian hieroglyph or
Chinese inscription, that they disappeared without even substituting
their own calendar for the Mesoamerican system that was so different
from those of the Old World? When we study the detailed arguments
propounded in favor of this theory, we note that the suggested similarities between Asiatic civilizations and that of the Olmecs are either
too general to enable us to draw conclusions from them—the one, for
example, based on the fact that Asiatics and early Mexican peoples
both had monarchic regimes—or else they result from highly doubtful
or erroneous interpretations of the facts observed. Thus, for instance,
Jairazbhoy (1974, p. 39) takes the cylindrical object held in the hand
of an Olmec statue to be a manuscript rolled up in the manner of an
Egyptian scroll. Moreover, this author has gone to considerable effort—to no avail—to come up with a plausible explanation of why the
Mesoamerican calendar and glyphs do not coincide with Egyptian or
Chinese models. And finally, it is obvious that one cannot jumble
together facts concerning Olmecs, classic Mayas, Quichés (extracted
from the *Popul Vuh*), and Aztecs, stemming from quite distinct civilizations and from periods separated by millennia, and then proceed
to link them to a supposed presence of African and Asiatic immigrants
around the middle of the third millennium B.C.

---

[14]The monuments in question are: no. 1 at Laguna de Los Cerros; no. 14 at La
Venta; D and N at Tres Zapotes. Bernal (1969, p. 105) concludes: "At this time . . .
it is not possible to reach a definite conclusion regarding sacrifice."

Betty J. Meggers's research is not entirely immune to similar criticisms. This archaeologist attempts to establish a parallel between the Shang civilization of China (1750 to 1200 B.C.) and Olmec civilization. She lists a number of traits such as the following:

—similarities between Shang Chinese characters and certain glyphs such as the "Olmec cross";

—the importance of jades, "a primary commodity of long-distance trade";

—individual dwellings grouped around ceremonial centers;

—a feline deity (the Chinese *t'ao t'ieh*);

—the worship of mountains, supposedly reflected in the pseudo-pyramid at La Venta.

According to Betty Meggers, it was a transpacific contact which explains what she calls the "quantum jump" that enabled the Olmecs to make their appearance as the first civilized people of Mexico. Her demonstration, however, is not convincing. A cross in a square or a rectangle is not a sufficiently original sign to make it necessary to call upon outside influence to explain it. Dwellings grouped about a center are too widespread a phenomenon; even the cult of a feline is not sufficiently conclusive proof, and what is more, it may have come not from China, but from South America. But above all, it would be necessary to explain not the similarities but the differences; not the presences but the absences. If there had been a cultural transfer from Shang China to Olmec Mexico, why were bronze and gold work both unknown to the people of La Venta? And why, essentially, were their symbols so different from Chinese characters?

David C. Grove (1976) was right to have doubts about the simplistic view, or the optical illusion, that would lead us to believe that Olmec civilization exploded, so to speak, *ex nihilo*, without passing through a formative phase. It cannot be regarded as having remained homogeneous, immobile, and identical throughout its entire duration. Jade carving appears only after 900 B.C. Writing and the calendar were late developments. Though he does not reject the possibility of contacts across the Pacific, he rebels against the comparative method that consists of "selective trait picking and choosing."[15]

Betty Meggers replied to this criticism by calling attention to "numerous striking parallelisms" and by denouncing—an argument worthy of note—the "double standard" that applies, depending on whether or not there exists an "oceanic barrier" between two areas of civilization. It is in fact true that there has been too marked a tendency to regard sea expanses as unbridgeable, though the migrations of the

[15] With regard to this controversy, see Meggers, 1975; Grove, 1976; and Meggers, 1976.

Polynesians, to cite but one example, are sufficient proof that early man was perfectly capable of crossing them.

The debate is not yet ended. It will be of interest and of scientific value only insofar as it is not limited to the fruitless confrontation of a priori supporters or adversaries of diffusionist or anti-diffusionist hypotheses. Dogmatism aside, the history of civilizations demonstrates that, depending on times and places, diffusion and independent invention, borrowings and the rejection of borrowings, expansion and withdrawals have taken place. What is of prime importance is to define precisely what we are speaking about, to refrain from comparing anything and everything from any and every period, to refuse to be satisfied with vague intuitions, to seek, on the contrary, the precise and incontrovertible facts that, simply because they are most unusual, may furnish the proof of a relationship between two cultures.

The relationships between Mexico and Andean America (see Lehmann, 1938; Krickeberg, 1956) are proven fact as far as a relatively late period is concerned, at the turning point between the classic era and the post-classic phase, when South American metallurgy was introduced into Mexico, first of all in the regions of Oaxaca and Michoacán bordering the Pacific Ocean. Tarascan depilatory tweezers, jewelry such as the Mixtec golden diadem of purely Peruvian style found in tomb no. 7 at Monte Albán, certain "stirrup-handled" vessels, clearly reflect the influence of Peru. But these are recent developments. A systematic comparative study of the entire panorama from 1500 to 1000 B.C. in Mesoamerica and in the Andes, embracing the two oldest civilizations, that of the Olmecs in the north, that of Chavín in the south,[16] could cast new light on the origin and the relations of the high cultures of the two parts of the continent.

If we grant that the orientation of the monuments of La Venta is related to a configuration in the heavens that could be observed in this region in the year 2000 B.C.,[17] we perhaps catch a glimpse of the distant point of departure of the formative phase that led to the flowering of Olmec civilization. Our knowledge of this period of around five centuries in the Gulf coast region is still almost nil. The key of many enigmas lies buried in the soil of the tropical expanses covered with forest and brush in the states of Veracruz and Tabasco.

The exciting search for the human past in this area of Mexico will undoubtedly turn up new finds that will lead to new syntheses. Hence the one presented in this book must be regarded as tentative.

[16] Krickeberg (1956, conclusions) emphasizes the similarities that exist between the representations of felines at Chavín and a bas-relief at Placeres de Oro (state of Guerrero).

[17] This is the hypothesis put forward by Marion Popenoe Hatch, 1971.

Perhaps discoveries that we do not even expect today will lead archaeologists to modify radically the views most widely accepted at present. What is certain is that this people that only yesterday was unknown to us was the creator of a great civilization, rich in original inventions that left their mark on this entire part of the world for the next three thousand years. It is the Olmecs who began the glorious procession that brought one city of Mexican antiquity after another into existence down through the centuries, until the invasion of the continent by Europeans. The Olmec heritage was perpetuated in the minds and in the art of the indigenous peoples down to the fall of Tenochtitlán, and still survives in part among the Indians, whose present is profoundly steeped in the past.

The touching continuity of indigenous Mexican civilization in spite of the often bloody upheavals of its history, and the indelible imprint still preserved in the depths of its nature despite the changes of the modern era, are ample justification for the attempt being made by archaeologists to return to the earliest sources of this autochthonous civilization. With the Olmecs we catch a glimpse of the decisive mutation that made Mexico and Mesoamerica a cultural high-pressure area: they in fact leapt beyond the mysterious threshold that other Indian peoples approached but never managed to cross. Pre-Conquest Mexico would not have been what it was—and even the Mexico of the twentieth century would not be what it is—if these men of long ago had not begun to erect their stelae and to sculpt their bas-reliefs in the depths of torrid jungles, more than three thousand years ago.

# Bibliography

⊠⊠⊠⊠⊠⊠⊠

AGRINIER, Pierre. 1973.
"Un completo cerámico, tipo olmeca, del preclásico temprano en El Mirador, Chiapas." *Sociedad Mexicana de Antropología. 13 ava. Mesa Redonda.* Jalapa.

ANTON, Ferdinand. 1969.
*Ancient Mexican Art.* Putnam's, New York. (Original German edition: *Alt-Mexiko und seine Kunst.* Leipzig, 1965.)

*Art olmèque (L'), source des arts classiques du Mexique.* Exhibition catalogue of the Musée Rodin, Paris, 1972. Introduction by Ignacio BERNAL.

*Arte olmeca (El).* In *Artes de México*, año XIX, no. 154, 1972. Articles by DE LA FUENTE, POHORILENKO, FONCERRADA de MOLINA, LAPORTE, BEVERIDO PEREAU. Mexico City.

BALSER, Carlos. 1958.
"Los 'baby faces' Olmeca de Costa Rica." *Actos del 33 Congreso Int. de Americanistas*, vol. 2, pp. 280–85. San José.

BALSER, Carlos. 1964.
"Some Costa Rican Jade Motifs." In *Essays in Pre-Columbian Art and Archaeology* (ed. S. K. Lothrup), pp. 210–17. Harvard University Press, Cambridge, Mass.

BARBA DE PIÑA CHAN, Beatriz. 1956.
"Tlapacoya, un sitio preclásico de transición." *Acta Antropologica*, Epoca 2, vol. 1, no. 1. Mexico City.

BASAURI, Carlos. 1928.
"Informe de los trabajos realizados . . . en los Estados de Chiapas, Departamento del Petén en Guatemala, Campeche, Yucatán y Territorio de Quintana Roo en el primer semestre del año de 1928." In PALACIOS, 1928, appendix III, pp. 197–203.

BASAURI, Carlos. 1931.
*Tojolabales, Tzeltales y Mayas.* Talleres gráficos de la Nación. Mexico City.

BAUDEZ, Claude F. 1963.
"Cultural Development in Lower Central America." In *Aboriginal Cultural Development in Latin America*. Smithsonian Miscellaneous Collections, vol. 146, no. 1. Washington, D.C.

BAUDEZ, Claude F. 1970.
*Amérique centrale*. "Archaeologia Mundi" series. Nagel, Geneva.

BAUDEZ, Claude F., and BECQUELIN, Pierre. 1973.
*Archéologie de Los Naranjos, Honduras*. Mission Archéologique et Ethnologique Française au Mexique. Mexico City.

BENSON, Elizabeth P. (ed.). 1968.
*Dumbarton Oaks Conference on the Olmec*. October 28, 1967. Dumbarton Oaks Research Library and Collection, Trustees for Harvard University, Washington, D.C.

BENSON, Elizabeth P. 1971.
*An Olmec Figure at Dumbarton Oaks*. Dumbarton Oaks, Trustees for Harvard University, Washington, D.C.

BERNAL, Ignacio. 1968.
"Views of Olmec Culture." *Dumbarton Oaks Conference on the Olmec*, pp. 135–42. Washington, D.C.

BERNAL, Ignacio. 1969.
*The Olmec World*. University of California Press, Berkeley.

BERNAL, Ignacio. 1975.
"Los Olmecas." In *Del nomadismo a las centros ceremoniales*, pp. 183–234. I.N.A.H., Mexico City.

BEVERIDO PEREAU, Francisco. 1972.
"Las ciudades." In *Arte olmeca*. *Artes de México*, pp. 83–92.

BEYER, Hermann. 1927.
"Bibliografía: Tribes and Temples." *El México Antiguo*, vol. 2, nos. 11–12, pp. 305–13. Mexico City.

BEYER, Hermann. 1928.
"A Deity Common to Teotihuacán and Totonac Cultures." *International Congress of Americanists*, New York, 1928, pp. 193–99. Spanish translation in *Mito y simbolismo del México antiguo*, pp. 365–68, Mexico City, 1965.

BLOM, Frans. 1929.
*Preliminary Report of the John Geddings Gray Memorial Expedition Conducted by the Tulane University of Louisiana*. New Orleans.

BLOM, Frans, and DUBY, Gertrude. 1957.
*La selva lacandona*. Editorial Cultura, Mexico City.

BLOM, Frans, and LA FARGE, Oliver. 1926–27.
*Tribes and Temples*. 2 vols. Tulane University Press, New Orleans.

BOGGS, Stanley H. 1950.
" 'Olmec' Pictographs in the Las Victorias Group, Chalchuapa Archaeological Zone, El Salvador." Carnegie Institution of Washington, notes on Middle American Archaeology and Ethnology, no. 99, pp. 85–92. Cambridge, Mass.

BOGGS, Stanley H. 1971.
"An Olmec Mask-Pendant from Ahuachapan, El Salvador." *Archaeology*, vol. 21, no. 4, pp. 356–58.

BORHEGYI, Stephan F. de. 1964.
"Ball-game Handstones and Ball-game Gloves." In *Essays in Pre-Columbian Art and Archaeology* (ed. S. K. Lothrop), pp. 127–51. Harvard University Press, Cambridge, Mass.

BREINER, Sheldon, and COE, Michael D. 1972.
"Magnetic Exploration of the Olmec Civilization." *American Scientist*, vol. 60, no. 5, September–October 1972, pp. 566–75.

BRÜGGEMANN, Jurgen, and HERS, M. A. 1970.
"Exploraciones arqueológicas en San Lorenzo Tenochtitlán." *Boletín del I.N.A.H.*, no. 39, pp. 18–23. Mexico City.

CAMPBELL, Lyle, and KAUFMAN, Terrence. 1976.
"A Linguistic Look at the Olmecs." *America Antiquity*, vol. 41, no. 1, January 1976, pp. 80–89.

CASO, Alfonso. 1942.
*Definición y extensión del complejo olmeca.* Tuxtla Gutiérrez. Reprinted as appendix in CASO, 1965, pp. 44–46.

CASO, Alfonso. 1947.
*Calendario y escritura de las antiguas culturas de Monte Albán.* Mexico City.

CASO, Alfonso. 1965.
"¿Existió un imperio olmeca?" *Memoriás de El Colegia Nacional*, vol. 5, no. 3, 1964 (Published, Mexico City, 1965).

CASO, Alfonso. 1971.
"Calendrical Systems of Central Mexico." In *Handbook of Middle American Indians*, vol. 10, pp. 333–48. University of Texas Press, Austin.

CASSIER, Jacques, and ICHON, Alain. 1978.
"Les Sculptures d'Abaj Takalik (Guatemala)." *Journal de la Société des Américanistes*, vol. 65. Paris.

CERVANTES, María Antonieta.
"Dos elementos de uso ritual en el arte olmeca." *Anales del Instituto Nacional de Antropología e Historia* (undated photocopy).

CERVANTES, María Antonieta. 1976.
"Olmec Materials in the National Museum of Anthropology, Mexico." In NICHOLSON (ed.), 1976.

CHADWICK, Robert. 1971.
"Archaeological Synthesis of Michoacán and Adjacent Regions." In *Handbook of Middle American Indians*, vol. 11, pp. 657–93. University of Texas Press, Austin.

CHAVERO, Alfredo. 1887.
*México a través de los siglos.* Vol. 1. Mexico City.

*Chefs-d'œuvre de l'art mexicain.* Exhibition, Petit Palais, Paris, April–June, 1962. Ministère d'État aux Affaires Culturelles.

CLEWLOW, Carl William, Jr. 1974.
*A Stylistic and Chronological Study of Olmec Monumental Sculpture.* University of California, Department of Anthropology, Berkeley.

COBEAN, Robert H., COE, Michael D., PERRY, Edward A., TUREKIAN, Karl K., and KHARKAR, Dinkar P. 1971.
"Obsidian Trade at San Lorenzo Tenochtitlán, Mexico." *Science*, vol. 174, pp. 666–71.

COE, Michael D. 1962.
"An Olmec Design on an Early Peruvian Vessel." *American Antiquity*, vol. 27, no. 4.

COE, Michael D. 1965.
"The Olmec Style and Its Distributions." In *Handbook of Middle American Indians*, vol. 2, article 29. University of Texas Press, Austin.

COE, Michael D. 1965.
*The Jaguar's Children: Pre-Classic Central Mexico.* Museum of Primitive Art, New York.

COE, Michael D. 1966.
*An Early Stone Pectoral from Southeastern Mexico.* Dumbarton Oaks, Washington, D.C.

COE, Michael D. 1967.
"Cycle 7 Monuments in Middle America: A Reconsideration." *American Anthropologist*, vol. 59, no. 4, pp. 597–611.

COE, Michael D. 1968a.
"San Lorenzo and the Olmec Civilization." *Dumbarton Oaks Conference on the Olmec*, pp. 41–78. Washington, D.C.

COE, Michael D. 1968b.
*America's First Civilization: Discovering the Olmec.* American Heritage, New York.

COE, Michael D. 1974a.
"Meso-American Civilization (History of)". In *Encyclopaedia Britannica*, 15th edition, vol. 11, pp. 933–46.

COE, Michael D. 1974b.
"Photogrammetry and the Ecology of Olmec Civilization." In *Aerial Photography in Anthropological Field Research*. Harvard University Press, Cambridge, Mass.

COE, Michael D. 1976.
"Early Steps in the Evolution of Maya Writing." In NICHOLSON (ed.), 1976, pp. 109–21.

COE, Michael D. 1977a.
"Archaeology Today: The New World." In *New Perspectives in Canadian Archaeology*. Royal Society of Canada, Ottawa.

COE. Michael D. 1977b.
"Olmec and Maya: A Study in Relationships." In *The Origins of Maya Civilization* (ed. R. E. W. Adams). University of New Mexico Press, Albuquerque.

COMAS, Juan. 1972.
*Hipótesis trasatlánticas sobre el poblamiento de América.* U.N.A.M., Mexico City.

COOK DE LEONARD, Carmen. 1967.
*Sculptures and Rock Carvings at Chalcatzingo, Morelos.* University of California Press, Berkeley.

CORDAN, Wolfgang. 1959.
*Geheimnis im Urwald.* Düsseldorf-Cologne. Translation: *Secret of the Forest.* Garden City, N.Y., 1964.

COVARRUBIAS, Miguel. 1942.
*Origen y desarrollo del estilo artístico "olmeca."* Tuxtla Gutiérrez. Reprinted as appendix in CASO, 1965, pp. 46–48.

COVARRUBIAS, Miguel. 1946a.
"El arte olmeca o de La Venta." *Cuadernos Americanos,* vol. 153, no. 79. Mexico City.

COVARRUBIAS, Miguel. 1946b.
*Mexico South: The Isthmus of Tehuantepec.* Knopf, New York.

COVARRUBIAS, Miguel. 1950.
"Tlatilco: el arte y la cultura preclásica del Valle de México." *Cuadernos Americanos,* año 9, no. 3, pp. 149–62, Mexico City.

COVARRUBIAS, Miguel. 1957.
*Indian Art of Mexico and Central America.* Knopf, New York.

DAVIES, Nigel. 1977.
*The Toltecs Until the Fall of Tula.* University of Oklahoma Press, Norman.

DAVIS, Whitney. 1978.
"So-called Jaguar-Human Copulation Scenes in Olmec Art." *American Antiquity,* vol. 43, no. 3, pp. 453–57.

DE LA FUENTE, Beatriz. 1972.
"La Escultura monumental." In *Arte olmeca. Artes de México,* pp. 6–34.

DE LA FUENTE, Beatriz. 1973.
*Escultura monumental olmeca: catálogo.* Universidad Nacional Autónoma, Instituto de Investigaciones Estéticas, Mexico City.

DE LA FUENTE, Beatriz. 1976.
"La proporción armónica en la escultura monumental olmeca." *XLII$^e$ Congrès International des Américanistes,* Paris.

DELLA SANTA, Elizabeth. 1959.
"Les Cupisniques et l'origine des Olmèques." *Revue de l'Université de Bruxelles,* n.s., 11$^e$ année, pp. 340–63.

DISSELHOFF, H. D. 1963.
*Les Grandes Civilisations de l'Amérique ancienne.* Arthaud, Paris.

DOCKSTADER, Frederick J. 1973.
*Indian Art of the Americas.* Museum of the American Indian, Heye Foundation, New York.

DORSINFANG-SMETS, A. 1973.
*L'Amérique précolombienne: Les civilisations du maïs.* Meddens, Brussels.

DRUCKER, Philip. 1943.
*Ceramic Stratigraphy at Cerro de Las Mesas, Veracruz, Mexico.* Smithsonian Institution, Bureau of American Ethnology, bulletin 141. Washington, D.C.

DRUCKER, Philip. 1943.
*Ceramic Sequences at Tres Zapotes, Veracruz, Mexico.* Smithsonian Institution, Bureau of American Ethnology, bulletin 140. Washington, D.C.

DRUCKER, Philip. 1952.
*La Venta, Tabasco: A Study of Olmec Ceramics and Art.* Smithsonian Institution, Bureau of American Ethnology, Washington, D.C.

DRUCKER, Philip. 1955.
*The Cerro de Las Mesas Offerings of Jade and Other Materials.* Smithsonian Institution, Bureau of American Ethnology, bulletin 157, pp. 25–68. Washington, D.C.

DRUCKER, Philip, HEIZER, Robert F., and SQUIER, Robert J. 1959.
*Excavations at La Venta, Tabasco, 1955.* Smithsonian Institution, Bureau of American Ethnology, bulletin 170. Washington, D.C.

EASBY, Elizabeth Kennedy. 1966.
*Ancient Art of Latin America: From the Collection of Jay C. Leff.* Catalogue of a special exhibition, Brooklyn Museum, November 22, 1966–March 5, 1967. Brooklyn Museum, Brooklyn, N.Y.

EKHOLM, Gordon F. 1973.
"The Archaeological Significance of Mirrors in the New World." *Atti del XL Congresso Internazionale degli Americanisti,* Rome and Genoa, September 3–10, 1972, vol. 1, pp. 133–35. Genoa.

EKHOLM, Susanna M. 1969.
*Mound 30a and the Early Preclassic Ceramic Sequence of Izapa, Chiapas, Mexico.* New World Archaeological Foundation, Brigham Young University Press, Provo, Utah.

EKHOLM-MILLER, Susanna. 1973.
*The Olmec Rock Carving at Xoc, Chiapas, Mexico.* New World Archaeological Foundation, Brigham Young University Press, Provo, Utah.

EMMERICH, André. 1963.
*Art Before Columbus.* Simon and Schuster, New York.

FERDON, Edwin N., Jr. 1953.
*Tonalá, Mexico: An Archaeological Survey.* School of American Research, monograph no. 16. Santa Fe.

FIELD, Frederick V. 1967.
*Thoughts on the Meaning and Use of Pre-Hispanic Sellos.* Studies in Pre-Columbian Art and Archaeology, no. 3. Dumbarton Oaks, Washington, D.C.

FLANNERY, Kent V. 1968.
"The Olmec and the Valley of Oaxaca: A Model for Inter-regional Interaction in Formative Times." *Dumbarton Oaks Conference on the Olmec*, pp. 79–118. Washington, D.C.

FONCERRADA DE MOLINA, Marta. 1972.
"La Pintura rupestre." In *El arte olmeca. Artes de México*, año XIX, no. 154, pp. 63–68. Mexico City.

FURST, Peter T. 1968.
"The Olmec Were-Jaguar Motif in the Light of Ethnographic Reality." *Dumbarton Oaks Conference on the Olmec*, pp. 143–78. Washington, D.C.

GARTH, Norman, V. 1973.
*Izapa Sculpture*. Part 1: Album. New World Archaeological Foundation, Brigham Young University Press, Provo, Utah.

GAY, Carlo T. E. 1967.
"Oldest Paintings in the New World." *Natural History*, vol. 76, no. 4, pp. 28–35.

GAY, Carlo T. E. 1971.
*Chalcacingo*. Drawings by Frances Pratt. Akademische Druck und Verlagsanstalt, Graz, Austria.

GAY, Carlo T. E. 1972.
*Xochipala: The Beginnings of Olmec Art*. The Art Museum, Princeton University, Princeton, N.J.

GAY, Carlo T. E. 1973.
"Olmec Hieroglyphic Writing." *Archaeology*, vol. 26, no. 4.

GENDROP, Paul. 1970.
*Arte prehispánico en Mesoamérica*. Ed. Trillas, Mexico City.

GENDROP, Paul. 1972.
*El México antiguo. Ancient Mexico*. Mexico City.

GIRARD, Rafael. 1969.
*La misteriosa cultura olmeca: Ultimos descubrimientos de esculturas pre-olmecas en Guatemala*. 3rd edition. Guatemala City.

GIRARD, Rafael. 1973.
"Nuevas esculturas líticas en el área maya." *Atti del XL Congresso Internazionale degli Americanisti*, Rome and Genoa, September 3–10, 1972, vol. 1, pp. 195–202 (ill.). Genoa.

GIRARD, Rafael. 1977.
*Origen y desarrollo de las civilizaciones antiguas de América*. Mexico City.

GORENSTEIN, Shirley. 1975.
*Not Forever on Earth: Prehistory of Mexico*. Scribner, New York.

GREEN, Dee F., and LOWE, Gareth W. 1967.
*Altamira and Padre Piedra: Early Preclassic Sites in Chiapas, Mexico*. New World Archaeological Foundation, Brigham Young University, Provo, Utah.

GRENNES-RAVITZ, Ronald A., and COLEMAN, G. H. 1976.
"The Quintessential Role of Olmec in the Central Highlands of Mexico: A Refutation." *American Antiquity*, vol. 41, no. 2, pp. 196–206.

GROVE, David C. 1968.
"The Pre-Classic Olmec in Central Mexico: Site Distribution and Inferences." *Dumbarton Oaks Conference on the Olmec*, pp. 179–85. Washington, D.C.

GROVE, David C. 1970.
*The Olmec Paintings of Oxtotilán Cave, Guerrero, Mexico*. Dumbarton Oaks, Washington, D.C. Spanish edition: *Los murales de la Cueva de Oxtotitlán, Acatlán, Guerrero*. I.N.A.H., Mexico City.

GROVE, David C. 1976.
"Olmec Origins and Transpacific Diffusion: Reply to Meggers." *American Anthropologist*, vol. 78, no. 3, pp. 634–37.

GROVE, David C. 1977.
"The Central Mexican Preclassic: Is There Really Disagreement?" *American Antiquity*, vol. 42, no. 4, pp. 634–37.

GROVE, David, and PARADIS, Louise I. 1971.
"An Olmec Stela from San Miguel Amuco, Guerrero." *American Antiquity*, vol. 36, no. 1, pp. 95–102.

GULLBERG, Jonas E. 1959.
*Technical Notes on Concave Mirrors*. Smithsonian Institution, Bureau of American Ethnology, bulletin 170, pp. 280–83. Washington, D.C.

GUZMÁN, Eulalia. 1934.
"Los relieves de las rocas del Cerro de la Cantera, Jonacatepec, Mor." *Anales del Museo Nacional*, 5ᵉ época, vol. 1, pp. 237–51. Mexico City.

HABERLAND, Wolfgang. 1971.
*Die Kunst des indianischen Amerika*. Rietberg Museum, Zürich. Atlantis Verlag, Zürich.

HAMMER, Olga, and D'ANDREA, Jeanne. 1978.
*Treasures of Mexico from the Mexican National Museums*. Exhibition catalogue, Armand Hammer Foundation, Washington, D.C.

HASLER, Juan A. 1959.
"Due teste litiche olmeche con capelli crespi." *Archivio Internazionale di Etnografia e Preistoria*, vol. 2, pp. 31–34. Turin.

HEIZER, Robert F. 1968.
"New Observations on La Venta." *Dumbarton Oaks Conference on the Olmec*, pp. 9–40. Washington, D.C.

HEIZER, Robert F. 1973.
"An Unusual Olmec Figurine." In *Studies in Ancient Mesoamerica* (ed. John Graham), pp. 199–201. University of California, Department of Anthropology, Berkeley.

HELLMUTH, Nicholas B. 1974.
*The Olmec Civilization, Art and Archaeology: An Introductory Bibliography.*
Foundation for Latin American Anthropological Research, Providence, R.I.

HENDRICHS, Pedro R. 1940–41.
"Datos sobre la técnica minera prehispánica." *El México Antiguo*, vol. 5, pp. 148–60, 179–94, 311–28. Mexico City.

HIRTH, Kenneth G. 1978.
"Interregional Trade and the Formation of Prehistoric Gateway Communities." *American Antiquity*, vol. 43, no. 1, pp. 35–46.

HOLMES, W. H. 1907.
"A Nephrite Statuette from San Andrés Tuxtla, Veracruz, Mexico." *American Antiquity*, vol. 9, no. 4.

ICHON, Alain. 1977.
*Les Sculptures de La Lagunita, El Quiché, Guatemala.* Editorial Piedra Santa, Guatemala City.

JAIRAZBHOY, R. A. 1973.
" 'The God-Kings and the Titans' by James Bailey." Book review. *The New Diffusionist*, vol. 3, no. 13, October, pp. 156–66. Sandy, Beds., England.

JAIRAZBHOY, R. A. 1974.
*Ancient Egyptians and Chinese in America* (Old World Origins of American Civilization, vol. 1). George Prior, London.

JIMÉNEZ MORENO, Wigberto. 1942.
"El enigma de los Olmecas." *Cuadernos Americanos*, año 1, no. 5, pp. 113–45. Mexico City.

JOESINK-MANDEVILLE, R. L. V., and MELUZIN, Sylvia. 1976.
"Olmec-Maya Relationships: Olmec Influences in Yucatán." In NICHOLSON (ed.), 1976.

JORALEMON, Peter David. 1971.
*A Study of Olmec Iconography.* Studies in Pre-Columbian Art and Archaeology, no. 7. Dumbarton Oaks, Washington, D.C.

JORALEMON, Peter David. 1976.
"The Olmec Dragon: A Study in Pre-Columbian Iconography." In NICHOLSON (ed.), 1976.

KAN, Michael. 1968–69.
"Notes on a Polished Greenstone Figure from Guerrero, Mexico." *The Brooklyn Museum Annual X*, pp. 152–58. Brooklyn, N.Y.

KAN, Michael. 1972.
"The Feline Motif in Northern Peru." In *The Cult of the Feline: A Conference in Pre-Columbian Iconography, October 31 & November 1, 1970* (ed. Elizabeth P. Benson), pp. 69–90. Dumbarton Oaks, Washington, D.C.

KELLEY, David H. 1966.
"A Cylinder Seal from Tlatilco." *American Antiquity*, vol. 31, no. 5, pp. 744–46.

KNOROZOV, Y. V. 1967.
*The Writing of the Maya Indians.* Russian Translation Series, vol. 4. Harvard University Press, Cambridge, Mass.

KRICKEBERG, Walter. 1956.
*Altmexikanische Kulturen.* Berlin.

*Kunst aus Mexico.* Exhibition catalogue, Villa Hügel, Essen, May 8–August 18, 1974. Verlag Aurel Bongers, Recklinghausen, West Germany.

KUNZ, George F. 1890.
*Gems and Precious Stones of North America.* Lippincott, New York.

LAFAY, Howard. 1975.
"Los Hijos del Tiempo." *National Geographic,* December 1975, pp. 3–41.

LAPORTE, Jean-Pierre, 1972. "La cerámica." In *Arte olmeca. Arts de México,* pp. 69–82.

LEE, Thomas A., Jr. 1969.
*The Artifacts of Chiapa de Corzo, Chiapas, Mexico.* New World Archaeological Foundation, Brigham Young University Press, Provo, Utah.

LEHMANN, Walter. 1938.
"La Antigüedad histórica de las culturas Gran-Mexicanas y el Problema de su contacto con las culturas Gran-Peruanas." *El México Antiguo,* vol. 4, nos. 5–6, pp. 179–208. Mexico City.

LISTER, Robert H. 1971.
"Archaeological Synthesis of Guerrero." In *Handbook of Middle American Indians,* vol. 11, pp. 619–31. University of Texas Press, Austin.

LOTHROP, S. K., FOSHAG, W. F., and MAHLER, Joy. 1957.
*Pre-Columbian Art.* Robert Woods Bliss Collection. Phaidon Publishers, New York.

LOWE, Gareth W. 1962.
"Algunos resultados de la temporada 1961 en Chiapa de Corzo, Chiapas." In *Estudios de Cultura Maya,* vol. 2, pp. 185–96. Mexico City.

McDONALD, Andrew J. 1977.
"Two Middle Preclassic Engraved Monuments at Tzutzuculi on the Chiapas Coast of Mexico." *American Antiquity,* vol. 42, no. 4, pp. 560–66.

MARQUINA, Ignacio. 1951.
*Arquitectura prehispánica.* I.N.A.H., Mexico City.

MEDELLÍN ZENIL, Alfonso. 1960.
"Monolitos inéditos olmecas." *La Palabra y el Hombre* (journal of the University of Veracruz), vol. 16, pp. 75–97. Jalapa.

MEDELLÍN ZENIL, Alfonso. 1971.
*Monolitos olmecas y otros en el Museo de la Universidad de Veracruz.* I.N.A.H., Mexico City.

MEGGERS, Betty J. 1975.
"The Transpacific Origin of Mesoamerican Civilization: A Preliminary Review of the Evidence and Its Theoretical Implications." *American Anthropologist,* vol. 77, no. 11, pp. 1–27.

MEGGERS, Betty J. 1976.
"Yes If by Land, No If by Sea: The Double Standard in Interpreting Cultural Similarities." *American Anthropologist*, vol. 78, no. 3, pp. 627–39.

MELGAR Y SERRANO, José María. 1869.
"Antigüedades Mexicanas." *Boletín de la Sociedad Mexicana de Geografía y Estadística*, 2 época, vol. 1, pp. 292–97. Mexico City.

MELGAR Y SERRANO, José María. 1871.
"Estudios sobre les antigüedades y el origen de la cabeza colosal de tipo etiópico que existe en Hueyapan del Cantón de Los Tuxtlas." *Boletín de la Sociedad Mexicana de Geografía y Estadística*, 2 época, vol. 3, pp. 104–9. Mexico City.

MELGAREJO VIVANCO, José Luis. 1975.
*El problema olmeca.* Jalapa.

*Mexikanische Tage.* Exhibition catalogue, April 19–June 1, 1975. Ingelheim-am-Rhein, West Germany.

*Mexikanischen Sammlungen des Museums für Völkerkunde (Die).* 1965, Vienna.

MORLEY, Sylvanus G. 1956.
*The Ancient Maya.* (Third edition, revised by George W. Brainerd.) Stanford University Press, Stanford, Cal.

NAVARRETE, Carlos. 1974.
*The Olmec Rock Carvings at Pijijiapan, Chiapas, Mexico, and Other Olmec Pieces from Chiapas and Guatemala.* New World Archaeological Foundation, Brigham Young University Press, Provo, Utah.

NICHOLSON, H. B. (ed.). 1976.
*Origins of Religious Art and Iconography in Preclassic Mesoameria.* U.C.L.A. Latin American Studies, series no. 31. U.C.L.A. Latin American Center, Los Angeles.

NOEL, Bernard. 1968.
*Mexican Art. 1: Beginnings to Olmecs.* Fernand Hazan, Paris; Tudor Publishing Co, New York (1979).

NOGUERA, Eduardo. 1939.
"Exploraciones a El Opeño, Michoacán." *XXVII^e Congreso de Americanistas*, vol. 1, pp. 574–86. Mexico City.

OCHOA, Lorenzo, and IVON HERNANDEZ, Martha. 1977.
"Los Olmecas y el Valle del Usumacinta." *Anales de Antropología*, 14, pp. 75–90. Mexico City.

ORELLANA, Rafael T. 1952.
"Zona arqueológica de Izapa." *Tlatoani*, vol. 1, no. 2, pp. 17–25. Mexico City.

ORELLANA, Rafael T. 1953.
"La cabecita del Mangala (Veracruz)." *Yan* (publication of the Centro de Investigaciones Antropológicas), no. 2, pp. 140–41. Mexico City.

PALACIOS, Enrique Juan. 1928.
*En los confines de la selva lacandona.* Secretaría de Educación Pública, Mexico City.

PALACIOS, Mario L. 1965.
*La cultura olmeca* (with the collaboration of Halina R. Cesarman). Instituto Indigenista Interamericano, Mexico City.

PARADIS, Louise Iseut. 1972.
*The Olmec Viewed from the Middle Balsas, Guerrero, Mexico.* Paper presented at the 31st Congress of the S.A.A., Bar Harbour, Fla.

PARADIS, Louise Iseut. 1973.
*Ecological and Cultural Marginality in the Tierra Caliente of Guerrero.* Paper presented at the 33rd Congress of the S.A.A., San Francisco.

PARADIS, Louise Iseut. 1974.
*The Tierra Caliente of Guerrero, Mexico: An Archaeological and Ecological Study.* Ph.D. dissertation, Yale University, New Haven, Conn.

PARADIS, Louise I., and GROVE, David C. 1971.
"An Olmec Stela from San Miguel Amuco." *American Antiquity*, vol. 36, no. 1, pp. 95–102.

PARSONS, Lee A. 1973.
"Iconographic Notes on a New Izapan Stela from Abaj Takalik, Guatemala." *Atti del XL Congresso Internazionale degli Americanisti*, Rome and Genoa, September 3–10, 1972, vol. 1, pp. 202–12. Genoa.

PEÑAFIEL, Antonio. 1885.
*Nombres geograficos de México. Catálogo alfabético de los nombres de lugar pertenecientes al idioma náhuatl. Estudio jeroglífico de la Matrícula de Tributos del Codice Mendocino.* 2 vols., incl. 1 album. Secretaría de Fomento, Mexico City.

PEÑAFIEL, Antonio. 1890.
*Monumentos del Arte Mexicano Antiguo*, vol. 1. Berlin.

PIÑA CHAN, Román. 1952.
"Tlatilco y la cultura preclásica del Valle de México." *Anales del I.N.A.H.*, vol. 4, pp. 33–43. Mexico City.

PIÑA CHAN, Román. 1955a
*Las culturas preclásicas de la cuenca de México.* Fondo de Cultura Económica, Mexico City.

PIÑA CHAN, Román. 1955b
*Chalcatzingo, Morelos.* I.N.A.H., Mexico City.

PIÑA CHAN, Román. 1958.
*Tlatilco.* 2 vols. I.N.A.H., Mexico City.

PIÑA CHAN, Román. 1964.
*Los Olmecas.* I.N.A.H., Mexico City.

PIÑA CHAN, Román. 1971.
"Preclassic or Formative Pottery and Minor Arts of the Valley of Mexico." In

*Handbook of Middle American Indians*, vol. 10, pp. 157–58. University of Texas Press, Austin.

PIÑA CHAN, Román. 1975.
"Los Olmecas aldeanos." In *Del nomadismo a los centros ceremoniales*, pp. 83–86. I.N.A.H., Mexico City.

PIÑA CHAN, Román, and COVARRUBIAS, Luis. 1964.
*El Pueblo del Jaguar: Los Olmecas arqueológicos*. Drawings by Miguel Covarrubias. Mexico City.

PIÑA CHAN, Román, and NAVARRETE, Carlos. 1967.
*Archaeological Research in the Lower Grijalva River Region, Tabasco and Chiapas*. New World Archaeological Foundation, Brigham Young University Press, Provo, Utah.

POHORILENKO, Anatole. 1972.
"La pequeña escultura." In *El arte olmeca. Artes de México*, pp. 37–62. Mexico City.

POPENOE HATCH, Marion. 1971.
"An Hypothesis on Olmec Astronomy, with Special Reference to the La Venta Site." In *Papers on Olmec and Maya Archaeology*, pp. 1–64. University of California Press, Berkeley.

*Pre-Columbian Art*. 1963.
*Handbook of the Robert Woods Bliss Collection of Pre-Columbian Art*. Dumbarton Oaks, Trustees for Harvard University, Washington, D.C.

*Pre-Columbian Art*. 1969.
*Supplement to the Handbook of the Robert Woods Bliss Collection of Pre-Columbian. Art*. Dumbarton Oaks, Trustees for Harvard University, Washington, D.C.

PROSKOURIAKOFF, Tatiana. 1954.
*Varieties of Classic Central Veracruz Sculpture*. Carnegie Institution, Washington, D.C.

PROSKOURIAKOFF, Tatiana. 1968.
"Olmec and Maya Art: Problems of Their Stylistic Relation." *Dumbarton Oaks Conference of the Olmec*, pp. 119–34. Washington, D.C.

QUIRARTE, Jacinto. 1973.
*Izapan-style Art: A Study of Its Form and Meaning*. Studies in Pre-Columbian Art and Archaeology, no. 10. Dumbarton Oaks, Washington, D.C.

QUIRARTE, Jacinto. 1976.
"The Relationship of Izapan-style Art to Olmec and Maya Art: A Review." In NICHOLSON (ed.), 1976.

RAMIREZ VASQUEZ, Pedro, et al. 1968.
*Le Musée du peuple mexicain: Art, architecture, archélogie, anthropologie*. French translation by Robert Victor. Introduction by Jaime Torres Bodet. Edita, Lausanne; Vilo, Paris.

ROBICSEK, Francis. 1972.
*Copán, Home of the Maya Gods*. Foreword by Gordon F. Ekholm. Museum of the American Indian, Heye Foundation, New York.

SAVILLE, Marshall H. 1900.
"A Votive Adze of Jadeite from Mexico." *Monumental Records*, vol. 1, pp. 138–40. New York.

SAVILLE, Marshall H. 1929.
*Votive Axes from Ancient Mexico*. Museum of the American Indian, Heye Foundation, vol. 6. New York.

SELER-SACHS, Cecilia. 1922
"Altertümer des Kanton Tuxtla im Staate Veracruz." In *Festschrift Eduard Seler*, pp. 543–56. Stuttgart.

SHARER, Robert J., and SEDAT, David W. 1973.
"Monument 1, El Portón, Guatemala, and the Development of the. Maya Calendrical and Writing Systems." In *Studies in Ancient America* (ed. John Graham), pp. 177–94. University of California Press, Berkeley.

SIMONI-ABBAT, Mireille. 1978.
"Les Olmèques." In *Civilisations précolombiennes: Mexique-Pérou*, pp. 31–35. Larousse, Paris.

SMITH, Bradley. 1968.
*Mexico: A History in Art*. Doubleday, Garden City, N.Y.

SOUSTELLE, Jacques. 1966.
*L'Art du Mexique ancien*. Arthaud, Paris. (Revised edition, 1977.)

SOUSTELLE, Jacques. 1967.
*Mexique*. "Archaeologia Mundi" series. Nagel, Geneva.

STIRLING, Matthew W. 1939.
"Discovering the New World's Oldest Dated Work of Man." *National Geographic*, vol. 76, pp. 183–218.

STIRLING, Matthew W. 1941.
"Expedition Unearths Buried Masterpieces of Carved Jade." *National Geographic*, vol. 80, pp. 277–302.

STIRLING, Matthew W. 1943a.
"La Venta's Green Stone Tigers." *National Geographic*, vol. 84, pp. 321–32.

STIRLING, Matthew W. 1943b.
*Stone Monuments of Southern Mexico*. Smithsonian Institution, Bureau of American Ethnology, bulletin 138. Washington, D.C.

STIRLING, Matthew W. 1947.
"On the Trail of La Venta Man." *National Geographic*, vol. 91, pp. 137–72.

STIRLING, Matthew W. 1955.
*Stone Monuments of the Río Chiquito, Veracruz, Mexico*. Smithsonian Institution, Bureau of American Ethnology, bulletin 157, pp. 1–24. Washington, D.C.

STIRLING, Matthew W. 1964.
"The Olmec, Artists in Jade." In *Essays in Pre-Columbian Art and Archaeol-

*ogy* (ed. S. K. Lothrop), pp. 42–59. Harvard University Press, Cambridge, Mass.

STIRLING, Matthew W. 1968.
"Early History of the Olmec Problem." *Dumbarton Oaks Conference on the Olmec*, pp. 1–8. Washington, D.C.

STIRLING, Matthew W., and STIRLING, Marion. 1942.
"Finding Jewels of Jade in a Mexican Swamp." *National Geographic*, vol. 82, pp. 635–61.

STONE, Doris. 1977.
*Pre-Columbian Man in Costa Rica*. Peabody Museum Press, Harvard University, Cambridge, Mass.

SWADESH, Morris. 1953.
*The Language of the Archaeological Huastecs*. Carnegie Institution. Notes on Middle American Archaeology and Ethnology, no. 114. Washington, D.C.

THOMPSON, J. Eric S. 1931.
*Archaeological Investigations in the Southern Cayo District, British Honduras*. Field Museum of Natural History. Anthropological Series, vol. 17. Chicago.

THOMPSON, J. Eric S. 1941.
*Dating of Certain Inscriptions of Non-Maya Origin*. Carnegie Institution, Washington, D.C.

THOMPSON, J. Eric S. 1950.
*Maya Hieroglyphic Writing: Introduction*. Carnegie Institution, publication 589. Washington, D.C.

THOMPSON, J. Eric S. 1962.
*A Catalog of Maya Hieroglyphs*. University of Oklahoma, Norman. Okla.

TIBON, Gutierre. 1973.
"La festa della pubertà femminile nel'archeologia mesoamericana." *Atti del XL Congresso Internazionale degli Americanisti*, Rome and Genoa, September 3–10, 1972, vol. 1, pp. 137–46. Genoa.

TOLSTOY, Paul. 1971.
"Utilitarian Artifacts of Central Mexico." In *Handbook of Middle American Indians*, vol. 10, pp. 270–96. University of Texas Press, Austin.

TOLSTOY, Paul, and GUÉNETTE, André. 1965.
"Le placement de Tlatilco dans le cadre du Pré-classique du bassin de Mexico." *Journal de la Société des Américanistes*, vol. 54, no. 1, pp. 47–91. Paris.

TOLSTOY, Paul, and PARADIS, Louise I. 1970.
"Early and Middle Preclassic Culture in the Basin of Mexico." *Science*, vol. 167, pp. 344–51.

TOLSTOY, Paul, et al. 1977.
"Early Sedentary Communities of the Basin of Mexico." *Journal of Field Archaeology*, vol. 4, pp. 91–106.

TOSCANO, Salvador. 1970.
*Arte precolombino de México y de la America central*. 2nd edition. Mexico City.

VAILLANT, Suzannah B., and VAILLANT, George C. 1934.
"Excavations at Gualupita." *Anthropological Papers of the American Museum of Natural History*, vol. 35, part 1, pp 1–135. New York.

WEAVER, Muriel Porter. 1972.
*Tlapacoya Pottery in the Museum Collections*. Museum of the American Indian, Heye Foundation. Indian Notes and Monographs, Miscellaneous Series, no. 56. New York.

WEAVER, Muriel Porter. 1967.
*The Aztecs, Maya and Their Predecessors: Archaeology of Mesoamerica*. Academic Press, New York.

WEIANT, C. W. 1943.
*An Introduction to the Ceramics of Tres Zapotes, Veracruz, Mexico*. Smithsonian Institution, Bureau of American Ethnology, bulletin 139. Washington, D.C.

WEYERSTALL, A. 1932
*Some Observations on Indian Mounds, Idols and Pottery in the Lower Papaloapan Basin, State of Veracruz, Mexico*. Tulane University. Middle American Research Series, vol. 4. New Orleans.

WICKE, Charles R. 1971.
*Olmec, an Early Art Style of Precolumbian Mexico*. University of Arizona Press, Tucson.

WIERCINSKI, Andrzej. 1971.
"Afinidades raciales de algunas problaciones antiguas de México." *Anales del Museo Nacional de Antropología e Historia*, 7 época, vol. 2, 1969 (published in 1971). Mexico City.

WIERCINSKI, Andrzej. 1972.
"Inter- and Intrapopulational Racial Differentiation of Tlatilco, Cerro de Las Mesas, Teotihuacán, Monte Albán and Yucatán Maya." *XXXIX^e Congreso Intern. de Americanistas*, Lima, 1970. Actas y Memorias, vol. 1, pp. 231–52. Lima, 1972.

WILLEY, Gordon R., et al. 1975.
*Excavations at Seibal, Department of Petén, Guatemala*. Peabody Museum Memoirs, vol. 13. Harvard University, Cambridge, Mass.

WILLEY, Gordon R. 1977.
"Origines et destin des anciens Maya." *La Recherche*, no. 82, pp. 861–75. Paris.

WILSON, Thomas. 1898.
*Prehistoric Art, or, the Origin of Art as Manifested in the Works of Prehistoric Man*. Report of the U.S. National Museum for the year ending June 30, 1896, pp 325–664. Smithsonian Institution, Washington, D.C.

WINNING, Hasso von. 1947.
"A Symbol for Dripping Water in the Teotihuacán Culture." *El México Antiguo*, vol. 6, nos. 9–12, pp. 333–41. Mexico City.

WUTHENAU, Alexander von. 1975.
*Unexpected Faces in Ancient America, 1500 B.C.–A.D. 1500: The Historical Testimony of Pre-Columbian Artists*. Crown, New York.

# Index

Abaj Takalik, 133, 135, 179

Agriculture (vegetation, plants), 4–5, 23, 24–25, 37, 86, 87, 88, 104, 105, 143, 150, 153, 170–71, 175, 186, 189; gods, 186, 187, 189. *See also* Maize

Altars, viii, 1, 12, 13, 20, 22, 24, 25, 32, 33, 34, 40–41, 43, 50, 73, 142, 147, 184; "Olmecoid," 126, 135, 140

Animal hunting, 3, 4, 5, 23, 24

Animal motifs, 52, 89, 132, 146. *See also* specific artifacts, kinds, sites

Architecture, 33–35, 71–72, 102, 104–5, 106, 108, 128, 137, 153

Arroyo Pesquero statuette, 175, 176–78

Axes, 10, 11, 14, 15, 37, 38, 42, 50, 78, 93, 134, 153, 171, 174, 175, 189; engraved, 20, 37, 58, 72, 78, 107, 108, 118, 126, 148, 171, 174, 175, 181, 182, 183, 184, 189; Humboldt, 174, 175; jade, 10, 15, 37, 38; "Kunz," 10, 11; votive, 10, 11, 14, 16, 20, 58, 72, 93, 107, 108

Ayotla, 78, 79, 80, 105

Aztecs, 1–2, 6, 14, 28, 29, 52, 53, 73, 82, 86, 108–9, 122, 145, 146, 149, 150, 161, 168, 185, 190, 191

"Babies" motif, 20, 26–27, 40–41, 58, 64–66, 76, 77, 85, 87, 92, 132, 134, 136, 140; jaguar-babies ("were-jaguar" babies), 20, 85–86, 128, 146, 147, 150, 169–70, 171, 185, 187, 189

Basalt, 20, 22, 24, 33, 37, 38, 40, 42, 44, 46, 47, 54, 58, 59, 71–72, 73, 93, 151. *See also* specific artifacts, sites

Bas-reliefs, 25, 26, 40, 42, 46–47, 49, 50, 53, 54, 59, 60, 63, 66, 68, 74, 80, 84, 85–93, 94, 97, 110, 118–22, 143, 148, 149, 153, 158, 161, 166, 185, 194; "Olmecoid," 74, 80, 84, 85–93, 94, 97, 110, 118–32 *passim,* 133, 135, 139. *See also* Engravings

Bernal, Ignacio, 23, 30, 31, 36, 60, 70, 77, 88, 102, 106–7, 108, 120, 126, 133, 134, 135n., 138, 179, 187, 191n.; and "Olmec III," 137

Beyer, Hermann, 13–14, 163–65, 190

Birds (bird motif), 23, 50, 52, 96, 120, 135, 166, 168, 170, 180, 187; masks, 15, 96, 120, 130, 190

Blom, Frans, 10–15, 33, 42, 44, 118, 163

Bonampak, 94–95, 146, 153, 163

Bouvier, Anna, 119, 124, 172, 174, 184

Bucklers, 52, 93, 118, 122, 130, 146, 158

Calendars. *See* Time calculation

Cárdenas, 111, 112, 114

Caso, Alfonso, 15–18, 19, 23, 104, 106, 118, 142, 143, 150, 171

Cave paintings, 26, 74, 84, 94–95, 148, 165, 170–71, 185

Ceramics, 54, 80, 91, 93–94, 108. *See also* Clay; Pottery; Terra cotta

Ceremonial bar motif, 85–86, 87

Ceremonial centers, 137, 140, 142–43, 147. *See also* specific sites

Cerro de Las Mesas, 32n., 68–70, 72, 106, 137

Chalcatzingo, 53, 85–93, 99, 105, 146, 148, 188; bas-reliefs, 26, 84, 85–93, 122, 153, 170–71, 188, 189, 190; mounds (tumuli), 89–93; vase, 175

Chiapa de Corzo, 114–15, 179; steal no. 2, 114–15, 136, 137, 139, 179

Chiapas, 110–11, 114–15, 118, 119, 120, 122, 133, 136, 137, 139, 149, 156, 158, 166, 179

Chieftains (princes, kings), 146–47. *See also* Priests

Clay, 2, 35, 37, 39, 40, 47, 75, 78, 151. *See also* Ceramics; Pottery; Terra cotta; specific artifacts, motifs, sites

Cloud motif, 86–87, 170, 171

Coe, Michael D., 21, 22, 49, 54, 74, 88, 94, 134, 139, 179, 180, 183, 186, 187, 188, 190

Colossal heads, viii, 1, 2, 4, 8, 9–10, 13–14, 20, 26, 27, 32, 33, 35, 40, 44–46, 49, 54, 56, 66–68; "Olmecoid," 121, 125, 131, 135–36. *See also* specific sites

Copán, 136, 138, 145

Covarrubias, Miguel, 19, 27, 77, 78, 97, 98, 185–86

Cross motif, 37, 50, 52, 61, 66, 86–89, 93, 95, 104, 120, 136, 163, 165, 169–70, 171–75, 180, 188, 192. *See also* St. Andrew's cross

Cruz del Milagro, 32, 63, 76; "Prince" statue, 32, 63, 65, 76, 170

Dates (dating), 18–19, 21, 22, 47–49, 54–56, 60–61, 68–70, 75, 78–79, 80–81, 86, 93–94, 102–4, 105–6, 108, 114–18, 166; carbon-14 method, 19, 21, 25, 108, 128; "Long Count" (*see under* Time calculation); Maya "zero date" and, 60, 68, 114–18, 137, 166–68; "Olmecoid" relics (Olmec influence) and, 75, 78–79, 80–81, 86, 93–94, 105–6, 114, 128, 136–37, 138; spoken language and, 28. *See also* Time calculation; specific sites

Death god, 186, 187, 190

De la Fuente, B., 32n., 42, 53, 66, 68, 187

Dots and bars (bars and dots) notation, 126, 162–65, 183

Drucker, Philip, 20, 21, 47n., 49, 153n.

Duck motif, 52, 166, 170

Dwarf motif, 50, 59, 70, 88, 190

Dwellings, 5, 49, 71–72, 102, 104–5, 143, 151, 152–53, 192

Ear ornaments, 38, 41, 44–46, 50, 71, 72, 96, 102, 105, 152

El Baúl, 135, 136, 137, 179

El Salvador, 111, 133–34, 135, 137, 149

El Sitio, 132–33, 183, 184

Engravings, 71, 72, 73, 93, 100, 148, 158, 171–75; glyphs (signs), 160–83 *passim. See also* Bas-reliefs

Etla Valley sites, 104–6; dates, 105–6

Feline motif (faces, figures, gods, masks), viii, 10, 14–15, 35, 40, 46, 47, 50, 52–53, 58–59, 60, 61, 64–66, 85, 87, 88, 95, 105, 108, 126, 130, 132, 133, 135, 140, 147, 150, 155, 170, 171,

# INDEX